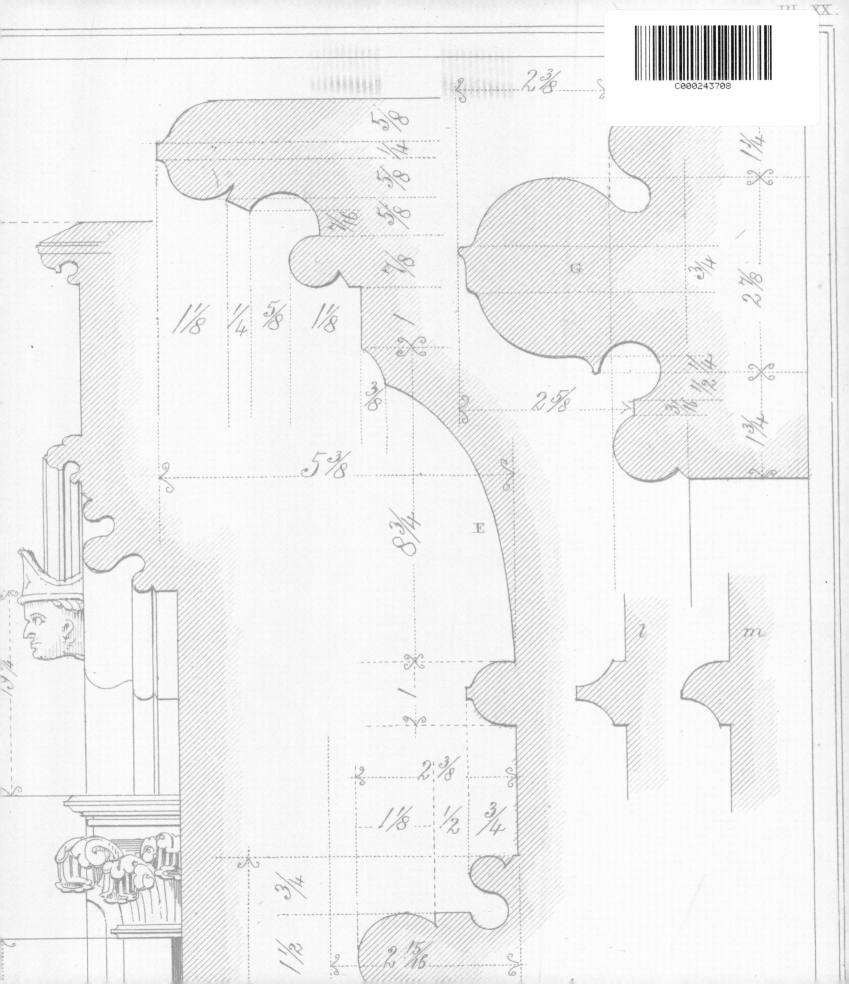

Pl. XX.

C000243708

DURHAM CATHEDRAL

Light of the North

DURHAM CATHEDRAL

Light of the North

John Field

New photography by **Malcolm Crowthers**

THIRD MILLENNIUM
PUBLISHING, LONDON

DEDICATION

In affectionate memory of Neville Walton, 1953–2006, Friend of Durham, who died too soon.
In memory of Jean Crowthers who loved Durham.

Copyright © Durham Cathedral and
Third Millennium Publishing Limited

First published in 2006 by
Third Millennium Publishing Limited,
a subsidiary of Third Millennium Information Limited

2–5 Benjamin Street
London
United Kingdom
EC1M 5QL
www.tmiltd.com

Hardback: Paperback:
ISBN 10 : 1 903942 51 9   **ISBN 10 : 1 903942 67 5**
ISBN 13 : 978 1 903942 51 2   **ISBN 13 : 978 1 903942 67 3**

British Library Cataloguing in Publication Data

A CIP catalogue record for this book is available
from the British Library.

All rights reserved

No part of this publication may be reproduced or
transmitted in any form or by any means, electronic
or mechanical, including photocopying, recording
or any information storage or retrieval system,
without permission in writing from the publisher

Text © John Field 2006
Photography © Malcolm Crowthers 2006
Designed by Matthew Wilson
Production by Bonnie Murray

Reprographics by Asia Graphic Printing Ltd
Printed by 1010 Printing International Ltd
on behalf of Compass Press Ltd

*Previous page: The Cathedral and the River Wear
through an arch of Framwellgate Bridge in April.*

All images are copyright © Malcolm Crowthers except for the
following:

British Library, 20, 53; British Museum, 121; Corpus Christi,
Cambridge, 27T; Brian Crosby, 158; Durham Cathedral
Library, 12, 25, 26, 27B, 30, 37, 59, 63, 72R, 105, 106, 112,
120, 137, 143, 147, 151, 152, 162; TUC Library (William
Lambeth), 150; Yorkshire Archeological Society, 50T

CONTENTS

PREFACE

A few years ago, listeners to BBC Radio 4 voted Durham Cathedral Britain's best-loved building. What is it about the Cathedral that draws out the affection of so many people?

It is undeniably a great building – one of Europe's greatest. It is set in one of Britain's most beautiful landscapes. But its appeal is about more than architecture and setting. Its close association with the saints of the north, especially through the shrines of Cuthbert and Bede, gives it a particular kind of 'spirituality' that speaks powerfully of the Christian history of these islands. There is, too, the sense – perhaps not unconnected with those well-earthed saints – that the Cathedral ultimately belongs not to bishops, deans or chapters but to the ordinary people of north-east England who are intensely proud and fond of it, something that is very obvious at the annual Miners' service. And finally, my experience echoes what others have told me, which is that despite its grandeur and nobility, the Cathedral has a capacity to 'enfold' us in a way that doesn't diminish or dwarf us but on the contrary, lends dignity and stature to our humanity. That strikes me as an eloquent image of how the grace of God meets us and embraces us.

It is the greatest possible privilege to spend this phase of my life living and working in and around this marvellous building. The next best thing to being here is having a book in your hands whose text and photographs capture the spirit of the place so well. We can all be grateful to author John Field, photographer Malcolm Crowthers and the publishers for creating a book that is both informative and evocative, and is also a thing of beauty in its own right.

MICHAEL SADGROVE
Dean of Durham

September 2006

The seal of the dynamic Antony Bek, Bishop of Durham 1284–1310 (see pp59–61). Warrior, international diplomat, friend of kings and popes, Bek established the impregnable authority of the County Palatine of Durham – the region ruled directly by the bishops of Durham until 1836.

THE POWER OF DURHAM

IT was a miracle, said the believers. It was nothing of the kind, said the sceptics. The dispute concerned the events of the early hours of 1 May 1942. In retaliation for R.A.F. raids which had destroyed the medieval German cities of Lübeck and Rostock, the Luftwaffe had been ordered out on 'Baedecker Raids' to bomb England's historic cities. At the end of April 1942, Exeter, Bath, Norwich and York were hit. At 2.33am on 1 May air-raid sirens sounded in Durham; German bombers were heard approaching. The sky was clear, the cathedral and town brightly moonlit. Then, according to some eye-witnesses, a white mist rose up from the river, blotting out town, castle, cathedral from aerial view. Bombers circled above; high explosives were dropped to the east at Belmont and Finchale. At 4am the all-clear sounded and the mist dispersed. One member of the Royal Observer Corps on fire-watching duty all that night recorded, on returning home, 'I shall believe to the end of my days that I witnessed a miracle.' Over the following days many explanations and interpretations were offered. It was a phenomenon regularly occurring in the Wear gorge. The cathedral tower was not obliterated by mist but remained visible. The German bombers knew well the landmark of Durham and could have bombed it then or on other occasions had they wished to. They were only seeking to shed their loads before crossing the North Sea to return home. But the long mythology of St Cuthbert's propensity to protect his people in times of peril had persisted. After all, had he not raised a mist in 1069 to confuse the forces of William the

Above: *The RAF Memorial Window at the west end of the North Nave Aisle depicts the mist rising from the river to protect the Cathedral from a bombing raid in 1942.*

Left: *The Memorial Cross to the officers and men of the Durham Light Infantry who were killed in the South African Campaign 1899–1902. It stands near the north-west corner of the Cathedral, and its style alludes to the traditions of Irish and Anglo-Saxon Christianity in which Durham is rooted.*

Castle, Cathedral, Framwellgate Bridge and the River Wear in April. The bridge was the first to be built across the River Wear to the peninsula, by Bishop Flambard in the early 12th century.

Conqueror advancing on Durham? The wartime report of the Friends of Durham Cathedral hedges its bets: 'Local patriotism declares that on nights when the cathedral had been selected for attack, a sudden mist (ascribed by the pious to St Cuthbert and by the profane to the Dean) arose from the Wear and shrouded it in safety.' But, to place the 'miracle' in a wider context, it is surprising that only a single bomb fell on Durham during the war, to explode harmlessly beside the sewage works.

The rising of the mist on 1 May might serve as a metaphor for the intrinsic power or powers that Durham continues to exert. When you step into the city, not through the back of a wardrobe but across one of its medieval stone bridges, you seem to be entering a separate universe operating by its own laws. It is in time and out of time. St Cuthbert raised a mist a thousand years ago, yesterday. It accommodates all shades of opinion in tolerant synthesis. The mist was natural; the mist was artificial; it was both. Nature and artifice in harmony make the experience of the place memorable, unsurpassed in all of Europe. The whole is greater than the sum of the parts, and the parts are world-class. Wedges of greenery, pasture, gardens, woodland, thrust into the heart of the

diminutive city. It is a synthesis of town and country, of land and water. The town clings to its sandstone whaleback as if fearful of sliding off into the river. It has depth; it has height. The central promontory has a circle of attendant hills: Windmill, Observatory, Aykley Heads, Frankland, Wharton Park, Elvet, Pelaw Woods, Mount Joy, all seemingly magnetized by the faerie vision at the centre into deferential genuflection. To complete the circle on foot would be an arduous task on a demanding switchback. At the centre, side by side, castle and cathedral, political, military, spiritual, another synthesis. In Durham they are inseparable: all sprang from Norman power, and the Norman desire to impose an unanswerable proof of regime change. If you looked at Durham at the end of the 11th century, only a generation after the Conquest, you would not doubt who was in command here. A *Times* leader in 1944, criticizing a proposal to build a new power station on the Wear, noted both the power of synthesis and the synthesis of power that Durham conveys: 'This is one of the sites on which buildings seem to grow out of their foundations, so that rock and structure form a unity … as a lesson in the significance of the Norman Conquest the group is without parallel in England.'

The quality of timelessness adheres to Durham as a pilgrimage town as to others along the world's pilgrim routes. Threading the narrow streets of the old town, many still cobbled, their patterns laid down in the Middle Ages, through the mix of costumes, tongues and accents that characterize a street crowd of students, residents and visitors, you are within imagination's reach of a pilgrim's experience and goal. If you have resisted the temptation to turn aside into the cosy claustrophobia of Rumbletum's tearooms or the cheery jumble of the Victorian covered market, a bazaar which would not be out of place in Aleppo or Samarkand, you round the narrow defile of Owengate to be struck for the first time by the great north flank of the cathedral, like a liner in dry dock, and the unexpected spaciousness of Palace Green. Here, with the castle at your back and Bishop Cosin's 17th-century library and almshouses on either side, you might easily be out of time, but for the compulsion of the authorities that abut

Timeless Durham: this view of the city in May 1978, when domestic fires were still the norm, seems to place it at any point in history.

on the Green to welcome the parking of vehicles there. Maybe one day, in a better world than this, aesthetics will triumph over economics and convenience, and both Palace Green and the College beyond the cathedral will be cleansed of cars.

Pilgrims and tourists alike travel in hope of finding little worlds at an angle to the everyday; those who over the centuries have been drawn to this place have generally been disposed to marvel. A few have dissented. 'A gloomy pile', wrote the not normally gloomy Tobias Smollett. He must have been there on one of Durham's bleak midwinter days. James Murray opined in 1828 that 'it would be a very fine place, were it not for the swarms of priests'. But Robert Hegge in 1626 was agog: 'he that hath seene the situation of the Citty, hath seene the Map of Sion, and may save a journey to Jerusalem'. Isaac Basire, a prebendary who converted his exile during the Civil War and Commonwealth into 14 years of adventuring in the Middle East, passed through the Holy Land and endorsed Hegge's hypothesis: 'this cittie is an absolute epitome of Jerusalem, nott only for the temple or cathedral standinge upon the highest hill in the town,

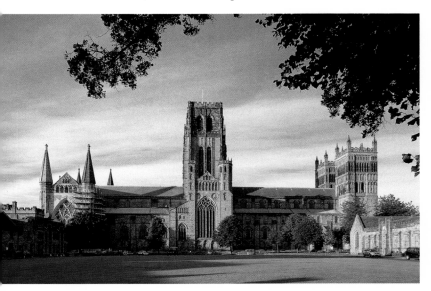

'A liner in dry dock': the north side of the Cathedral and Palace Green, early morning in August.

like Mount Sion, but the skirts of the town resemble Jerusalem, and nott only that, but the country about resembles the country about Jerusalem, beinge, as the Scripture saith, a hilly country'. One of the seven wonders of the world, judged John Ruskin, of the view of Durham from the railway station. Architects who have recently judged the power of the building to be up there with the Parthenon and the Taj Mahal should not be derided for partiality.

On Durham's acropolis the cathedral stands both in time and beyond it. Its history and fabric are time-defying continuities, some stretching back to an age before Durham even existed. In the Treasury, St Cuthbert's pectoral cross of the 7th century appears new-minted. Manuscripts from in Lindisfarne days, the great Gospels and the *Liber Vitae*, were preserved through centuries of restlessness when they were carried by the early monks to and fro across the north in attendance upon St Cuthbert's coffin. Durham became their home for centuries more, it is presumed, before the British Library assumed their guardianship. But they were back

The monastic brewhouse, fireplace intact, now serves as the workshop for stonemasons.

in Durham in 1987 for the 1300th anniversary of Cuthbert's death, and will perhaps be seen there again. Manuscripts given by William of St. Calais, founder of the Benedictine monastery in 1083, remain in the Chapter Library; in 2005 the 13th-century John Auckland Bible, originally from Durham, was brought home with celebrations after centuries of truancy.

Even at the Reformation, when despoliation of monasteries was common, Durham escaped lightly. Bishop Tunstall remained bishop; Prior Whitehead became the first dean. Continuity of personnel guaranteed continuity of the monastery buildings.

Above left: *'In Principio', the opening of St John's Gospel, in the Durham Gospels manuscript from the 7th or 8th century. A.II.17*

Above right: *The first page of St Mark's Gospel from a manuscript of the mid-7th century and therefore older than the more widely known Lindisfarne Gospels. A.II.10*

Below: *A decorative detail from the Magnificat in the Durham Gospels manuscript. A.II.17*

Above: *St Cuthbert's pectoral cross from the 7th century found in his tomb when it was opened in 1827. It is made of gold inlaid with garnets and a Mediterranean shell.*

Nowhere else in England have so many domestic monastery buildings survived to be found new roles. The 20 separate houses now in the College all had monastic functions. In addition, in the Clerk of the Works' yard, monastic barns and haylofts have acquired modern uses and, finest of all, the monastic brewhouse, complete with fireplace and shelves for barrels of ale, serves admirably as a workshop for stone carving. The most fundamental continuity at the western extremity of the peninsula is that the monastic reredorter, from which medieval effluent was conveyed in a shaft to the river, is still the location of visitors' lavatories.

The Deanery, an architectural palimpsest and one of the most distinguished continuously inhabited residences in England, was already 400 years old when James VI of Scotland stayed there in 1603 on his way to become James I of England. The tester bed in which he slept is still in the house. There must be something preservative about the Durham air, and not only for saints. Those appointed to positions in the College may confidently anticipate long lives and favourable insurance policies. Longevities are the lifeblood of the place. Prior Fossor lived to nearly 90, having survived the Black Death; George Cliffe, the last former monk to be translated to a prebendal stall, outlived four bishops and lived until 1596. Shute Barrington was still bishop in 1826 at the age of 91. The plaques listing bishops,

Top: *The south flank of the Cathedral and the deanery seen from the top floor of a house in The College, in March with clear light and leafless trees.*

Above: *An exotic bird from the Chinese wallpaper in the Solarium, a reception room in the Deanery.*

Right: *The tester bed in the Deanery, occupied by James VI of Scotland on his way to assume the English throne in London.*

priors and deans display a goodly measure of long service, but the most preserving post of all is that of Master of the Choristers. Their carved record, behind the organ in the South Choir Aisle, lists only 21 incumbents between 1541 and 2006. Take away one name that appears twice (Mr Browne), two names of men who held office for only one year apiece and two who served for only three years, and a remarkable statistic emerges: 16 Masters of the Choristers span 457 years, averaging nearly 30 years in the office.

'The best thing to happen in the last ten years', said one devoted, and female, member of the Durham community, 'was the appointment of the first woman canon.' First impressions of the cathedral are that it is an insistently masculine place: the pillars are like stone giants. Being a Benedictine monastery there was, very properly, no place for women within the precinct. Even Henry VIII's snooping commissioners, sent to spy out abuses, could find no evidence of impropriety. Under the pretext of Cuthbert's supposed misogyny, the practice continued of restricting women, even Queens of England, to the Lady Chapel and the extreme west end of the Nave behind the taboo line of blue-grey marble snaking across the stone pavement. And at first glance it is the record of men in monuments and memorials that appears to prevail. The Miners' Book of Remembrance in the South Nave Aisle: 'Kimblesworth Colliery. 18.11.46 H. Atkinson 21; 22.12.47 W. Slowther 21; Lambton Colliery 3.2.62 W. Robinson 64.' In the South Transept the Miners' Banner from Haswell recalls the lost way of colliery life, one of equal heroism and inhumanity. There are the soldiers too: the Chapel of the Durham Light Infantry, the record of service, suffering and death in the Peninsula Campaign, the Crimea, South Africa, Burma, the two

The 19th-century plaque in the South Choir Aisle chronicling Durham's bishops, priors and deans since 993.

Left: Forbidden space: the line of blue-grey marble set into the stone floor at the west end of the Nave marked the limit of access for women in the early centuries. St Cuthbert was reputed to be unsympathetic to women, though there is no evidence in Bede's early Life of Cuthbert *to support the tradition.*

Below left: This youthful angel keeps fitting vigil above the altar of the Durham Light Infantry Chapel where hundreds of young men who died in war are commemorated.

Below right: The Durham Light Infantry Cross was erected on the battlefield of the Somme as a tribute to the men of three battalions lost in an attack on the Butte de Warlencourt in November 1916. It stood there for ten years before being brought home to Durham in 1926.

world wars. In the Middle Ages the only yielding of exclusive masculinity was the burial of Alice Neville, wife of Ralph of Raby Castle, in the Neville Chantry. Not until after the Restoration did women begin to be allowed burial within the cathedral. Mrs Dorothy Greye in 1662, below a black marble slab in the Galilee Chapel, a skull and crossbones framing the family coat of arms. Dulcibella Morton in 1682, wife of Prebendary Morton, deserving her slab in the Nave on the strength of her exquisite name alone. Then in the first decades of the 19th century, in the Chapel of the Nine Altars, virtually empty of tombs but for the medieval bishops Antony Bek and Richard Bury, families arrived. Children and grandchildren of the precinct: Emily Cadogan, aged five; Elizabeth Davison, buried where she had spent her happiest hours; Elizabeth Mowbray, daughter of Prebendary Gray, 'who expired under the paternal roof at the Rectory, Bishopwearmouth'. At the other end of the cathedral, in the Galilee, Jane Underlock of Old Elvet, sister to the late Brass Crosby, Alderman of London. In 1832 Anne Colberg, housekeeper to the late Bishop Barrington, was interred in the principal Nave aisle, but mysteriously dispatched into anonymity some years later when her commemorative slab was inverted. Perhaps processions are at risk of tripping over inscriptions.

From the burial of the first woman in the cathedral to the appointment of the first woman canon, over 600 years elapsed. But amends have been made: the inauguration of the altars and icons of St Hild and St Margaret in the Chapel of the Nine Altars, the involvement of women members of the laity in services and in the governing and day-to-day management of the place have belatedly enriched Durham with a power it had previously lacked. St Cuthbert has so far expressed no displeasure.

AIDAN AND CUTHBERT

THE COMING OF CHRISTIANITY

A pagan king sowed the Christian seed in the north. Conflicts between the kingdoms of Bernicia, north of the Tees, and Deira, between Tees and Humber, were settled by battle in 616. Edwin of Deira defeated and killed Aethelfrith of Bernicia, and ruled both kingdoms. Aethelfrith's three sons took refuge in Argyll with Bernicia's Celtic allies, and, coming into contact with the monks of Iona somewhere in the west, received an education and were converted to Christianity. Meanwhile the ambitious Edwin sought a dynastic marriage with the royal house of Kent. It was agreed, on condition that Edwin accepted Aethelburh as a Christian wife. In 625 she brought north as her chaplain

Paulinus, a Roman bishop who had been a companion of Augustine in Canterbury. He seized his opportunity with missionary zeal: in 627 Edwin and his court were baptized at York, and a small basilica was built to create a see for Paulinus. The new religion caught on: Paulinus spent 36 days preaching and baptizing 'from dawn to dusk' at the Northumbrian royal stronghold of Yeavering at the northern extremity of the Cheviot Hills.

Suddenly all seemed lost. Instability and violence interrupted. An alliance of pagan Welsh and Mercians attacked Northumbria in 633, Edwin was killed in battle near Doncaster, and Northumbria was broken in two again, 'ravaged by ghastly slaughter' by Cadwallon of Gwynned and Penda of Mercia. But within a year the see-saw of political fortunes improbably tilted, and Christianity was restored, this time in perpetuity. Oswald, second son of Aethelfrith killed 18 years earlier, returned from Iona to claim his kingdom, and defeated Cadwallon in battle at Hefenfelth, appropriately translated as Heavenfield, on the uplands north of the Tyne and near the line of the Roman Wall. It had been a crusade: Oswald reputedly displayed a wooden cross before his fighting men on the battlefield. Northumbria was now reunited under a committed Christian ruler. The dramatic consequences were to shape the culture of the region for centuries to come.

Right: *St Cuthbert amid the ruins of Lindisfarne Priory: a bronze cast (2000) of the original elm sculpture by Fenwick Lawson (1983).*

Left: *St Aidan watches over the ruins of Lindisfarne Priory from the churchyard. The sculpture is by Kathleen Parbury (1958).*

Above: Northern England and Scotland in the 9th century.

Top left: From Thrush Island, the tiny islet which was St Cuthbert's first retreat, can be seen the Priory ruins and, on the right, the raised rib of hard black dolorite stone called The Heugh, on which the cells of the first monastery were probably built in the 7th century.

Left: The ruins of the 12th-century Lindisfarne Priory and, on the left, the parish church of Holy Island.

LINDISFARNE AND AIDAN

Close to the royal fortress at Bamburgh, Oswald founded a religious community as the springboard for consolidating a Christian kingdom. He turned to Iona, where he had been brought up, for support. Aidan, an Irish-born monk, journeyed to Northumbria, and in 635 they selected Lindisfarne, a low-lying sandy partial island with a spine and outcrops of hard dolorite rock which the incoming tide cut off from the mainland twice a day. For seven years king and monk, now the first bishop, worked in missionary partnership. Bede's account is attractive: 'The king always listened humbly and readily to Aidan's advice, and diligently set himself to establish and extend the church of God throughout his kingdom. And while the bishop, who was not yet fluent in the English language,

preached the Gospel, it was most delightful to see the king himself interpreting the word of God to his thanes and leaders; for he himself had obtained perfect command of the Scottish tongue during his long exile.'

The proximity of Lindisfarne to the two royal strongholds of Bamburgh and Yeavering underlines the alliance between royalty and monastery which gave Christianity in the north its secure foundation. Throughout the great age of Northumbrian culture in the late 7th and 8th centuries, religious communities remained in close alliance with the royal house. In 737, for example, King Ceolwulf gave up both his throne and his wife to enter monastic life.

The tradition Aidan brought with him from the west was Irish. Great simplicity, to the point of austerity, characterized Irish monasticism. It is

Bamburgh Castle stands on the rocky site of the palace of the early kings of Northumbria, including Oswald and Ecgfrith. Inner Farne beyond was the place chosen by St Cuthbert for his hermitage in 677, and where he died in 687.

probable that his community on Lindisfarne lived in small 'beehive' stone huts on the exposed Heugh, the raised rib of hard dolorite stone to the south of the ruins of the 12th-century church which magnetize visitors to Holy Island in modern times. Irish Christianity also possessed a strong missionary vocation, and Bede depicts Aidan travelling widely, attracting followers by his gentleness, compassion and acts of charity: 'He used his priestly authority to check the proud and powerful; he tenderly comforted the sick, he relieved and protected the poor … if he ever received gifts of money … he would distribute them for the use of the poor or for the redemption of those who had been unjustly sold into slavery.' Such words and

deeds must have amazed a savage land. It seems that people were drawn to his light: 'If anyone met him on the road, they ran to him and bowed, eager to be signed by his hand or receive a blessing from his lips. Whenever he spoke, he was given an attentive hearing, and people flocked to the churches and monasteries, not to obtain food but to hear the word of God taught.'

So fervent a movement was strong enough to survive the death of Oswald in 642, when he fell in battle at Oswestry against the aggressive Penda and his Mercians. He had again raised a cross on the battlefield, but was cut to pieces where he fell. Soon, however, there were tales of miracles at the place of his death, and his effective canonization by popular acclaim ensured his lasting influence. Again Northumbria was divided, but Aidan's work went on in both Bernicia and Deira, where he found another royal partnership with its king Oswine. By the time of Aidan's death at Bamburgh in 651, the model he had fashioned at Lindisfarne, of simple discipline and missionary endeavour, had been replicated across the north, at Melrose, Hexham, Coldingham and Hartlepool, a convent for nuns. After his death Whitby, Wearmouth and Jarrow were founded, and Aidan's monastic legacy was triumphant.

Bamburgh Castle, seen from the causeway to Lindisfarne, floats in a shimmer of marine light behind Thrush Island, marked by a wooden cross. The line of poles in the sea marks the safe walking route to Lindisfarne from the mainland.

Two illuminations from the 12th-century Life of St Cuthbert, probably from the Durham Scriptorium: The dying Boisil instructs St Cuthbert and prophesies his future achievements (above) and the death of St Cuthbert (left). From Yates Thompson 26 Bede Manuscript (British Library)

Right: Puffins, summer visitors to the Farnes, hold a May meeting on the rocks of Inner Farne, the place of St Cuthbert's hermitage from 677 and where he died in 687.

CUTHBERT

Aidan was the great forerunner; Cuthbert, through a vision, his lineal successor. On the night of Aidan's death, Cuthbert, a young Northumbrian Saxon, a shepherd in the Lammermuir Hills south-east of Edinburgh, had a vision of angels bearing a soul to Heaven. Learning shortly afterwards that the vision coincided with Aidan's death, he recognized it as a calling and presented himself at the monastery at Melrose, where he was received by the prior, Boisil, a man of celebrated spirituality, and the Abbot, Eata, the teachers who most influenced his life. With the exception of an abortive assignment in 654 to assist with the foundation of the monastery at Ripon, Cuthbert remained at Melrose, first as a monk and then as Prior, until after the contentious Synod of Whitby in 664, where the conflicts between Irish

Christianity, which had prevailed in Northumbria, and the Roman Christianity adopted further south, chiefly about the date of Easter and the shape of the monastic tonsure, symbols of deeper differences of religious practice and organization were resolved in favour of the Roman form. The Irish bishop of Lindisfarne, Colman, took himself back to Ireland in a huff, but not before appointing Abbot Eata of Melrose to serve also as Abbot of Lindisfarne. Eata, needing Cuthbert's support for his divided responsibilities, asked him to be Prior at Lindisfarne.

And so Cuthbert came to the island. It seems he was adept at healing the conflict of loyalties between rival religious traditions provoked at Whitby, and diplomatically fostered a Roman orthodoxy without rejecting the traditions of the Irish Church that were represented by manuscript illumination and the

solitary spiritual life. In addition to his patient and devoted work as head of the monastic community, he pursued his missionary vocation on the mainland with such intensity that he gained a reputation as a worker of miracles, healing the sick and casting out devils by the power of his prayer.

Yet, perhaps because of the very intensity of his faith, he was increasingly drawn back to the strongest strand of Irish Christianity, the life of the hermit. At first he took himself regularly to a cell on the tiny Thrush Island, now known as Cuthbert's Island, only a few yards offshore from the monastery but, like Lindisfarne itself, isolated by the flood tide. It proved an insufficient haven for a man of his widespread fame, and in 676, aged in his early 40s, he chose as his refuge the 16-acre island of Inner Farne, five miles as the gull flies to the south of Holy Island. The island was believed to be uninhabitable because of the presence of demons, which Cuthbert first had to drive away. Here he built a stone cell, dug a well, planted barley and rebuked the birds for stealing it, and developed an intimate relationship with the sea and its creatures, otters, dolphins and eider ducks, still known locally as Cuddy's ducks. Even here he still attracted visitors: monks brought him bread and pilgrims visited for his teaching and power of consolation. Given the prevailing weather conditions for much of the year they must have been very determined. His fame compelled him to make rare reluctant visits away from Farne. In 684 he had a meeting with Aelfflaed, Abbess of Whitby

Top: *The pele tower and chapel on Inner Farne, foreground, the site of the monastic cell dependent on Durham Priory until its dissolution in 1537, with Bamburgh Castle behind.*

Above: *An eider duck, known locally as Cuddy's ducks because of its association with Cuthbert, patrols the harbour at Seahouses.*

and sister of Ecgfrith, then King of Northumbria, on Coquet Island. He had earlier secured a miraculous cure of her wasting disease with the gift of a silk girdle. There were important consequences of the meeting: Ecgfrith appointed Cuthbert as Bishop of Hexham in 685, and even visited him on Farne in an effort to persuade him to leave his hermitage. His reluctance to leave his territory led to an exchange of sees with his old friend Eata, who had become Bishop of Lindisfarne in 678. Cuthbert was consecrated bishop in York on Easter Day 685, but resigned his brief episcopate 18 months later and retired to Inner Farne to die.

Cuthbert fell ill in March 687, and was attended by monks from Lindisfarne. He wanted a plain burial on Farne. Bede has him presciently say to them: 'I think that it will be more expedient for you that I should remain here, on account of the influx of fugitives and guilty men of every sort who will perhaps flee to my body because, unworthy as I am, reports about me as a servant of God have nevertheless gone forth, and you will be compelled very frequently to intercede with the powers of this world on behalf of such men, and so will be put to much trouble on account of the presence of my body.' As his death neared, however, he deferred to the wishes of the monks: 'If you wish to set aside my plans and take my body back there, it seems best that you entomb it in the interior of your church, so that while you yourselves can visit my sepulchre when you wish, it may be in your power to decide whether any of those who come thither should approach it.'

He died on 20 March 687. News of the death was signalled to Lindisfarne by a fire, and his body was brought home to the monastery. Instead of the simple burial on Farne that he had desired, he was enshrined opulently in the church on Lindisfarne, in fine vestments and winding sheets, with jewels and in a stone sarcophagus. In the years following his death the Lindisfarne Gospels were inscribed and illuminated in his honour by Eadfrith, bishop of the see. Their richly elaborated Irish design is a tribute to the ousted tradition Cuthbert had come to embody.

On the 11th anniversary of his death in 698, the monks undertook the ritual of elevating of the remains from below ground to a raised shrine appropriate for veneration. When they opened the sarcophagus, they discovered that the body was uncorrupted, an unchallengeable confirmation of his sainthood. Not only uncorrupted, but still giving every impression of suspended animation. In Bede's account: 'The skin had not decayed nor grown old, nor the sinews become dry … but the limbs lay at rest with the appearance of life and were still moveable at the joints. For his neck and knees were like those of a living man: and when they lifted him from the tomb they could bend him as they wished.' In that moment of revelation, the long

'The Journey': an elm-wood carving (1999) by Fenwick Lawson in Lindisfarne Parish Church next to the priory ruins. Six clerks of St Cuthbert's community carried the saint's coffin on its journeyings across the north in the 9th century.

history of Durham is implicit, though still nearly 300 fraught and perilous years distant.

But to how much, if any, of this extraordinary story should we give credence? Cuthbert's fame prompted the writing of three early lives of the saint. The first, by an anonymous writer, was written around 700, shortly after the discovery of the miracle of the body, and emphasizes Cuthbert's skill as a worker of miracles. This was followed by two lives by Bede, one in verse, the other in prose. Both were in existence by 720. Bede we know to have been a scrupulous historian, who sought out eye witness accounts wherever possible. His narrative of Cuthbert's death and elevation is derived partly from conversations with Herefrith, Abbot of Lindisfarne at the time. So although there are standard recurring features in early lives of saints, and although Bede's excitement may have led him to elaborate some aspects of the narrative, he was undoubtedly recording what observers believed they had witnessed. Bede placed his emphasis on Cuthbert's pastoral skills in his triple role of prior, hermit and bishop – fertile and varied ground for the subsequent cult.

CUTHBERT AND NORTHUMBRIA

But one truth is beyond question. The influence of Aidan and Cuthbert, and their association with royal houses, made possible the golden age of Northumbrian civilization of which the Lindisfarne Gospels are the most celebrated surviving example. After Ecgfrith had been killed in battle near Forfar in 685, he was succeeded by Aldfrith, his illegitimate half-brother, who, like Oswald 50 years earlier, had been in exile on Iona. He proved to be an enlightened patron of Northumbrian culture, and the historical scholarship and artistic achievements at the monasteries of Lindisfarne, Jarrow and Monkwearmouth flourished under his rule. Late in the seventh century, St Willibrord undertook a mission from Northumbria to Germany, and 100 years later Alcuin, educated at York, was influential in the court of Charlemagne. Alcuin's death in 804 marks the end of Northumbria's period of greatness, during which it exercised wide influence and set standards in religion, art and scholarship, the fruits of a short-lived but settled and

A damaged 14th-century statue in the shrine of St Cuthbert. The saint is holding the head of Oswald, King of Northumbria and also a saint. Oswald's head was a relic interred in Cuthbert's coffin.

widely connected aristocratic culture at the cross-roads of Northern Europe.

As a defining idea, and from time to time as a political reality, the kingdom of Northumbria, rooted in pre-Roman times, endured until at least the 12th century. After the Romans left it was revived under Saxon kings in the 6th century, and was sufficiently robust to survive destructive invasions from Scandinavia from the 8th to the 11th centuries, and even the arrival of the Normans after 1066. In the still undefined border regions, Northumbrians, though increasingly squeezed between their greater neighbours, owed no necessary allegiance to either Scotland or England except when self-preservation was at stake.

In precarious times, saints have often been the focus of social identity. St Cuthbert's cult proved an exceptionally successful bond across a wide swathe of the north, as the large number of churches dedicated to him in the border region and southern Scotland testifies. Adopted as the saint of the region soon after his death, he had a powerful unifying effect upon a territory with varied ethnic groupings and cultures. He was associated too with the political aspirations and separatist instincts

St Cuthbert with the head of St Oswald under his arm, from a Durham Priory manuscript of the late 14th century. A.I.3

of Bernicia and Northumbria. The presence of the uncorrupt body, especially when on the move, attended by his own guardians, the Community of St Cuthbert, holding their offices by hereditary succession, was the talisman that chiefly held together both the monastic tradition of Lindisfarne and the identity of wider Northumbria during times of danger and upheaval.

Even in Cuthbert's lifetime the Lindisfarne community had received generous gifts of land, from Ecgfrith of Bernicia and Oswine of Deira, in Cumbria and Yorkshire as well as Northumberland. In the 9th century, Bishop Ecgred of Lindisfarne added lands in Durham. The territories possessed by Lindisfarne were known as the Patrimony of St Cuthbert, and those who lived in them were the 'haliwerfolc', the holy man's people. The combination of popular devotion and landed wealth gave the Community a political and economic leverage which persuaded successive invaders to reach accommodation with it. It is no accident that the Cuthbert Community survived through an anarchic and destructive time in which other foundations, including Bede's at Jarrow, were lost.

Between the first Viking raid on Lindisfarne in 793 and the settling in Durham in 995, two tendencies provide some coherence in a time of confusion. One is the steady southward migration of the Community, prompted at least as much by the need to manage its widespread lands from a central location as by flight from danger. The other is the highly developed instinct

for survival which led the Community to seek alliances with any power that seemed likely to guarantee its privileges and independence. So we find it leagued successively with the royal house of Northumbria, the Scandinavian kings of York, the rulers of Wessex, and the noble house of Bamburgh. The diplomatic skills of the Community in presenting itself as politically indispensable, well practised in the 9th and 10th centuries, continued to serve it well in Durham, where it was required to adapt, in rapid succession, to Danes, Picts and Normans. In more modern times, small countries with powerful neighbours have followed a similarly pragmatic course.

THE COMMUNITY UPROOTED

In just over 100 years, there were three waves of Scandinavian incursion. The first was for plunder. The island refuge, secure for its first 150 years, suddenly found itself in the front line. Lindisfarne was raided by Vikings in 793, and the monks fled before them. Subsequent chroniclers milked the event in tabloid terms. *The Anglo-Saxon Chronicle* 100 years later recorded fiery dragons flying through the air. By the time the Durham monk Symeon narrated the event, 300 years of oral history had created raw melodrama: 'The pagans from the northern regions ... trampled the holy places with polluted feet, dug up the altars and seized all the treasures ... they killed some of the brothers; some they took away with them in fetters; many they drove out, naked and loaded with insults; and some they drowned in the sea.' However, when the monks returned they found Cuthbert's shrine intact, so we should assume a measure of exaggeration. But innocence was lost and the community unsettled. In 835 Bishop Ecgred moved both Aidan's wooden church and Cuthbert's body inland to Norham, on the Tweed, but by 875 both may have been back on the island, to meet a stronger Danish tide which had begun to flow in the 860s. This time they came to settle, not just for plunder. The influx brought Northumbrian culture to an end, with the destruction of monasteries and the intellectual and cultural life vested in them. In 875 Bishop Eardwulf of Lindisfarne led the exodus of the monks, either from Norham or from their island, carrying with them all their treasures: the Lindisfarne Gospels, their relics and the body of Cuthbert in his coffin, to which the head of King Oswald was added for the journey. For the next seven years the Community of St Cuthbert was on the move, travelling widely across the north, to Lancashire, Cumbria and Galloway with their curious burden. During these same years the rampaging Danish leader Halfdan led the destruction of the Northumbrian monasteries. Yet despite the chroniclers' tales of woe, the Community grew in wealth and landed possessions during this time, and also travelled towards the centres of Danish power rather than away from them. Since the Danes had come to stay, there was an inevitable interaction with them, and it seems that the Lindisfarne people reached some understanding with the fierce immigrants.

So rather than pitying the monks as fugitives, we should think of them as doing the round of their estates, both boosting morale and proving their right to possession by manifesting the body of Cuthbert on the progress, their authority reinforced by the addition of the head of a royal saint. In the iconography of medieval Durham, in stone, glass and wall painting, the most popular image was of Cuthbert holding Oswald's head in his hands, and a damaged 14th-century statue of the subject stands by the shrine in the Cathedral today. So the chronicler's tale of the random 'wanderings of St Cuthbert' is almost certainly more symbolic than real, and enabled the elaboration of the episode into a myth in which the saint's miracles are prominent. An attempted escape to Ireland by ship was thwarted by a storm that Cuthbert raised, and a precious Gospel lost overboard was recovered undamaged on a Galloway shore. Certainly the Community preserved its wealth and political importance during its travels, and even visited its estate at Crayke just outside York, the heart of Danish power.

Two of the apostles carved on St Cuthbert's oak coffin of the late 7th century, and now displayed in the Cathedral Treasury.

CHESTER LE STREET

The strongest evidence of political dexterity on the part of the church belongs to the year 883. The dreaded Halfdan died, and Cuthbert's relics were transported to a pagan ritual at which his successor, Guthred, was initiated, and which the Bishop of Lindisfarne and Abbot of Carlisle attended. One account even has Cuthbert select Guthred by appearing in a dream to the Abbot of Lindisfarne, commanding him to locate and free a Danish slave, who turned out to be Guthred. Whatever the circumstances, the Community picked up yet more land south of the Tyne. The decision in the same year to settle at Chester le Street was shrewd: the location was convenient both for Guthred's protection and patronage and for the management of their new estates. Guthred was awarded the saint's protection against the pagan Picts and was duly rewarded: Cuthbert destroyed them with an earthquake at the point of battle.

The saint and his attendants remained at Chester le Street for just over a century. It had been the site of a bishop's residence before 883, so it was not unknown territory. There were the remains of a Roman fort which made it defensible in a crisis, and a timber church as at Lindisfarne was probably constructed in the centre of the fort, on a site still occupied by the town's present church.

Instability in the north was compounded by a third invasion early in the 10th century by Vikings from Norway, and for a time conflict raged between the two groups of Scandinavians. The Norwegians captured York in 919, and set up a kingdom stretching from east to west between York and Dublin. It came to an abrupt end in 954 with the death of Eric Bloodaxe, the Viking lord of York, in battle with Northumbrians at Stainmore, in the Pennines.

There was a vacuum of power, filled by the overlordship of Wessex, an important step towards the incorporation of Northumbria with the south. Wessex exercised indirect control through the hereditary Earls of Northumberland based at Bamburgh, to whom the Community now turned for protection. The reward for the clients of Wessex was the acquisition of regalities, privileges and liberties exempting them from taxation or obligations of loyalty to southern kings: Tynedale, Redesdale and the Liberty of Durham among them. Such a network of semi-independent lands preserved in a partial form the old kingdom of Northumbria. The tenacity of Northumbrian identity against all the political odds was remarkable. But it was a tenacity paralleled by, and not wholly separable from, the survival of the Community of St Cuthbert.

The death of Guthred in 895 removed their protector. New manoeuverings were now needed to secure their wealth and influence, and the Community turned to Wessex, resurgent under King Alfred, for an alliance. The West Saxons were eager to confront the Scandinavians, and Cuthbert of course provided Alfred with miraculous assistance. So for a time Saxon Wessex and Northumbria were in opposition to Danes and Picts. The link with Wessex was fruitful: gifts poured into the shrine at Chester le Street. Athelstan arrived on pilgrimage around 934, when the tomb was opened for him, and a list of gifts (a 'testamentum') was placed on the saint's head. A richly illuminated *Life of Cuthbert* by Bede, one of these gifts, survives at Corpus Christi College, Cambridge. Ten years later Edmund visited the shrine and placed two gold bracelets on the body, before confirming the rights and privileges of the Community, doubtless what it was angling for. Later in the century there was a visit from Archbishop Dunstan, who recorded that Cuthbert's body was 'not only unspoiled and whole, but even pleasantly warm to the touch'.

Top: *Athelstan presenting a Gospel book to the shrine of St Cuthbert in 934. Corpus Christi College Cambridge MS 183.*

Left: *The figure of Peter the Deacon, about five inches in height, from the silk and gold embroidered maniple found in Cuthbert's tomb in 1827. It is dated by an inscription on the reverse to 909–16, and is thought to have been presented to St Cuthbert's shrine by King Athelstan in 934. The maniple and a stole also found in the tomb are the only surviving pieces of Anglo-Saxon embroidery depicting human figures.*

THE FOUNDATION OF DURHAM

THE CHOICE OF DURHAM

The recorded history of Durham begins in 995. The body of St Cuthbert and its attendant community took up permanent residence on the summit of the wooded peninsula almost encircled by the River Wear. The 70 years before the arrival of the Normans were both active and perilous. A church was built to house the saint's shrine, pilgrims began to arrive to venerate him, and a sequence of alliances was formed for protection in violent and lawless times. By 1066 the Cuthbert tradition was firmly rooted in what was to be its enduring territory 'inter aquas', between Tyne and Tees.

There are two versions of the choice of Durham, the practical and the mythic. Chester le Street was menaced by the real or rumoured presence of Danes over-wintering by the Tyne and threatening to establish settlements. After a brief retreat to Ripon, the monks turned north again in search of security. There had been a timely alliance between the daughter of Aldhun, the bishop, and Uchtred of the House of Bamburgh. Uchtred, it is said, assisted the Community in preparing the site by impressing all able-bodied labourers between the Tees and the Coquet. The new settlement was quickly and judiciously fortified, for in 1006 a Scottish raid laid siege to the place, and Uchtred and his men had to repel them. The Community had its necessary protector, but there was gain for Uchtred too: his defence of Northumbria against Scots in the north and west and Danes in the south was buttressed by his close association with the saint.

The mythic version of the arrival, fashioned over 100 years later by Symeon, a Benedictine monk and chronicler of Durham, begins with a visionary warning to Aldhun of a Danish attack. After the escape to Ripon, while on the road back to Chester le Street, at 'Wrdelau', east of Durham, the cart bearing Cuthbert's coffin halted and could not be moved. Aldhun ordered three days of fasting, prayer and vigil in the hope of a miraculous sign of the saint's intention, since he clearly had no wish to return to Chester le Street. A holy man named Eadmer was vouchsafed the command to translate the body to 'Dunholme' (hill island), and then the cart moved easily onward again. Symeon's blending of vision and miracle furnished the settlement at Durham with an appropriate and dignified foundation myth, though he is realistic enough to mention also the site's natural defences.

Not included by Symeon, and not appearing in print until *The Rites of Durham* of 1594, is a further embellishment of the foundation myth presumed to have belonged to oral history for some centuries. Cuthbert is supposed to have instructed his clerks, in a vision, to settle in Dunholme, though without telling where Dunholme was to be found. But a milkmaid was overheard telling another that a stray cow had been found at Dunholme, and the mystery was solved when the milkmaid led the community to the hilltop. The

The ceremonial entrance to Bishop Hugh du Puiset's Great Hall in Durham Castle. Of the mid-12th century, it is the most elaborate Norman stonework in the city. It is located on the first floor of the castle, and is now enclosed by the Tunstall Gallery, added by Cuthbert Tunstall in the first half of the 16th century.

tale is commemorated in a bas-relief sculpture at the north-east corner of the exterior; the present version, thought to be a replacement for an older, eroded carving, was put in place during the restorations at the end of the 18th century.

Symeon asserts that the peninsula was a virgin site. Given its strategic attractions, this is unlikely. A handful of Roman artefacts from the hilltop may have belonged to a late or post-Roman farm, and though there is insufficient evidence for continuous occupation before 995, remains of wooden houses of the mid 10th century have been excavated, turning up leather and pottery fragments. So it is probable that there was a small agricultural settlement somewhere among the trees, with some clearances for cultivation.

With the help of Uchtred and his enforced workers, more timber was cleared and building began. The saint was first housed in 'a little church of boughs of trees', next in the 'Alba Ecclesia', the White Church, a larger structure of wattle and daub, and then in 998 Aldhun's 'Ecclesia Major', a substantial church of stone, was consecrated. The location of this church has not yet been established but the best guess is that it stood to the south of the present cathedral, across the cloister garth, for until the dissolution of the monastery in 1539, a tomb and statue of Cuthbert on the east side of the garth was believed to mark his first resting place.

ANGLO-SAXON DURHAM

By the time of Aldhun's death in 1016 or 1017 the church was complete and already pilgrims were visiting. Visitors brought money and needed food and shelter; a market was set up and trades began to flourish. Durham began to turn into a town; the age of tourism was under way. By the middle of the century, tales of Cuthbert's miracles were drawing pilgrims from a distance: a group of monks arrived from Sherborne. Durham's allure for pilgrims was shrewdly promoted by the unscrupulous

sacrist Elfred Westhou in the first two decades of the 11th century. He travelled widely and with intent around the religious houses of the north, and succeeded in purloining a large number of holy bones: hermits, bishops, at least two abbesses, St Boisil from Melrose and, most triumphantly, the skeleton of Bede from Jarrow in 1022. All these relics were added to Cuthbert's shrine to give Durham a monopoly of venerable remains in the north. It is a mystery why his reputation as a body

A battle scene from the Book of Maccabees in the Puiset Bible of the mid-12th century. The forceful soldiers in Norman armour may be a reminder of The Harrying of the North by troops of William the Conqueror in 1069–70. A.II.i Vol.3

The full range of the castle, lit by a shaft of sun, seen from the Cathedral tower.

snatcher did not go before him as he sought out hospitality, and why he was not searched when he departed with more baggage than he brought. 'Pious theft' was widespread in Europe by agents who appointed themselves to enact the supposed 'decisions' of saints about where they wished their remains to rest.

The authority of the House of Bamburgh was weakened by the struggles against Northumbria's enemies, and the Durham Community prudently sought a bond with the Danish court of Wessex. Aldhun's successor Edmund, chosen in 1020, was confirmed in his office by Cnut at Winchester, 'much loved and honoured by the king'. It suited Cnut also to foster an alliance with the Community to benefit from its status and influence in the north. So around 1031 he made a barefoot pilgrimage from Garmondsway, near modern Trimdon, to Durham, a distance of five miles, where he confirmed the privileges of the Community and presented still more lands. Such an ally was a blessing in these violent years, for the opportunist Scots were a constant threat. In 1040 Duncan besieged Durham, only to be driven back north, where he was murdered by Macbeth. Between 1058 and 1061 Malcolm Canmore, exploiting the

growing political disarray of Northumbria, raided regularly. On a particularly destructive spree in 1061 he captured slaves and booty, ravaged what remained of Lindisfarne and briefly laid siege to Durham itself.

The misery of Northumbria deepened in the mid century, when it was ruled with great severity by two outsider earls. Siward, a Dane from York, killed the son of Earl Uchtred of Bamburgh and claimed the title, outrageously marrying into the family whose kinsman he had murdered. Though Siward repelled the Scots and rooted out brigands, providing a temporary peace from which Durham benefited, his strong-arm tactics provoked instability and resentment. He insulted the Community in Durham when he appointed another outsider, the Peterborough monk Aethelric, as their bishop without consulting their views. (Aethelric and his brother Aethelwine had been invited to Durham by Bishop Edmund, who wanted to learn more about monastic life in a Benedictine community.) Siward died in 1055 and Aethelric, deprived of his patron, resigned the see and fled back to Peterborough. But Siward was succeeded as earl by Tostig of Wessex, younger brother of Harold Godwinson, destined to die in battle at Hastings. He too refused to allow Cuthbert's monks a

The Norman Chapel in Durham Castle, the oldest surviving structure above ground in the city, completed by 1080. Its fine state of preservation is accounted for by the construction of a larger chapel immediately above it in the 12th century when it became redundant.

voice in the selection of their bishop, and crassly appointed Aethelwine to the position. The Community took its revenge for both insults by claiming that both the brothers were villains who had robbed Cuthbert's church. Resentment of outsiders and the earl's trampling on their traditional rights may be closer to the reason why the last two Anglo-Saxon bishops of Durham passed into history vilified by later chroniclers.

Tostig over-reached himself. He murdered several members of the rival House of Bamburgh, including the popular Cospatric, and greedily tried to exact a punitive tax which the Northumbrians believed infringed their traditional privileges. It was doubly resented as a move to incorporate Northumbria into the kingdom of Wessex. There was an uprising: Tostig's residence in York was sacked and he fled to Flanders. Because of their dislike of Aethelwine and the manner of his appointment, the Durham monks were deeply implicated in the revolt, led by the redoubtable old relic-snatcher Elfred Westhou, still sacrist. In March 1065, in a deliberately provocative act, they put on display in Durham the body of King Oswine of Deira, murdered in parallel circumstances to Cospatric nearly 400 years earlier.

As the Anglo-Saxon era neared its close, the Community of St Cuthbert in Durham had established itself as a wealthy and influential political and religious force in the north of England. It had learned to survive and even prosper at times of extreme political instability through a sequence of shrewd alliances with powerful groups and individuals. The monks had preserved and extended their estates; rulers had come to them on state visits. Their rights and possessions had been repeatedly confirmed. Above all they had maintained their independence, so that every aspiring ruler of the north had to begin by coming to a reckoning with Cuthbert's people as indispensable allies. Now it was the turn of the Normans.

Capitals in the Norman Chapel: a mermaid flanked by two vividly carved beasts.

NORMAN DURHAM

'This city is famous throughout Britain, on its steep foundation, wondrously rising up about a rocky base. The Wear flows round it with a strong current in whose waters live many kinds of fish …. In the city too, famous among men, lies Cuthbert the holy and blessed.'

An Anglo-Saxon poem written at Durham in the 11th century captures the marvel of the new settlement as experienced by its early inhabitants. The tranquillity conveyed in part be attributed to poetic licence: the times were unstable as well as unhygienic. Between 1065 and 1080 the city and district were riven by episodes of ultimate violence. William the Conqueror inherited challenges in the north which he failed to understand, and compounded them by making just about every mistake an occupying power can make. There was a great deal of shock and awe but no effective control of insurgents for at least 15 years. The king appointed unsuitable agents, two of whom were assassinated and one he had to execute himself. He failed to grasp that 'the leaders of the North thought of it as a separate territory' and were therefore hostile to outsiders, especially those from the South who used repressive tactics and tried to exact unjust taxes. He provoked the Northumbrians into becoming a swarm of angry bees that posed a greater threat to the survival of Durham than the Normans themselves. His blunders were the direct cause of bloodshed and suffering excessive even by the standards of the age, and, during the 'harrying of the north', of what would now be classed as genocide. His policy for ultimate control of the north hinged upon the development of Durham as his provincial capital and garrison town. So the city with its religious community is at the very heart of the Norman endeavour to seize control of the north, and both, by the end of the century, were to be wholly transformed by it.

William at first tried to govern through native deputies. But his choice of Copsig, who had been implicated in the rule of the loathed Tostig, was a disaster. He too tried to exact a severe tax to help William pay his chiefly mercenary soldiers, so it was easy for Osulf, of the House of Bamburgh, to mount guerilla warfare from the hills, especially after the provocation of William's promotion of Copsig to the earldom of Northumbria, which the Bamburgh house regarded as theirs. Osulf trapped Copsig feasting at Newburn in March 1067; Copsig took refuge in a church which was set on fire, and as he fled, Osulf beheaded him. William sold the earldom later in the year to another Cospatric, who proved little more than a glorified brigand of dubious loyalty.

William now turned to a Norman baron, Robert Cumin, appointed Earl of Northumbria towards the end of 1068, and sent north with 700 greedy soldiers. He reached a suspiciously quiet Durham in January 1069, to be greeted by the despised Bishop Aethelwine with a warning of danger. Cumin shrugged it off, and released his men to plunder the town for a day. Just before dawn, almost certainly with the assistance of the citizens, a Northumbrian force which had strategically withdrawn broke through the city gates. Making skilled use of the narrow alleys of the town, they took the Normans unprepared, satiated with excess, and there was a general massacre. Cumin himself was cornered in Aethelwine's palace, which was fired. He and his bodyguard were cut down as they tried to escape. 'All save one were killed … the streets were filled with blood and carcasses.' Cuthbert delivered a timely miracle by changing the direction of the wind just as the flames were poised to engulf his church. A second miracle bought precious time: William sent a reprisal squad north at once but it was lost in the thick fog with which Cuthbert draped Northallerton, near the boundary of the diocese, and was forced to withdraw.

The slaughter of the Normans in Durham was the trigger for a widespread rebellion in the north, and for a time it seemed that the land north of the Humber would become a breakaway kingdom. There were other predators around: Swein with 240 Danish ships landed in 1069, capturing York and killing the garrison there. An alliance between him and the Northumbrians would place the north beyond Norman control. William's response was first deft, then brutal. He dealt with the Danes by a bribe: they might freely plunder the east coast over the winter on condition they went home in the spring. Now the north was in his sights. In the winter of 1069–70 he moved north, spent a cheerless Christmas in the ruins of York and then set his men on to lay waste much of Yorkshire, both as punishment for the rebellion and to scorch the earth to reduce its capacity to attract or support the Danes. Guerilla bands were hunted down in the hills; villages, their stock and supplies were burned and the peasants killed or sold into slavery. Famine awaited any survivors since it was winter. The chroniclers record wholesale destruction and slaughter, as chroniclers are paid to do. The *Historia Regum Anglorum* describes a land 'deprived of anyone to cultivate it for nine years, an extensive desert prevailed on all sides. There was no village inhabited between York and Durham; they became the homes of wild beasts and robbers, and were a great source of fear for travellers.' The Domesday survey of 1086 provides evidence to support this grim view of the harrying in Yorkshire. Over half the villages in the North Riding and more than a

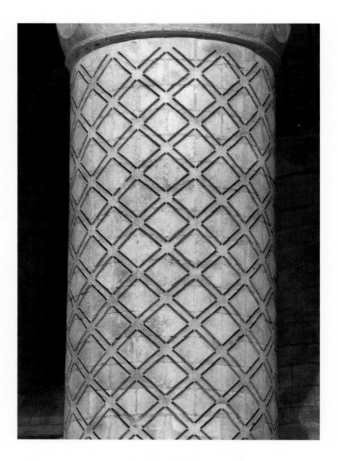

third in the East and West Ridings were still wholly or partially waste, and recorded populations were minuscule: 2,362 in the East Riding, 2,014 in the North.

William reached Durham in January 1070. The previous month, hearing of his purpose, the Cuthbert Community had thought it prudent to convey themselves and Cuthbert's body out of range of Norman wrath, fearing that 'on account of both the slaughter of the earl (Cumin) and of the Normans at York, the king's sword should despatch equally the innocent and the guilty in indiscriminate slaughter.' So they returned to Lindisfarne after a 200-year absence. The folk memory had failed. Confounded by the presence of the sea barring access, they turned to Cuthbert for help, and the sea miraculously parted to allow them across. Once news reached the island that William had gone on his way south, the Community

Three different patternings of the circular pillars in the Nave.

The Conqueror was in Durham for the second and last time in October 1072 after chasing the Scots. He visited Cuthbert's shrine, in the tradition of Saxon and Danish kings. In all probability, the event was arranged for the benefit of the Cuthbert Community, so that William could learn something of the history of their church, present gifts and, most importantly, confirm privileges. Symeon, however, presents a sequence which proclaims Cuthbert's power and William's failure. The king wished to see whether the saint's body was really present in the shrine, and vowed to execute 'all those of superior rank throughout the city who had presumed to impose upon him' if it were not. During All Saints' Day mass, William was struck by a sudden fever, left the church in haste and galloped south until he was safe beyond the Tees.

crept back to Durham in March, rededicated the plundered church and returned Cuthbert to his shrine.

William's Yorkshire clearances had savagely terminated all possibility of a unified northern rebellion and, *pour encourager les autres*, he arranged some token marauding by his men as far as the Tyne. Now he could make a fresh start in Durham with a new bishop and earl. From Liège in Lorraine he summoned Walcher, a secular cleric rather than a monk, to be bishop, replacing the hapless Aethelwine, who had resigned his see and headed south, only to be either murdered or starved as a prisoner in Wessex. The new earl was Waltheof, son of Siward, the earl who had bullied Northumbria before the Conquest. To ensure his loyalty, William bound him to his own family by marriage.

While in Durham, the king had ordered Waltheof to begin building a castle. With the massacre of Cumin and his men still fresh in the memory, William hoped it 'might be a place to keep the bishop and his household safe from the attacks of assailants'. But it was also a symbol of Norman authority, a fortress strong enough to deter any thoughts of rebellion, and a palace suitable for the king's representative. Waltheof began the work – a curtain wall, mound and moat, and the east and west ranges – but building continued under Walcher and his successor bishops for over 100 years before it acquired its formidable profile on the cliff above the Wear. By the end of the 12th century Durham was a fortress city.

Marriage was insufficient to guarantee Waltheof's loyalty. In 1075 he was implicated in a Norman plot

Each pillar was ingeniously constructed from a single template of stone: the squared, the chevron and the spiral templates are pictured here.

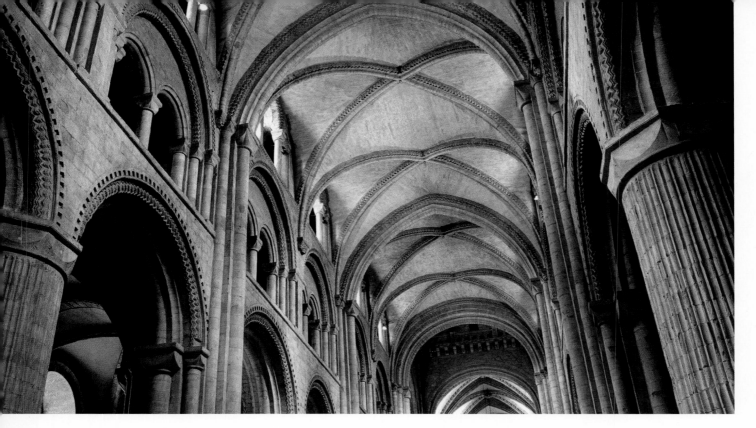

The rounded Norman arch at the east end of the Nave was succeeded by the early Gothic pointed arches as the building progressed westwards in the first quarter of the 12th century.

against the king, and though he had warned Archbishop Lanfranc of the threat and carried a load of treasure to William in Normandy in expiation, there was no forgiveness, and he was executed on his return to England, a Saxon scapegoat. William now sold the earldom to Walcher, whose uniting of political and religious roles was unique in England: he became the prototype Prince-Bishop of the north. His dual role and his wielding of a ruthless private army did not endear him to Northumbrians, and their opportunity to strike at the Norman regime arose from a dispute on Walcher's council. Leobwin, a relative of Walcher and his archdeacon, contrived the murder of Ligulf, a Northumbrian magnate, and his family. Walcher was entangled in a blood feud further poisoned by racial conflict. He was enticed by the Northumbrians to a meeting at Gateshead, at which the bloodthirsty Northumbrians cut down most of his company. He and Leobwin fled into St Michael's Church, but it was set on fire. 'When he was able no longer to bear the heat of the raging flames, he commended his soul with prayers to God, and went to the door, making the sign of the cross with his fingers and covering his eyes and head with the pall he was wearing. Alas! Alas! on the very threshold he was pierced through and through with spears, and many

sword wounds were even inflicted on his dead body.' In triumph the Northumbrians swept on to attack Durham, but its defences held. William's response was predictable: he sent his half-brother, Odo of Bayeux, on another punitive expedition directed against both Durham and Northumbria, and for the second time in a decade the diocese was 'reduced to a wilderness'.

With Walcher's murder and Odo's reprisal it must have seemed that William's attempts to control the north were mired in a cycle of violence. His best hope of pacification, the colonizing of the area with Norman barons, had been thwarted by the extent of the devastation he had created. Neither Durham nor Northumbria was included in the Domesday survey of 1086, indicative that the region was still not incorporated into England and was therefore under no obligation to the English exchequer. But from 1080 for about 50 years, as the Scots were driven back by a mixture of negotiation and military defeat, Norman settlers moved into the north, largely displacing Anglo-Saxon landowners. By 1135 the district was effectively colonized as far as the River Tweed, though the Patrimony of St Cuthbert remained inviolate. The great castle was rising in Durham as the practical and symbolic centre of Norman power. In 1080 William's son Curthose had built New Castle, just across the Tyne from the scene of Walcher's murder, affirming the extension of power to the enemy's heartland. The next step in the consolidation of the Norman empire in the north was the reform of the church in Durham. The fever raised by Cuthbert could only be allayed by destroying the Northumbrian foundation of Cuthbert's church and appropriating its status in the service of the new regime.

FOUNDING OF THE MONASTERY

Benedictines had led a renewal of the monastic ideal in the south of England before the Conquest. Soon after 1066 their influence began to spread north. Curiosity about the holy places of Northumbria had been aroused by the reading of Bede, whose *History* was widely known. Around 1073 Aldwin, a monk from Winchcombe in Gloucestershire, collected two friends from neighbouring Evesham, Elfwy and Reinfred ('who was ignorant of letters'), and they travelled north on foot, with one donkey to carry their holy baggage, to take up residence on the Tyne, at Monkchester. Bishop Walcher of Durham invited them to return to the ruins of Bede's Jarrow, to renew the great tradition there. Walcher intended to found a Benedictine house at Durham, and in 1075 began to build a dormitory. The Norman Undercroft, on the south side of the present Cloister, is Walcher's work.

In November 1080 William of St. Calais was appointed the first Norman bishop of Durham in succession to the murdered Walcher. He was an abbot who had caught William's eye for the political dexterity he had displayed in Maine, and had the makings of an ideal courtier-bishop. Within two years of his arrival in Durham he had supplanted the Community of St Cuthbert by a Benedictine monastery adjacent to the saint's church. It was a project requiring all his manipulative skills.

An illumination from an 11th-century Commentary on the Psalter by St Augustine. The figures, from top to bottom, are Christ, William of St. Calais, founder of the monastery, and Robert Benjamin the monk, possibly the illustrator. B.II.13

The Community which had founded Durham was well established, wealthy and highly regarded as the lineal successors of the sacred Lindisfarne tradition, and closely bound up with regional identity. But its members were not monks as the Normans knew them. They did not practise celibacy nor live communally. They lived privately with wives and families, held land individually and inherited their offices. 'Clerks' is a more accurate term for them than 'monks'. They were ruled by a dean; there were seven senior clerks, descendants of the original seven bearers

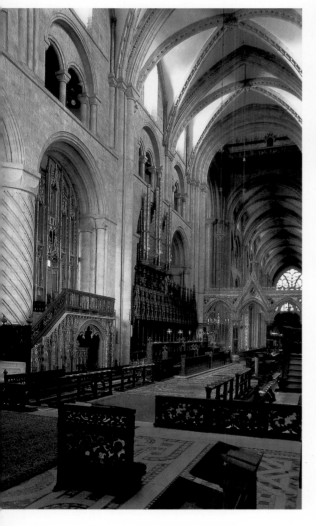

Left: *The Quire, looking south-west. The vaulting here is of the late 13th century, and replaced the original Norman round arched vaulting, which had become structurally unsound.*

Above: *A 13th-century corbel on the north side of the Quire, of one animal devouring another.*

Above right: *A piece of oak shuttering still in place in the South Triforium gallery. Wooden shuttering was used to support arches while the rubble and mortar infill solidified. This piece proved impossible to remove afterwards.*

What he wanted was the nationalization, or perhaps 'Normanization', of the most influential native religious body in the occupied land. He prepared the ground carefully. On a journey to Rome on behalf of the king in 1082 he secured papal blessing for his project, and letters of anathema against all who obstructed it. He may also have picked up from Lanfranc the regulations he had devised for his Benedictine foundation at Canterbury, and gained his support. By now he also had 23 Benedictines waiting in the wings at Jarrow and Monkwearmouth, whom he summoned to Durham. By Whit Sunday 1083 all was ready for the takeover. St. Calais installed the Benedictines, entrusting to them the church and shrine of St Cuthbert. Within a week a chapter had been formed and monastic offices assigned. Aldwin from Winchcombe was made the prior, and the Patrimony of St Cuthbert was shared out between the bishop and the priory. The clinching argument for the move was one beloved of bureaucrats down the ages, rationalization: the district could not support more than one monastic foundation.

Of the fate of the traditional clerks, we know little. One of their number, the dean, may have joined the new order, though the requirement of celibacy must have excluded most. They seemed to have been exiled from Durham, either pensioned off or simply cast off. There is no historical record of protest. Our

of Cuthbert's body when they left the island, and a larger number of junior clerks. So they must have seemed anomalous to the Normans, both as a religious order and politically because of their affiliation with Northumbrian independence. William of St. Calais had to displace them while retaining the status of the cult without alienating its regional devotees.

Two wild boars on a pew end in the Durham Light Infantry Chapel: an oak carving of 1934 in memory of Colonel Wilson.

knowledge of what really occurred is obstructed rather than clarified by the closest primary source, that of Symeon the chronicler, who had become a monk *c.*1090, written between 1104 and 1107 when he was a member of the priory. His task was to justify the change by conveying to posterity a wholly approving account of the organization to which he himself belonged and of which he had been a founding member. His narrative is specious enough to make him a distinguished member of the polemical fraternity.

Symeon's arguments are well rehearsed and deficient in historical foundation. He claims the Lindisfarne community had fallen away from its original purity and 'followed the allurements of a laxer mode of life'. For the division of the land between bishop and monks he invented a precedent in the earlier history. To these tendentious claims that the new monastery represented a return to the spirit and practice of the Lindisfarne community, he added the spurious element of Cuthbert's misogyny, ideologically convenient at a time when the habit of married clergy was being subverted. Women were banned from approaching the shrine, and the prohibition continued when the new cathedral was built.

The political adroitness of St. Calais and Symeon's subsequent polemic succeeded in presenting apparent change as continuity with the past. The clerks of St Cuthbert were discredited and ousted, but their tradition was honoured and taken over by 'worthier successors'. The system of land ownership which had linked the Cuthbert community with its locality was dismantled, though the sharing of lands between the bishop as titular head of the priory and the priory itself was to prove contentious later on, when ambitious bishops without St. Calais' tender feelings for his own foundation succeeded to power.

St. Calais, like many later bishops, was often absent for long periods on royal business. He took a leading part in the drawing up of Domesday Book, and frequently figures as a witness to the royal seal on legal documents. He implicated himself, or was implicated by others, in a coup attempt against William Rufus by Odo and Curthose in 1088, was tried for treason at Old Sarum and exiled to Normandy for three years. In his absence, work on the monastic buildings continued: to the early buildings at the south end of the east cloister, which may have been the first dormitory for the monks, was added the Refectory on the south.

Returning to Durham in 1091 he brought many gifts: treasures for the altar and precious manuscripts, some of which remain in the Library today. His time in Normandy had been fruitful: its architecture apparently gave him the inspiration to replace the Anglo-Saxon minster, less than 100 years old, with a more magnificent Romanesque cathedral. It would be the architectural equivalent of the displacement of the Cuthbert Community, a religious statement finally dissevering the saint's cult from its native roots, and a political affirmation of the triumph of Norman power in the north. 'Here we are; this is what we do; we are here to stay.' The Normans needed the saint and the allegiances he commanded, and here was the perfect way to show how highly they valued him. The consequence was to be, within an extraordinarily short span of 40 years, the completion of the Durham acropolis substantially as we still know it, 'as a lesson in the significance of the Norman Conquest without parallel in England'.

Far left: *A view into the North Transept from the South Nave Aisle.*

Above: *The length of the Cathedral seen from the gallery below the west window. In the foreground is the towering font cover commissioned by Bishop Cosin after the Restoration.*

THE NEW CATHEDRAL

'It was begun on Thursday 11 August in the year 1093 of our Lord's incarnation, the 13th of William's time as bishop, the 11th since he had brought together the monks at Durham. On that day the bishop and Prior Turgot … with the other brothers laid the first stones in the foundations. Shortly before [that is, on Friday 29 July] the bishop and prior after saying prayers with the brothers and giving their blessing had begun to dig the foundations. While the monks were responsible for building the monastic buildings, the bishop carried out the work on the church at his own expense.'

The only first-hand account of the building of the greatest icon of the Norman Conquest is by Symeon, who probably participated in the rituals and on this topic had presumably less pretext for distortion. St.

Calais had ordered the demolition of the Anglo-Saxon church before the new work began, but it is probable that at least the east end containing the shrine was left standing until Cuthbert's translation, the move from the old shrine to the new, in 1104. In any case, there was plenty of other stone to hand from the quarries along the Wear gorge, a sandstone known as Low Main Post, or Cathedral Sandstone. It was as if the peninsula was producing an exotic growth out of its own roots.

Other Saxon cathedrals in England had been swiftly replaced by Romanesque as a consequence of regime change: Canterbury in 1070, Lincoln 1072, St Albans 1077 and Winchester 1079, but at Durham the architectural triumph was more colossal not only by English but also by European criteria. The sheer bulk of the cathedral was bold enough: it raised the stakes for aspiring church builders across the Continent. Finer still was the master mason's solution to the challenge of crowning the interior space by a ribbed stone vault, the oldest surviving in Europe. Like other pilgrimage churches – St Albans, Bury, Winchester – the cathedral had an extended eastern arm to accommodate the shrine. But the determination of such churches to outdo one another in splendour may have prompted William to order a building with higher vaults and a more elaborate scheme of decoration than any other in England. If exile in Normandy had given him the inspiration for the work, his earlier visit to Rome also seems to have influenced his imagination. Not only is the plan of Durham virtually identical with Old St Peter's, but there are Roman precedents for Durham's patterned columns, harmoniously alternating with still more massive main piers. Pope Gregory III in the 8th century had added to the spiral columns first placed in St Peter's by Gregory the Great 200 years before, signalling the approach to a place of exceptional sanctity.

William of St. Calais died in 1096, with much of his wonderful conception still only in his mind's eye. But the momentum with which he had imbued the project was unflagging. Prior Turgot continued the work for the next three years before Ranulf Flambard arrived as the new bishop, by which time the walls of the east end and transepts had been raised.

Flambard was an expert in vacant bishoprics. Of humble birth, the son of a priest in Bayeux, he was an adroit and unscrupulous manipulator of money as minister and treasurer to William Rufus. 'Wherever there was money to be had, there was Flambard.' While sees were vacant, their incomes were diverted to the royal coffers. In 1097 Flambard had 16 such milch cows in his grasp, and had produced the revenue to enable Rufus to build the first Westminster Hall, the supreme space of royal self-glorification in Europe at that time. While in Rufus's service he had acquired the nickname he retained for the rest of his life: Flambard, 'the fiery one' or the flamboyant. Early in his time as royal procurator he had made so many enemies among the powerful by his arrogance that he was lured aboard a boat on the Thames in an assassination attempt, which he evaded through sheer bravado of manner. He had, naturally, made profits for himself as well, and he recognized the lucrative possibilities of Durham. He may even have bought the office from Rufus in 1099 as a solid gold investment. But at the height of his hitherto brilliant career, the heavens fell upon him. The still unexplained death of Rufus, struck down by a random or well-aimed arrow while hunting, removed Flambard's patron and accomplice. Within a fortnight he found himself arrested, deprived of his see and imprisoned in The Tower by Henry I, the new king. He was the ideal scapegoat for the old order. He was also a bold adventurer, a swashbuckler, driven by tempestuous energy. Episodes following the death of his master included his breaking out of The Tower by means of a rope too short to reach the ground (and he was a bulky man), and flight to Normandy in 1101, where he incited Robert Curthose to an invasion in an attempt to topple Henry. The most improbable of all outcomes, Flambard's reconciliation with the king and restoration of his bishopric, is only explicable on the assumption that he had agreed to act as Henry's agent and spy against Curthose in Normandy, where Flambard spent more time in the next few years than in Durham. The deal paid off: in 1106 Henry overran Normandy and locked up Curthose. But it was the end of Flambard's eventful career at the centre of affairs,

Above: *13th-century capitals and corbel at the south-east end of the North Quire Aisle.*

Middle: *Capital of cat face or mask in the Norman Chapel of Durham Castle. 11th century.*

Bottom: *A cat-like corbel, maybe a demon with pricked ears, on the west wall of the South Transept. 12th century.*

and he was now forced to apply his energies on the periphery. But second-best for Flambard was glorious for Durham.

A kind of James Bond of the medieval episcopate, Flambard laid no claim to spiritual gifts and took little heed of morality. His private life was disreputable and extravagant; his use of power corrupt. He filled a variety of positions in the diocese with his own relatives, known as 'nepotes episcopi' (though he had no hesitation in admitting to his own sons), and assigned to them monastic lands he had filched from the priory. Only the quick thinking of a niece, Christina of Markyate, averted his attempt to rape her, but his own quick thinking averted his dismissal for incontinence by a papal legate who had arrived in Durham to wield the hatchet. The legate was enticed into bed by a more acquiescent niece and publicly shamed.

Far left: *Looking west from the central tower to the Early English west towers, completed in the 12th century. Contrasting Norman stonework is clearly identifiable below the level of the parapet.*

Left: *The magnificent Norman door and arch give access to the Cathedral from the north-west cloister. The elaborately patterned ironwork on the door itself is original, from the early 12th century.*

Flambard used Durham money to try to buy back the king's favour, and failed. He had enormous wealth, and was able to act generously as a builder on behalf of cathedral, monastery and city. His dynamism in the construction business was unsurpassed. By the time of his death in 1128 the cathedral was complete but for the nave vault and western towers. He directed a massive expansion of the castle, adding the north wall and towers, a great hall and new gatehouse. He created Palace Green, by making 'as clear and level as a field the space between the Cathedral and the Castle, which had been invaded by numerous dwelling places, lest the church be soiled by their filth or emperilled by their fires'. In 1112 he founded the Hospital and Church of St Giles as a hostel for pilgrims, and around 1120 built Framwellgate Bridge across the Wear, one of the first stone arched bridges in England, to connect Bishop's

Borough to Old Borough, stimulating trade and happily providing the bishop with profitable tolls. In 1121 he built the first castle at Norham, on the Tweed, to challenge the Scots, as part of a strategy to make himself the ruler of a semi-independent territory. His appointment of two sheriffs to direct secular affairs and two archdeacons to rule on ecclesiastical matters marks the inception of what later came to constitute the Palatinate of Durham. Symeon knew him personally: he was 'impatient of leisure; he went on from labour to labour, thinking nothing done unless new enterprises pressed on the heels of those already accomplished'.

The fulfilment of St. Calais's vision occurred on 4 September 1104, when the saint's coffin was translated from the old church to the new. We can assume that by this year the vaulting and roof of the choir and maybe also the transepts were complete. Before the enshrining, Prior Turgot took the opportunity to report on Cuthbert's remains. He found two coffins, one inside the other. Within a chest covered with hide was a wooden coffin with scraps of linen cloth attached. There were two lids with iron rings, the lower resting on transverse bars, with a copy of the Gospel of St John placed upon it. The lower lid was lifted and a linen covering removed. The witnesses 'smelt an odour of the greatest fragrancy; and behold, they found the venerable body of the blessed Father: laying [sic] on its right side in a perfect state, and, from the flexibility of its joints, representing a person asleep rather than dead'. He was surrounded by relics: the head of Oswald, the bones of Bede and other saints, the prizes of Westhou's forays. The monks removed the body from the coffin, when it bent in the middle like a living man. The relics were taken out and the body replaced while Te Deum was quietly chanted. Twice more the body was exhibited in response to doubters, once to all the monks in the middle of the choir, laid out on robes and tapestries. To dispel all suspicion of conspiracy, it was shown also to the visiting Abbot of Seez, who could vouch for its preservation to the sceptics.

Then it was time for the ritual translation. A procession passed from the old shrine to the new, through 'the immense crowd waiting for it which from very joy burst into tears and fell flat on the ground, rendering it almost impossible for the procession to advance; all the while the voices of the singers were drowned by the strong cries of the praying, the exulting and the weeping for joy'. The procession halted outside the east end of the cathedral, and Flambard began his sermon. Now the narration turns from ecstasy to an endearing grumpiness: 'He kept preaching on, touching many points not at all appropriate to the solemnity and fairly wearing out the patience of many of his hearers by the prolixity of his discourse.' But even the mighty Flambard had to yield to a Cuthbert miracle. There was a sudden torrent of rain out of a clear sky. The monks broke off the sermon by seizing the coffin and hurrying it into the new church. At once the rain ceased, and 'nothing it had touched was in any way injured by it'.

At the end of his life in 1128, Flambard repented of at least some of his misdeeds and placed a ring on the altar as a token of his returning to the monks the estates he had stolen from them. His impact on Durham had

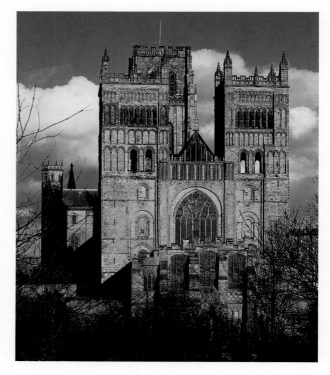

Above: *The West Towers and West Front from South Street, just before sunset in early April.*

Right: *The tomb of the Venerable Bede in the Galilee Chapel. His remains were stolen from Jarrow in an act of 'holy theft' in the 11th century and placed in Cuthbert's tomb. Then in the 12th century he had his own sanctuary near to Cuthbert's shrine. In the 14th century he was placed in the Galilee. The present tomb has a 19th-century slab placed on earlier stonework.*

been spectacular, and after his death he was celebrated nostalgically by Lawrence, a monk and one of the community's most stylish writers, who had joined the priory during Flambard's reign. 'His was a spirit worthy of Durham, worthy of riches, worthy of honour, dispensing hospitality with the best. That was our golden age, under Ranulf our bishop …. Durham demands such a man – great in spirit, liberal in spending – for Durham is no empty shell for the man who holds it.'

Within five years of his death the western towers up to roof level and the nave vaulting with its pointed transverse arches, again the earliest surviving example in Europe, were finished. Cuthbert had a shrine in a cathedral fit to amaze pilgrims (and attract their money); the equal of any pilgrimage church in Europe.

WAR AND PEACE 1136–1350

SCOTTISH RAIDS

There was to be little repose for either the monks or citizens of Durham. Between the arrival of the Scots in 1136 and the Black Death in 1349, monastery and town were in thrall to continual confrontation, conflict and actual or imminent violence. Over 500 years of intermittent border warfare intensified in the 12th and 14th centuries; masterful bishops were at war with the priory. In the midst of the turmoil a crisis in the lucrative pilgrimage business compelled the remarketing of Durham as a pilgrim destination.

Two kingdoms eyed the unclaimed lands in the north, in the midst of which sat the diocese of Durham and the Patrimony of St Cuthbert. Effective boundaries were undefined until the mid-12th century, and north of the Tees authority was uncertain. Any perceived weaknesses on either side acted as a magnet for the other: for the Scots, the weak presence of the Normans and the hostility to them of Northumbrians in the 11th century; the political anarchy of the rival reigns of Stephen and Matilda in the 12th; the incompetence of Edward II and the distraction for England of the French Wars in the 14th; for the English, the political vacuum arising from the disputed Scottish crown at the end of the 13th century.

The Normans had wanted to plant settlers in the disputed lands from the start, but it was only during the 12th century that Norman barons began to take up lands as far as the Tweed. They were reluctant to colonize oat-growing areas, for their refined palates preferred bread made of wheat flour. Still, in Northumbria and Durham many new towns were planted between 1100 and 1200. The arrival of barons with their castle-centred societies, however, did not necessarily improve the defences of the region against highly mobile raiders conducting guerilla warfare: they simply by-passed the castles. Additionally, Scotland held most of the advantages: greater population and prosperity, and proximity to the substantial city of Edinburgh. In contrast the bishops of Durham and the border barons were largely abandoned by their remote centre of government to fend for themselves. The north of England was also disunited, riven by a patchwork of semi-independent fiefdoms known as franchises, not only Durham itself ('the lordship of the blessed Cuthbert'), but also Redesdale, Tynedale, Hexhamshire, Tynemouth, Islandshire, Norhamshire and Bedlingtonshire.

Durham, as seat of the bishopric, garrison town and centre of the Cuthbert cult, was in the very eye of the turbulence. Yet the Haliwerfolc felt their primary allegiance was to their saint and patron, not to either of the kingdoms hemming them in, to neither of which did they feel they belonged. Moreover, many Scots felt great devotion to Cuthbert. The Scottish kings Malcolm III and Alexander I were present in Durham, the first for the rituals attending the laying of the foundation stone in 1093 and the second for the translation of Cuthbert to the new shrine in 1104. Donations and gifts of land came as readily from Scots as from English and

The ruined nave of the 12th-century Lindisfarne Priory. The patterning of the sandstone pillars embodies its kinship to the mother church in Durham, completed a generation before.

St Cuthbert's tomb, east of the Quire, High Altar and Neville Screen. The shrine was demolished in 1538 by order of Henry VIII's commissioners, and the saint's body disinterred. It was reburied in the original place four years later. The lines traced on the stone floor mark the shape of the first Norman apse of the Cathedral.

The pair: Wall paintings of a king and a bishop face one another on the east wall of the Galilee Chapel. The formalized figures probably represent Richard I and Bishop Hugh du Puiset, and mark the dedication of the chapel in 1189. But they also allude to an older pairing of king and bishop in the 7th century: Oswald of Northumbria and Cuthbert.

Northumbrians. Unitl the 14th century, Durham was spared the worst of the raiding just because it was Cuthbert's home. It was Edward I's aggression towards the Scots after 1296 that finally extinguished the long-cherished idea – part tradition, part dream – of a kingdom of the north. Thereafter Scottish allegiance to Cuthbert waned, as did gifts in his honour. He was now only a north of England saint, so that during the worst of the Scottish raids in the early 14th century, Durham escaped plunder only by bribery: the cost of eight truces between 1311 and 1327 amounted to over £5,000 (£1.6m) in Scotgeld.

The aim of border warfare in the 12th century was, for the Scots, to push the de facto border as far south as possible, ideally to the River Tees. In 1136 King David of Scotland invaded. He had been brought up at the Norman court, was brother-in-law to Henry I, and had served him as a marcher lord until he gained the Scottish crown in 1124. He was also uncle to Matilda, rival of Stephen for the crown of England, and the opportunity to advance his niece's interests alongside those of his country was irresistible. David swept down to the Tees largely unopposed, and there inexplicably lost the Battle of the Standard, which he had been expected to win. In the absence of a military explanation, Cuthbert was credited with the outcome, since the battle was fought on his land.

The anticipated emergence of a new Kingdom of the North was only half-achieved: by the Treaty of Durham in 1139 Stephen conceded the earldom of Northumbria to the Scots, and David named his son Henry as earl. North of the Tyne, Northumbria was now under Scottish control.

The next move was predictable. The Scots boldly tried to seize the bishopric for themselves, and were prevented, after a three-year struggle, only by the resolve of Prior Roger and his monks. William Cumin, the chancellor of Scotland, had been captured in 1138 and took up residence in Durham with Geoffrey Rufus, the bishop and an old friend and patron of Cumin. In 1141 Rufus was on his deathbed, and Cumin, who may have been his chosen successor, seized his chance. With Scottish backing he was able to take the castle and hold the town against attack. With a nucleus of support in the monastery, he claimed the see. But Prior Roger and other monks feared for the independence of the Patrimony of St Cuthbert if the Scots took over the see, and insisted on their right to choose their own bishop. No holds were barred in the battle for the bishopric. Cumin forged a papal letter naming him as bishop; Roger slipped secretly out of town and sent an embassy to Rome to acquire a genuine letter from Innocent II authorizing an election. Though Cumin imprisoned as many electors as he could, in 1143 William of Sainte-Barbe from York was chosen.

The desperate Cumin tried still more force. Sainte-Barbe's approach to the city was blocked by armed men supplied and led by local barons. Land deals had no doubt been offered as an incentive. The Teesside baron Roger de Conyers led forces which supported Sainte-Barbe and escorted him to Durham. Cumin and his men broke down the doors of the cathedral in order to fortify it: 'Mailed men with drawn swords charging between the altars … the whole cathedral was filled with roaring and shouting and tumult … they lit fires so that the smell of the meat they were cooking rose up in place of the scent of incense …' In this extremity the Scots acknowledged that Cumin's cause was lost, and Earl Henry upheld the canonical election of Sainte-Barbe. Cumin and his men took their revenge upon the locality with torture and destruction. But again Cuthbert's church had shown its resilience in surviving an ordeal of conflicting and violent pressures from powerful would-be exploiters, preserving its valued independence and insisting on its rights. By 1157 Northumbria was English again: Malcolm IV of Scotland met Henry II at Chester, and gave up the Scottish claim to Northumberland and Cumbria. From this time the Tweed became the established boundary between the kingdoms, despite a wobble when the hard-pressed Richard I was ready to hand Northumbria to the Scots for £10,000 (£3.5m) at the end of the century, a property deal that would have benefited his successor, King John, opposition to whom was led by the barons of the north.

The second wave of border warfare after the Battle of Bannockburn in 1314 was not about borders so much as Scottish independence, plus the temptation to harass the Auld Enemy in the rear at times when England was preoccupied with wars in France. Robert Bruce led the raids in the early 14th century and took Durham briefly in 1315, though the city managed to buy itself out of the misery that afflicted much of the surrounding district for the next 30 years.

Top: A Norman thief at Durham Cathedral: a drawing from the Oxford MS provides an impression of St Cuthbert's shrine.

Above: A medieval stained glass image of a soldier in a panel of fragments in the south wall of the Galilee Chapel.

Relief, and a 40-year breathing space was achieved, naturally enough, by St Cuthbert, who by now had long practice in looking after his own people. Back in 1091 when Durham was awash with Haliwerfolc seeking refuge in the no-man's-land between two armies, one advancing from the south, the other from the north, fervent prayers to the saint had gained the miracle of a simultaneous double retreat. Now in 1346, with the Scottish army camped just beyond the town at Bearpark, originally called Beaurepaire, the prior's country residence which they had ravaged as only marauding Scottish armies of the time could, Cuthbert intervened. He appeared to King David of Scotland on the eve of battle, requesting him, politely, not to invade his lands. He identified the battle site in advance, the high ground to the west of the town which became known as Neville's Cross. In yet another vision he commanded Prior Fossor and a group of monks to fix St Cuthbert's Banner, the cloth reputedly associated with him which had hung beside his shrine for 200 years, to the end of a spear and to carry it to the battlefield. For a good view they stood on top of an ancient earthwork, the Maiden's Bower, and watched the beaten Scots fleeing north after fierce hand-to-hand fighting. A further miracle protected the monastic party from harm. Prior Fossor wrote of what he had seen to Bishop Hatfield: 'At that hour [nones, or 2pm] to the greater joy of the people of the English Church, both sides fought strenuously, bitterly and very fiercely. However God Almighty, in whose hands lay the cords of the kingdom, provided the English with a miraculous victory over the Scots, restoring to those inhabitants of the northern parts, whom the Scots long oppressed, the joy of freedom for which they had yearned.'

In the 14th century the north of England had at last begun to attract the interest from royal government it had hitherto lacked. The Scottish wars had given it a

The Rose window in the Chapel of the Nine Altars, viewed from a high gallery.

strategic significance previously unheeded. The political and military situation advanced the powers of the County Palatine ruled by the Prince-Bishop, but simultaneously promoted the importance, wealth and influence of the chief land-owning dynasties who were to become his equals. Northern power in the 14th century began to crystallize around two families, the Nevilles of Raby and the Percys of Alnwick, and was to remain with them until the failure of the Rising of the North in 1569. In 1377 Henry Percy was made Earl of Northumberland by Richard II, inadvertently creating a power base in the north for the dynastic change that would see the king deposed in 1399.

THE CUTHBERT CULT

The cult of St Cuthbert is remarkable both for its continuity and its intensity. The cults of two other Anglo-Saxon saints, Etheldreda of Ely and Edmund of Bury, had also survived the Conquest and were thus competitors, but Cuthbert's popularity exceeded theirs, not only locally but all over Britain and mainland Europe, where his feast days were celebrated in monasteries. Many manuscript copies of the *Life of Cuthbert* survive: Bede was widely known and his influence was decisive for the extension of the cult. Until the compulsive surge of pilgrims to Canterbury following the murder of Thomas Becket, Durham was the major shrine in England, and, through shrewd marketing of itself, continued to prosper even in the years of Canterbury's great popularity.

The modern fixation with celebrity may be the best analogy as we try to comprehend the cults of saints in the Middle Ages. The popular hysteria which accompanies the appearances of musicians and film actors or even that which arose at the time of the death and funeral of the Princess of Wales in 1997 bore some similarity to the events surrounding the translation of St Cuthbert in 1104. The Cuthbert cult was fervent and obsessional. It had, as celebrities (and cathedrals!) still have in present-day culture, its fair share of both possessors and possessed. The sacrist, Elfred Westhou, used to trim Cuthbert's nails and hair, and hold conversations with him. The superiority of Cuthbert to his rivals in Ely and Bury was, self-evidently to his devotees, the flexibility of his body. Ever more relics were gathered around him, including a tooth and hair of Queen Margaret of Scotland, the comb and some finger-nails of St Malachy, and a rib bone of St Bernard of Clairvaux. Cuthbert's banner, placed by the shrine in the 1150s, was a talisman in wars against the Scots, usually carried to the battlefield by a posse of monks, as at Neville's Cross in 1346 and Flodden in 1513, both

A marriage ceremony: medieval glass in the west wall of the Galilee.

English victories. Its last recorded use was on the Pilgrimage of Grace in 1536. It was also taken out of the cathedral into the city when help was needed in extinguishing fires.

Tales of Cuthbert's miraculous powers were wide-ranging, at least until the end of the 12th century. We have already noted his readiness to protect his people, the Haliwerfolc, in the face of danger, but there are other unifying strands. His sojourn on Inner Farne had awarded him special powers over weather and the sea. He could raise or quell storms, protect seafarers, and command the wind to blow in two directions at once. For centuries 'Cuthbert' was the most popular name given to ships built in the north. Farne had given to him the propensity to manage animals and birds. He released prisoners, fed the hungry at times of famine

St Cuthbert's Gospel, formerly known as the Stonyhurst Gospel, is the oldest bound book in Britain. It may have been the saint's own copy of St John's Gospel, and was found in his tomb when his body was translated to its new shrine in 1104. British Library.

and performed an impressive range of miraculous cures, from madness, blindness and dysentery to bad colds, boils and toothache. No fewer than 83 churches in the north of England were dedicated to him. In Durham itself the copy of St John's Gospel (now in the British Library) found in his coffin in 1104, and brandished by Flambard in his sermon at the translation, was kept in a leather bag within a reliquary by the shrine. As a mark of honour for eminent visitors it was taken out and hung around their necks by a cord. It was no surprise that miracles should be reported, especially on Lindisfarne and Inner Farne. Around 1120, the monk Edward,

began to build a new church on Lindisfarne, and marked Cuthbert's supposed first burial place with a new tomb. Crowds gathered on the island on the saint's feast days, and sat down to a festive picnic.

For monastery and city, pilgrims, like modern tourists, were a necessity, not an optional extra. They were the lifeline providing income and stimulating trade. Between 1170 and 1175 this lifeline was suddenly threatened. The response of bishop and monks to the challenge was decisive and spectacular. Durham was so successfully publicized that the flow of visitors and their wealth was sustained for another 300 years, at least until 1500.

The threats to Cuthbert's cult came from a murder, a hermit and women. Cuthbert's popularity, accumulated over five eventful centuries, was jeopardized by the murder of Thomas Becket, Archbishop of Canterbury, in his own cathedral in December 1170. The shrine rapidly set up at the scene of the horror predictably began to draw crowds of the devout and the prurient. As Chancellor as well as Archbishop, Becket was the celebrity of his age. Also dying in 1170 was St Godric, the hermit at Finchale, just

St Cuthbert was famed for his sympathy with creatures. This black horse has chosen to pose in front of Cuthbert's Island at a time of day when it is cut off from Lindisfarne by the rising tide.

outside Durham, where he occupied a hermitage under the patronage of Bishop Flambard. He was reputed to be 105 years old at his death, a direct link with the Anglo-Saxon world. In 1172 the first Godric miracle was reported at Finchale, and he was soon St Godric. Local people, especially women, began to flock to Finchale rather than Durham. Unlike Cuthbert, whose misogyny had been foisted upon him by the Benedictines as a political tactic, Godric was a unisex miracle worker at a time when women were excluded from the cathedral and monks' cemetery at Durham as well as from Inner Farne and Lindisfarne, though not from the parish church there.

THE GALILEE CHAPEL

During the 12th century, the cult of the Virgin Mary swept across Europe. A Lady Chapel, generally at the east end of the original building, was the indispensable accessory for cathedrals seeking to keep up with fashion. Here was Durham's chance to woo back women to the cult of Cuthbert. In 1175 work began on a Lady Chapel to the east of Cuthbert's shrine. But the masons quickly met problems. The rock of the peninsula is further below the surface at this point, and it is likely that they could not lay down adequate foundations. Responsibility for the debacle was conveniently shifted to Cuthbert. The saint's misogyny would not permit the construction of a Lady Chapel so near to his resting place. Hugh du Puiset, the masterful bishop, defiantly moved the site of his chapel from east to west, a restricted site beyond the west doors perched on the very edge of the river gorge, but one where the rock sat on the surface to provide a foundation. A further advantage of the location lay in its being the only place, furthest from the shrine, where women were allowed to gather in search of the saint's help. It was the spot on which a blind woman found her sight restored with a vision of Christ crucified high on the west front. So a Lady Chapel here, dedicated to the

Virgin Mary, would also provide shelter for those previously left in the cold. It was completed in 1189 and a contemporary charter names it as the Galilee: the place of departure for Christ's journey to Jerusalem was a fitting name for a space in which processions began and ended. It was also a chapel in which women were allowed for prayer and worship, though they were still not permitted to advance closer to the shrine than the line of dark blue marble set into the floor on the nave on the line of the North Porch, the main entrance to the cathedral today. From the 14th century it also served as the bishop's consistory court.

The chapel itself is a miracle of architecture and decoration. The delicacy of the arcading of its five aisles and the play of light upon it on a winter afternoon or summer evening has few, if any, European rivals. Slender pillars in quatrefoil clusters, gnarled Purbeck marble north and south, smooth sandstone east and west, support the roof and, as the visitor moves around it, appear to change places in a slow and formal dance. Enough of the early wall painting survives for the imagination to sense the place flooded with vivid images. Across the spandrels and the arcading of the north side of the second aisle from the north scenes of horror are frozen into faded delicacy: James and Paul beheaded, Peter and Andrew crucified, John the Evangelist boiled in oil, Christ's crucifixion with Adam at the foot rising from his grave in his shroud, bearing the chalice of the Saviour's blood. Below one, a little group of Benedictine monks huddles, kneeling, gazing east to what was once a circular image of the Coronation of the Virgin. On either side of the altar beneath her stand the best-preserved full-length iconographic figures of a king and

Above: *An angel playing a trumpet: medieval glass in the west wall of the Galilee Chapel.*

Right: *The Early English Galilee Chapel, built at the west end of the Cathedral as a Lady Chapel between 1175 and 1189. It was threatened with demolition at the end of the 18th century.*

bishop in 12th-century dress, maybe Puiset and Richard I, but also invoking Cuthbert and Oswald five centuries before. The risk of their vanishing into the stonework has been reduced by recent stabilization.

When Cuthbert's popularity seemed at risk, there chanced to be on hand in the monastery a first-rate publicity agent. The monk Reginald had been compiling for some years an anthology of stories illustrating the saint's miracles. The practice was to display such collections at a shrine to honour the saint and endorse his powers, rather like the crutches left behind at Lourdes. An urgent and additional aim after 1170 was to promote Cuthbert's efficacy over that of St Thomas (St Godric's cult was less of a threat, for the monks had taken over the running of it).

Reginald's 141 episodes cover 300 years from around 875 to 1175. The earlier miracles are widespread geographically, but the more recent ones, especially after the murder in Canterbury alluded to in story 112, are understandably centred upon cathedral and city. The testimonies offer us intimate vignettes of contemporary life in Durham. A youth is injured when a clapper falls from a bell in the tower; Brother Robert of St Martin throws his psalter at Cuthbert's shrine in frustration at his failure to learn to read; a boy is harassed by evil spirits who toss him to and fro like a ball; a pushy knight rides up to the church door disparaging Cuthbert's powers, but his horse tumbles and he is rolled in the mud; a sick Norwegian boy chooses Durham in preference to Canterbury and is cured. Reginald's Cuthbert is generally compassionate rather than fierce, though there remain resonances of the retributive saint: a little girl strays into the cathedral and loses her wits as a punishment. Important in Durham's makeover was the absorption of Godric's reputation, so Reginald went on to compile another anthology of 200 of Godric's miracles. And St Godric's beard was now added to the jumble of relics at Cuthbert's shrine.

Wall paintings in the Galilee include the Crucifixion, right, and beside it the inverted crucifixion of St Peter.

The remarketing of Durham was successful: the flow of pilgrim traffic stayed healthy. The shrine also did business as a place where oaths were sworn and crosses dedicated at the start of crusades. There were royal visits by Henry VI in 1448, Richard III in 1483, and Margaret Tudor in 1503. Canterbury had challenged Durham but not triumphed over it. So Durham, just before the Reformation, was 'accoumpted to be the richest churche in all this land … so great was the rich Jewells and ornaments, Copes,

Vestments and plaite presented to holy St Cuthbert by Kinges, Queenes, Princes and Noblemen as in theis days [1593] is almost beyonde beleife.'

Until 1280 the shrine was reached by a flight of stone steps beyond the monks' choir. Pilgrims disrupted services and caused congestion. The appearance of 'fissures and fractures' at the east end of the church, where Puiset had had his difficulties with the Lady Chapel, was the opportunity for a grand architectural solution. Bishop Richard le Poore had the idea of the Chapel of the Nine Altars; Prior Melsonby initiated the work in 1242 after Poore's death, but it took 40 years to complete – as long a time as the entire Romanesque cathedral. Revenue for the chapel was raised nationwide from indulgences. In 1235 the Bishop of Ely offered a 30-day remission of penance for contributions to Bishop Poore's Chapel of the Nine Altars at Durham; the last known date of such fund-raising for this cause is 1279 from Norwich. Poore's intention was to glorify the setting of one of the two greatest shrines in England, and the spur may have been a recent enhancement of the shrine at Canterbury. The east end of Fountains Abbey, where more altars had been needed for its expanding community of Cistercians, furnished the design and the architect–mason was Richard of Farnham, whose relative Nicholas had succeeded Poore as bishop. The discovery of a source of fine marble at Frosterley in the Wear Valley enabled the masons to incorporate jewel-like shafts which appear as fresh today as on the day of dedication. With the chapel at last complete in 1280, Cuthbert's shrine was embellished upon a raised platform behind the high altar, accessible and viewable through the choir aisles and from the spacious new transept four feet below the level of the main floor, a feature which magnifies the grandeur of the shrine on its stone platform. The new shrine was 'exalted with most curious workmanship, of fine and costly green marble, all limned and gilted with gold, having four seats convenient underneath, for the pilgrims or lame men sitting on their knees to lean and rest on in the time of their devout offerings and fervent prayers to God and holy St Cuthbert for his miraculous relief and succour'.

TEMPESTS WITHIN

Relations between bishop and monks were destined to be stormy. Lanfranc's constitutions obtained by St. Calais, named the bishop as abbot of the priory, and thus the prior's superior. Bishops of Durham were rarely monks themselves, but rather diplomats, courtiers and administrators, busy in royal service and generally winning the Durham appointment as a reward for that service. Their spiritual gifts were of little or no relevance, and some monks were justified in feeling that such worldly magnificoes were improper superiors or exemplars of the supposed monastic ideals. Moreover, they tended to be absent from Durham for months or years at a time, so the priors and monastic officers acquired a welcome independence in managing affairs themselves. Durham was also a plum diocese, given its income and estates, and bishops were often ambitious and greedy men: why else accept the posting? The division of St Cuthbert's Patrimony between bishop and priory defined a frontier of continual attrition as each party sought advantage over or suspected duplicity by the other. On five occasions, in 1260, 1274, 1311, 1316 and 1333, the monks hoped for greater harmony by electing bishops from within their own community.

The monks were entitled to elect their bishop, though the royal will was invariably conveyed north before the election, and monastic chapters knew that their own interests lay in taking note of it if possible. Besides, they needed a strong man as their champion against the habitual claims of Archbishops of York to wield supreme authority in the Durham diocese, and the predatory impulses that underlay that claim. So, paradoxically, the powerful bishops they sought to defend the long independence of the church in Durham were also those most likely to trample on the rights of the monastery.

Bishop Hugh du Puiset was a formidable contender. His family were powerful barons from Chartres; his patron was his uncle Henry of Blois, Bishop of Winchester and brother of King Stephen, who created Puiset Archdeacon there when he was only 14 years old. He easily won the election as Bishop of Durham in 1153, when the Archbishop of York excommunicated the principal electors beforehand, and remained bishop for 42 years. Magnificent was his style and high-handed his methods. He commanded armies in battle. He had a portable private chapel requiring several horses to draw it, and when he made preparations to go crusading in 1189 he assembled so much luggage that a private fleet was needed to convey it. 'The great ship of the Bishop of Durham' had a crew of 32. But he never got round to setting out. In Durham his chief delight was to build. 'The more Hugh was anxious to build on earth, the more remiss he was in building in Heaven' was the tart appraisal of a contemporary chronicler. As well as the Galilee Chapel he was compelled to rebuild much of the castle when it was destroyed by fire. He built Elvet Bridge connecting the peninsula to the east bank of the Wear, and bestowed a charter on the swelling borough below his walls. He 'never slumbered where money was in question' and his role as bishop has been described more as shearer than shepherd. His disputes with the priory about revenue were legion. At one point he seized all the lands, churches and revenues of the monks and returned them only at a death-bed repentance similar to Flambard's. His tendency to behave like Flambard forced the monks into forging charters in an attempt to validate their rights and privileges. The dismissal of Prior Thomas in 1162 characterized his authoritarian conduct and soured relations with the priory for the rest of his over-long episcopate.

Worse was to follow. Philip of Poitou, Puiset's successor in 1197, had a dispute with the monks so violent that he besieged them in the cathedral with his private army, fired the doors, cut off supplies of food and water and destroyed the fish ponds. When he was refused admission to the Chapter House he excommunicated the prior and all his chapter and attacked the cathedral during the St Cuthbert's Day rituals. His end was fitting: he fell out with the Pope and died excommunicate himself. The nine-year vacancy in the bishopric that followed both swelled the royal exchequer and gave the prior and his brethren a disposition to independence – and an indisposition to bishops. Richard Marsh, bishop from 1217 to 1226, was accused by the monks of murder, simony, adultery, sacrilege, perjury and, what is more, neglect of church property. A long legal wrangle steered by bribery and evasion concluded dramatically. On his way to another ecclesiastical court in London and halting overnight in Peterborough, he was found dead in bed in the morning, having retired in apparently perfect health. He left the diocese with debts of over £10,000 (£3.5m).

So the first task of Richard le Poore, who came from Salisbury to Durham in 1228, was to try to cleanse the bad blood that had been flowing for 100 years. He and Prior Kerneth came to an agreement in 1229 known as Le Convenit. Its most important terms named the bishop as nominal rather than functional abbot, and although the prior was to do canonical obedience to the bishop, he was to be ranked equally with him in the bishopric with the status of an abbot. The allocation of spoils was also defined: wrecks at sea washed up on the prior's land were to be shared between prior and bishop; all customs on the Tees were to go to the bishop alone, and though prior and monks were forbidden to raid the bishop's forest, they were granted the not over-generous right of free watercourse through the bishop's lands.

The seal of Bishop Antony Bek, c.1300. As Patriarch of Jerusalem he was entitled to have depicted on his seal both the Crucifixion and the Resurrection.

BISHOP BEK

There was peace for a while, but peace is the natural condition of very few communities, religious or secular. Dissension seems the first law of their existence. The election of the mighty Antony Bek as their bishop was to drag the monks into a seven years' war within the priory and with the bishop, a comic and desperate struggle from which Bek, as he had to, emerged victorious, but only just, and only through the greatest of good fortune.

Bek came from a Lincolnshire family of royal administrators and saw royal service as a young man in the household of Prince Edward, soon to be Edward I, with whom he went off crusading for two years in 1270, an aspect of his curriculum vitae which was to prove an asset in years to come. While gathering overdue taxes for Edward in the north in 1283, he was called into a dispute between Durham and York and was able to be a mediator. Their recurrent antagonism had flared in 1281, when the Archbishop tried to impose his right of visitation at Durham and was driven away by force. Bearing the grudge of indignity he sallied north again in 1283 on the death of Bishop Robert, and caused uproar by excommunicating prior and monastic officers before fleeing home. Bek seemed the very man to keep the Archbishop in his place, and he was elected defender of Durham in July 1283. He already held prebends at Exeter, Southwell, Lichfield, Lincoln, York and Ripon.

Bek was a warrior-bishop. He was actively involved in Edward I's Scottish wars, for as bishop in Durham he was the chief royal spy upon Scottish politics, and both rivals for the Scottish throne in 1290, John de Balliol and Robert Bruce, were Bek's tenants. When Edward invaded Scotland in 1296, Bek led a Durham-gathered force of 1,500 across the Tweed at Norham to the siege of Berwick. The seal of Scotland was surrendered to him at Brechin after the Battle of Dunbar,

and again in 1298 he led the siege of Dirleton Castle on the Firth of Forth and took his men to battle and victory at Falkirk. His passion for soldiering brought him into conflict with the men of Durham, who resisted Bek's military levies on the ground that as Haliwerfolc they were required only to protect their saint and were not obliged to serve out of the Palatinate. Apparently they were over-ruled.

Bek was a busy man and after his election took over two years to find his way to Durham. He had been consecrated at York in 1284 in the presence of the king and queen. At once the archbishop ordered him to excommunicate the prior of Durham and his officers. His reply would have heartened the priory: 'Yesterday I was consecrated their bishop: and shall I excommunicate them today? No obedience will induce me to it.' But even before his arrival he was in dispute with the monastery about the payment of taxes required by the king, and refused to meet the detachment of monks who had gathered to greet him when he reached the town. Dissension marked his enthronement on Christmas Eve 1285. The prior and a cleric from York disputed the right to preside, so Bek took charge himself and asked his brother Thomas, Bishop of St David's, to do the honours. Within two days he had sacked the Prior, Richard de Claxton, and appointed his man Henry de Horncastre in his place until a successor had been chosen: Hugh of Darlington, briefly. Richard de Hoton, the sub-prior, was bitterly offended at this insult to his position. This notoriously fractious man was at once rusticated to the dependent cell at distant Lytham, in Lancashire. The monks saw Bek's tactics as threatening their privileges and responded by electing Hoton as their prior.

His period of office began badly. On 4 September, the feast of the Translation of St Cuthbert, it was traditional for the Nevilles of Raby Castle to present a stag to the monks and join them at the feast. In 1290 Ralph Neville brought his entire household to enjoy the prior's hospitality. Consternation: 'the honour due to the saint was turned into a burden and a loss' (i.e. short rations all round). Hoton refused the gift, but the Raby people took it to the kitchen and had a fracas with the servants there. The fight spread to the cathedral. Neville's men attacked the monks serving at the altar who warded them off by using the large wax candles as truncheons. Both parties next turned to litigation, but Neville's action against Hoton collapsed when one William of Brompton, a bishop's justiciary, admitted that he had begun the affray, 'for being but a youth, he loved blowing the horn and coming in with the Lord of Neville', and that when the stag was presented he had said 'Come into the abbey, and let us there sound our horn.' Peace was grudgingly accepted, but there were no more stags from Raby on Cuthbert's Day.

Over the next ten years Hoton strengthened his position. Bek was mostly away in Scotland. Whenever the king passed through Durham, Hoton ingratiated himself and in 1300 persuaded Edward to reconfirm the charters of the priory, notably the rights of the prior to manage estates on the community's behalf. Hoton had been doing so already, bestowing land and benefices on his relatives and exiling to distant cells those he perceived to be his enemies, just as he had been exiled after Bek's arrival. The indignant exiles now complained to Bek who headed north at speed, having announced a formal visitation of the monastery for May 1300. Seven years of subsequent conflict expanded from a technicality: whether the bishop's visitation should be accompanied by outsiders. 'What mighty contests rise from trivial things.'

Highlights include, beside the predictable cut and thrust of excommunications, deprivations and resisted appointments: a blockade of the priory for several months to prevent appeals to York or Rome; the water supply cut off and the priory mill disabled; Hoton's occupying the prior's stall in the cathedral for three days to prevent Bek's chosen successor from sitting in it, before being dragged from it to the monastic prison; Hoton's journey to Rome, where he spent much of the remainder of his life appealing to the pope (or rather popes, since a quick succession of papal deaths required him to present his case three times); a game of hide-and-seek for the priory seal, hidden by the monks when they heard rumours of Hoton's return; two journeys by Bek to Rome to see two popes, both of whom were bowled over by his magnificence and agreed with all he said. On his second visit, to Clement V in 1305, he brandished his crusading credentials and was created Patriarch of Jerusalem with a church in Rome, precedence over the Archbishop of Canterbury, and the right to wear his patriarchal pallium in any cathedral in Europe. Rivalry between king and pope now prompted Edward I to take Hoton's part and send him trekking again to Rome to press his claims. Clement reversed his earlier judgement and ordered Hoton's restoration. But at the moment of his triumph Hoton, worn out by travel and litigation, suddenly died. The parallel death of Edward I who was scheming Bek's downfall, ensued his triumph instead. Bek was now able to take legitimate control of the priory and ask his friend Pope Clement to nominate the new prior; he was also able to exploit his long-standing friendship with the new king, Edward II, to restore his position in Durham and at court. He visited Durham to absolve in person many of the monks in person in a ceremony at the castle in 1310, earning himself an improbable reputation for magnanimity. In his last years Bek's authority and that of the Palatinate he commanded was impregnable. He died at Eltham in

East end of the Cathedral from Whinney Hill at sunrise in March.

March 1311 and his body was interred in the Chapel of the Nine Altars by the Archbishop of York in May. It was the first burial within the cathedral. Though Bek had been hugely in debt to Edward I, his son forgave the sum, 'for the good and laudable service which the patriarch and bishop showed our father, and for the great affection he had toward us, and also for the immense gifts liberally given to us by the same patriarch and bishop while he lived.' So passed a man hailed as 'the most valiant clerk in Christendom'.

After Bek, ecclesiastical life in Durham reverted to the ordinary. Bishop Louis Beaumont was ambushed on his way to the city and held to ransom at Mitford Castle. The unhappy prior had to sell treasures to raise the sum asked for the still unenthroned prelate. And when he finally arrived he was far from grateful and proved wholly unsuitable. He possessed neither Latin nor English (not required for a cousin of Queen Phillipa), threatened Cuthbert at his shrine and was unusually greedy: 'A spendthrift he is, and eager to get, nor particular how he gets it.' His message for the monks was ' Pray for my death, for whilst I live you shall have no favours from me.' He selected a burial place inside the altar rails under what was the largest brass in medieval England. His successor, Richard d'Aungerville, known as Bishop Bury, was a papal choice in preference to Edward III's candidate, Graystanes, a historian and chronicler who, having already been elected, consecrated and enthroned, had to step down in favour of the papal chaplain. Bury was a diplomat (and friend of Petrarch) who largely ignored his diocese to spend his time in France. When a Scottish invasion threatened he dealt with it by ordering Prior Fossor to remain in Durham to do all that was necessary. It was the same Fossor who, after Bury's death, wrote joyously of witnessing the English victory over the Scots at Neville's Cross in 1346, and heralding a time of happiness. Three years later the Black Death reached Durham.

MONASTIC LIFE 1083–1539

THE MONKS

The Benedictine community founded by William of St. Calais had a continuous existence of 456 years. With the exception of a cursed time in the first half of the 14th century its life was generally prosperous, scholarly and tolerably harmonious. With nine outlying dependent cells its influence and responsibilities ranged over a great swathe of the north. The Patrimony of St Cuthbert had endowed it richly with lands; it had, together with the bishop, virtually total economic and legal sway over the city that had grown up below it. But what made it unique was its custodianship of St Cuthbert, his shrine, his church and the long tradition, part Irish, part Anglo-Saxon, accruing to the saint. The monks were 'mynistres of Saynt Cuthbert', their books the 'libri Sancti Cuthberti', and the rights and traditions they tenaciously defended in their vocation were Cuthbert's, not theirs. Devotion to the saint's service was the unifying focus both of the community in Durham and its colony of cells. Upon their responsible custodianship of their sacred charge the prosperity of the monastery and city depended. The continuing conviction of Cuthbert's sanctity and his power over individuals and events was the very heart of the community's purpose. Remote from other major foundations, with a prestige acquired through a long history, guarding a tradition that pre-dated the Norman Conquest, the Durham community had every reason to think highly of itself. Even the potential crisis of legitimacy which might have arisen in 1083, when southerners usurped Northumbria's bond with Cuthbert, had been deflected by the building of the greatest new cathedral in Europe as a fitting home for him and by Symeon's dextrous propaganda which discredited the former clerks of St Cuthbert, only one of whom became a Benedictine, and substantiated the claims of the Benedictines to be their rightful successors.

The number of monks who met daily in the Chapter House to hear a reading of a chapter of the Benedictine rule and then to deal with monastic business was seldom fewer than 65, and at its maximum, usually when revenues permitted expansion, it was well over 100. At the Dissolution in 1539 there were

Above: 'Carried by angels into Abraham's bosom': a 13th-century boss above the west end of the Quire.

Right: The Death of a Monk, from the Durham Priory Obit Roll of the 15th century. B.IV.48.

66. Around 40 of these would be in residence at Durham, and the rest distributed around the daughter houses and cells. The monks in Durham would have been greatly outnumbered by the tradesmen and servants they employed, for the priory kitchen expected to feed between 200 and 300 mouths each day.

The *Liber Vitae*, a manuscript book placed on the high altar, listed the names of those who joined the community as well as benefactors to be commemorated in prayers. The range of Christian names was small; of 139 names recorded between 1383 and 1446 all but seven share six names: John, William, Thomas, Robert, Richard and Henry. Many needed a toponymic which identified their place of origin. Two-thirds were from Durham or the surrounding district, and most of the rest from Northumberland and North Yorkshire, Cuthbert's traditional lands. A handful came across the Pennines. To be accepted into the monastery a novice had to be both legitimate and freeborn; nearly all came

from yeoman families, not the gentry. Their family occupations tended to be craftsman and merchant, a social class known as 'valecti' or varlets. The usual age of joining was 19 to 23, and the life expectation of a monk was higher than outside the priory; the average length of service before death was 40 years. Old age was provided for. There were 19 rooms in the infirmary, each with a fireplace, and after death, burial was in the monks' cemetery east of the Chapter House. Ten shillings (£175) were distributed to the poor as alms for the departed soul.

Novices were prepared for their vocation by a two- to three-year preparatory education in the West Cloister, founded upon grammar, biblical commentaries and patristic texts. They would attend all the monastic offices in the church and eat in the monastic refectory. Each at his noviciate was provided by the chamberlain with appropriate clothing: two undershirts, two pairs of drawers, two head caps, one pair of gaiters, two pairs of

Right: The 12th-century arch above the Chapter House door in the East Cloister.

Below: The well-worn iron door handle and keyhole on the medieval door of the North Porch.

slippers, two pairs of blankets, one hood, one cowl, one monk's robe, one white-and-black tunic and two pairs of boots. Tailors employed in the priory made up the garments from lengths of worsted and linen bought as far away as York and Boston.

MONASTIC OFFICES

The prior ruled the community. His social and economic standing was second only to the bishop's, and his more frequent presence in Durham added to his authority. He was an important public figure, keeping open house with a lifestyle comparable to that of a great landowner. He entertained brethren from the priory, local magnates and the commanders of the many detachments of soldiers occupying or passing through the garrison town. Lavish hospitality was the norm. At Christmas 1430 the prior's table finished off two boars, seven cattle, 26 sheep, 44 legs of pork and four loads of fish. Administration of the monastery devolved upon the prior, who was always elected by the monks as a whole, a right fiercely defended against those bishops who tried to impose their own nominees. The prior appointed the obedientiaries (those who held positions of responsibility for the various divisions of monastic activity), postings to distant cells and the selection of novices. Since there were over 20 'obediences', over half the monks resident at any one time would be office holders. Eleven of these managed estates in order to fund their activities and were required to present annual accounts to the chapter. Beside the Bursar, chief financial officer, there was the Terrar (the monastic land agent), the Hostillar who looked after guests, the Cellarer who provided food and drink and looked after the kitchen, the Granator who purchased malt, barley and wheat, the Chamberlain who was responsible for clothing, the Almoner who oversaw charitable provision for the sick and the poor, the Commoner who administered the common room beneath the dormitory,

The Spendement, a secure end off the Cloister built to house monastic manuscripts, and still the home of the library's precious books. The iron grille is original 15th-century work.

the Master of the Infirmary, the Sacrist who looked after the fabric of the cathedral and the vestments, candles, incense, bread and wine needed for rituals, and the Feretar who held particular responsibility for St Cuthbert's shrine and the revenue it generated. A secondary range of obediences involved deputies for the principal office-holders and monks responsible for the organization of rituals in the cathedral.

THE DAILY ROUND

'Idleness is the enemy of the soul; the brethren, therefore, must be occupied at stated hours in manual labour, and again at other hours in sacred reading.' This extract from the Rule of St Benedict underlies both the detailed and inflexible routine of the monks and, with the substitution

The Crucifixion: medieval stained glass in the west wall of the Chapter House.

also attended by individual monks who celebrated mass at each. Every Sunday a procession of the whole brotherhood visited each altar to sprinkle it with holy water. For the chief rituals there was music too, an organ and singing boys, skilled in 'playnsonge, prikenot, faburdon, dischaunte and countre'. The precincts were always frequented by large numbers of boys, some accepted members of the Almonry school where a basic education was given to the singing boys and to poor boys deserving of charity: 'certaine poor children onely maynteyned and releyved with the almesse and Benevolence of the whole house, which were cauled the childrine of the aumery going daily to the fermery schole being all together maynteyned by the whole Covent with meate drynke and lerninge'. But there were unwelcome urchins too, the 'pueri nudipedes et inhonesti' who scavenged for food. The precinct would have been neither peaceful nor clean, being a combination of farmyard and building site, awash with carts, animals and feral boys, the cries and shouts of workmen, the creaking of winches, percussion of hammers, and the grating and rasping of saws and adzes.

A committee of monks met to make regular reports on the condition of the monastery and listed their 'diffinitions' in a complaint book for the prior's notice. The three commonest topics for grousing about were the misconduct of servants, the menace posed by gangs of predatory boys, and inadequate provision for sickness and old age. We learn little about individuals unless they misbehave and are liable to discipline. Henry Helay, a disputacious man, slandered a fellow monk and kept animals, money and goods for his own benefit when prior at Lindisfarne; William Partrike when prior at Lytham in 1431 sought to make his little cell independent of the mother house and was recalled to Durham where he could be watched, and where he festered in suspicion and resentment: 'We have a new prior, and he luffyd me neuer and Robert Westmorland and John Gatished and Richard Bell are cheff wit hym, and none of them luffis me.' Monks wounding one another with knives were not unknown, but in 1420 one John Tynemouth lost control and murdered William Warner.

of sport for manual labour, the monastic life's reincarnation in the 19th century as the public school. The Horarium at Durham differed little from the regime of other religious houses. Matins at midnight, to which the monks processed by the night stair direct from their interrupted sleep in the dormitory. Prime at 6 am, Chapter Mass at 9, followed by the Chapter meeting at 10. High mass at 11, dinner at noon, Nones at 2 pm, Vespers at 4, supper at 6, followed by Compline before bed. In addition there were daily masses of the Holy Spirit, Our Lady (in the Galilee), and de Cimeterio for the dead. At more than 20 altars prayers for the living and the dead were offered by individual monks, and the chantries of Bishops Langley, Hatfield, Skirlaw, Prior Fossor, Richard of Barnard Castle and Lord Neville were

The rigour of the monastic round was relieved by 'ludi', periods of festivity around Advent and Christmas, and after Lent and Easter when the prior entertained the brethren at his country residence outside the city, called Beaurepaire, anglicized as Bearpark. Here was the springtime opportunity to let the tonsure down and go in for a spree of unmonastic indulgence out of sight of the town. Meat-eating was one joy. In 1440 'thirty seven lambs were bought for the expenses of the Prior at Beaurepaire for the Easter holidays', we learn from the Cellarer's roll. In 1438 John Oll, steward of the Prior's Hall, laid out money for the solace and amusement of the Prior and his brethren. The sum of 65s 1d (£1,200) is spent for their 'playing and taking holiday at Bearepayr for eleven weeks and four days', probably a total for the year. Sometimes there are hints that the carnival may have got out of hand, with music, acting, dancing, minstrels, jugglers. 'For the Minstrel of my Lord the Duke, with a youth dancing in my Lord Prior's room, 6s 8d (£100); for a man who played on a loyt (lute) and his wife who sang with him, 2s (£30).' Thomas the Prior's Fool is on hand to amuse guests for 20 years; there is also mention of ferrets, an ape, a goshawk, and dogs for coursing hares. And no getting out of bed at midnight for Matins in a cold cathedral.

CELLS

Durham inherited that gene of Irish Christianity which favoured the solitary life of devotion to God in remote places. Cuthbert's example alone ensured that the eremitical tradition would enter the bloodstream of the community and endure until the dissolution. The Rule of St Benedict also endorsed the practice. It held up two patterns for a monk's life, the cenobite and the anchorite, the latter 'after long probation in a monastery goes out well-armed from the ranks of the community to the solitary combat of the desert'. As the spiritual heart of the Durham history, Lindisfarne cried out for repossession, and a priory was refounded there after a cenotaph church to mark Cuthbert's gravesite had been constructed in the 1120s. The 12th-century priory church was manifestly a daughter house of Durham, echoing on a smaller scale the patterned pillars of the mother cathedral. Yet its endowment was small and it was never able to support more than a tiny community. It was vulnerable to Scottish raids and in the troubled 14th century it even had to be fortified. Inner Farne as the place of Cuthbert's own ascetic life and death issued a more compelling summons and, beginning with Aelric in 1150, a line of Durham monks resided there again until just before the Dissolution, in a small cell generally manned by two residents. Other outlying houses were Coldingham Priory, Jarrow, Monkwearmouth, Lytham, Stamford, Finchale close to the home base and the study house for monks in Oxford. Most were sources of trouble more often than not. Coldingham, north of the Tweed, was resented by the Scots and coveted by the diocese of St Andrews. Its eventual surrender was a blow to the bipartisan strand in the history of Cuthbert's church. Finchale was well endowed and popular, with eight residents, some on sabbatical, some elderly and put out to grass. Ease of contact with Durham softened the perception of exile. But apart from Finchale, postings to cells were not always popular, so discipline might be lax and morale low. Most groups were too small for a flourishing community life, and priors tended to use them for the rustication of troublesome members of the main priory. Disciplinary lapses were predictable: frequenting of taverns and keeping low company. Thomas Brogham in Oxford preferred alcohol and archery to prayer and theology. The isolation of Farne broke some: 'many tymes you tak a boote and roith unto

Durham's medieval glass was famous for its golden light. Two birds from the west wall of the Chapter House prove the point.

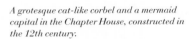

A grotesque cat-like corbel and a mermaid capital in the Chapter House, constructed in the 12th century.

the land at thin own liberty', and John Harom had to be expelled from the island for rambling about on the mainland, dirty and in rags. An annual Chapter Meeting of representatives of all the cells was held on the first Monday after Ascension Day, a favourable time for travelling, when small payments were handed over by the satellites to the main house, and envious eyes roved over the blessings of Durham.

SCHOLARSHIP

William of St. Calais' benefaction of some 50 books to his fledgling community is a measure of his aspirations for its intellectual life. Twenty of the 50 remain in Durham, among the finest productions of their age and in which scribes and illuminators match the quality of the fine white parchment they were invited to use. A commentary on the Psalms contains an image of Bishop William and Benjamin the illustrator within the elaborate initial. In all, some 350 books from the monastic library still survive at Durham; others known or presumed to have been there, including the Lindisfarne Gospels, have

wandered elsewhere down the years, as books do. The high survival rate is a tribute to successive monastic chancellors whose responsibility the books were. An inventory of the late 14th century records around 1,000 volumes, some kept in book cupboards in the Cloister for daily study, but the manuscripts were kept in a 'strong howse' known as the Spendement, on the south side of the door to the Dormitory in the West Cloister. A further 'libraria' was built by the devoted Chancellor Wessington between 1414 and 1418. He was rewarded by his election as Prior in 1416. He modelled it on the college libraries he had known in Oxford, and it was sited at first-floor level in the east cloister between the Chapter House and the South Transept. It is now used as the song school for choir rehearsals.

Interaction with the university in Oxford was a powerful stimulus to intellectual life in Durham, which together with Canterbury became the only Benedictine houses to establish their own colleges there. A small colony of Durham monks was planted in Oxford in the 1280s and 100 years later Bishop Hatfield amplified it

The Dean, about to go on sabbatical leave in 2006, tries to instruct Leofric in cathedral administration. He is seated in the Cloister Garth on a part of the monks' stone wash-basin made of Eggleston marble, from Teesdale.

of around 80 early printed books from the period 1480–1530 can only be accounted for by the influence of Oxford as a centre of European learning. The name, though not the institution in Oxford, was to be a casualty of the Reformation: in 1555 Sir Thomas Pope incorporated Durham College into Trinity College, dropping from its dedication the theologically unfashionable Blessed Virgin Mary and St Cuthbert.

THE MONASTIC ECONOMY

Durham was one of the wealthiest monasteries in the land. At its most prosperous it had an income of over £3,000 (£1m) a year, and at the Dissolution it still had £1,572 (£370,000). It was seldom out of the top ten, though its reputation for opulence certainly outran the reality. In the early 14th century the Pope was told that wealth had driven the Prior and Chapter of Durham mad, so in consequence they obeyed neither bishop nor archdeacon. The chief sources of income were rents and tithes. Rents came from agricultural land, fisheries, forests, mills and coal pits. Coal, though abundant, was not a major money-spinner because the Wear was not navigable, and successful arable farming by tenants was the greatest resource. Around one-third of the income vanished on overheads: repairs, monastic servants and agents who collected rents. Expenditure was about £1,400 (£500,000) a year. The Bursar shopped widely for necessities: cloth from York for garments both for monks and for 'generosi', valets and servants who wore a livery; wine and metal from Newcastle; white fish, lobsters, crabs and lampreys from the fish quays at Shields at the mouth of the Tyne. 'Dogdraves' were the fish most frequently eaten; in 1523 Percival Conyers of Hartlepool supplied 690 of them for £17 13s 4d (£700). The Cellarer and the Granator bought in provisions. In a typical week there passed through the Priory Kitchen five cattle, 22 sheep, two calves, 13 piglets, a cartload of fish, 22 hens and 400 eggs. The monastery had its own granary, mill and brewhouse; consumption of ale was heavy, though its potency was not high. Prices for standard items were reassuringly stable year in, year out: wax 6d (£9) a pound; boots 3s 4d (£55) a pair, socks 2d (£3), Spanish iron 8d (£12) a stone.

into Durham College and endowed it with a legacy of £3,000 (£1m). In the early years of the 15th century it expanded rapidly, with a quadrangle, chapel, library and gatehouse, demonstrating the exact debt owed to the monastic cloister by colleges of the ancient universities. Over a third of Durham's monks spent time there for periods of three to six years, generally when they were young. Eight student monks were nominated by the monks to study philosophy and theology as well as participate in the full round of monastic offices. In addition, eight secular students selected by the Durham Chapter from their own estates were sent to study grammar and theology. The quality of monastic administration in Durham, dominated by monks with a university training, was notable, and the merits of the Durham library, shaped by experience of intellectual life at Oxford, turned the monastery into a little university of the north. The existence in Durham

The prosperity of Durham town depended almost entirely on the monastery and its visitors. Unlike most cathedral cities it did not see the rise of an independent class of prosperous merchants, so castle and monastery between them ruled the town. Bishops built the bridges that enabled separate hamlets to coalesce into a city, and founded the twice-yearly St Cuthbert's fairs to stimulate trade. Le Convenit of 1229 insisted on the use of standardized units of weights and measures in each of the five boroughs. In three of these the overlords were obedientaries of the priory. The bishop was overlord in the Bishop's Borough, inevitably the most prosperous, and Bishop Flambard also seized from the priory that part of the town which became Old Borough, and handed it back only when on his death-bed. In the boroughs all tolls, rents and profits from law courts went to the overlords. A policy of buying up freeholds as they became available intensified the monks' economic dominance of the town. The bishop and the priory also had a monopoly of water mills on the river and sandstone quarries around the gorge.

The economic stability implied by this summary was often at risk – from bad weather and poor harvests, Scottish raids, and disease. In 1400 Flambard's Framwellgate Bridge was destroyed by a flood, and Bishop Langley had to rebuild it with fortifications to deter raiders. 1315 was the start of a particularly miserable time for everyone. There were bad harvests and murrain among the beasts. Food prices were high; there was famine and dysentery in the town; the priory was in debt. Then the Scots arrived: 'They plundered almost the whole stores of the house.' They chased the Prior all the way from Bearpark back to Durham and then ransacked his country residence, taking the long cart with horses and furnishing, altar vessels, table linen, 60 mares and 120 cattle. In the summer, floods brought in plague and yet more starvation. 'Such numbers died every day that hardly could living suffice to bury the dead.' The distress of Durham was compounded in 1316 by the death of Bishop Kellawe and the choice, against

The 14th-century tomb of Bishop Thomas Hatfield in the Quire, incorporating, in the gallery at the head of the staircase, the highest bishop's throne outside Rome.

the wishes of the monks, of the poisonous and ignorant Louis de Beaumont as his successor. Barely had the place begun to recover from these ordeals when the Black Death devastated it in 1349, wiping out 52 monks within a year, and leaving only 46 alive. It was the greatest single disaster to afflict the priory, and one which heralded still more decades of struggle and economic hardship beset by returning epidemics of plague. It was well into the next century before full prosperity returned.

SANCTUARY

In 883, supposedly, when Cuthbert's community assisted Guthred the Dane to become King of Northumbria, in gratitude he gave them both lands in Durham and the right of sanctuary. The privilege accorded to holy places was a feature of Saxon law, and the clerks of St Cuthbert claimed that the right was confirmed by King Alfred during their flirtation with the power of Wessex. This dramatic dimension of life in the Durham precinct continued under Norman rule.

The Saxon code offered protection in a church for seven days, extended by 30 if the fugitive surrendered his weapons. The right was open only to someone accused of a crime, not to one who had already been found guilty. It was often preferable to submit to the law and gain a breathing space during which deals might be done rather than fall victim to the medieval equivalent of gangland vengeance, the guardians of family honour. A crucial safeguard was a tariff of fines for any pursuer violating the area of sanctuary, the church and churchyard, the maximum being £96 (£20,000) for the killing of a fugitive. The practice at Durham was highly ritualized. The sanctuary-seeker sought admission at the north door, rousing the porters in the watchroom above by means of the formidable Sanctuary knocker. Once he was admitted the Galilee bell was tolled to alert the community. Immediately he made a confession before witnesses at Cuthbert's shrine, tolled a second bell to register his begging for protection and put on a black gown with the yellow cross of Saint Cuthbert sewn onto the left shoulder. He was given bedding, sleeping space on a wooden frame by the south door of the Galilee, and food and water for 37 days.

Far left: *The Sanctuary Knocker on the North Door. The original, of which this is a copy, is displayed in the Treasury.*

Left: *The smaller picture shows the original, which can be seen in the Treasures of St Cuthbert, before the substitution.*

The commonest crime confessed was murder. Rival woodmen attacked one another with their axes; poachers caught in the act killed bailiffs and park-keepers. Weapons listed, beside the common dagger and sword, included arrows, forest bills, Carlisle axes, pikestaffs, iron-fork shafts, lances, stones and turf spades. There were cattle thieves, corn thieves, horse stealers, debtors and house breakers. Fugitives often arrived at night; the refectory tables next morning must have buzzed with the prurience of tabloid-style tales.

A Bishop's visitation

From time to time there was an episcopal visitation of the priory, when monks were questioned individually about the order of the community. Their grievances were listed by the bishop and sent to the prior and a committee of senior monks, who were required to respond. Monastic politics and personalities were obviously at their most sensitive at such events, as we saw when Bishop Bek attempted to make his visitation in 1300. In 1441 Bishop Robert Neville was enthroned, and the following year made a visitation. He was the son of the Earl of Westmoreland; he, Puiset and Beaumont were the only bishops to gain office because of their aristocratic lineage. Neville was nominated by Henry VI: 'his birth and kynsmen ye which been of right greet and notable estat'. His election by the monks was in effect a formality, 'an act

The supplicant subsequently made a second confession before a coroner and a vow of abjuration, 'to abjure the land of England, haste me to a port, not deviating from the highway. To diligently seek for passage but one flood and ebb. If there is none, to enter the sea daily up to my knees essaying to pass over.' On his journey through parishes and boroughs to the nearest port his safety was guaranteed by a series of constables, who handed him on like a baton in a relay race; once at the port he had 40 days' grace to be gone.

Two 'Green Men' bosses, one from the 11th-century chapel in the castle, the other from the North Cloister, date uncertain.

of consent to the king's choice'. He had little learning and sought to wrest gains from the priory estates for the further aggrandizement of himself and his family. The list of 46 complaints supplied in depositions by monks ranges from slackness of worship through inadequate food and provision for the aged and infirm, failure to pursue monks who have absconded, the severity of the prior and his excessive gifts to minstrels and fools, disturbance of study ('the cantors sing lay and tripartite songs in the Chapter House, to the great inconvenience of those sitting in the Cloister') to the more basic pollution by large numbers of dogs who befoul the choir, refectory and other places.

The responses of the prior and his committee are models for any civil servant seeking to deflect attention from inflammatory material. What is alleged is not true, or not exactly true; in any case the rules forbidding such excesses are in place, and if misbehaviour occurs, it does so behind our backs. And, above all, the prior does treat his brethren gently and does not give anything to fools and only gives to minstrels exactly as his predecessors have done. So thank you for your interest, Bishop Neville, and goodbye until the next visitation.

MONASTIC BUILDINGS

By the middle of the 12th century the essential range of domestic buildings was complete. Bishop Geoffrey Rufus had built the Chapter House, Bishop William of Ste Barbe the first purpose-built dormitory. But with the fervour and energy of early colonists, new projects or rebuildings were continually under way as bishops and priors sought to leave their own monuments. The priory had to finance its works from its own income, which was swelled by pilgrims' donations to the pyx at Cuthbert's shrine. And sometimes bishops made contributions, especially if they needed favours from the community. But all building work had been halted during the time of conflicts within and disasters and disorder without, from the completion of the Chapel of the Nine Altars in 1280 to the visitation of the plague in 1349.

The election of Prior Fossor in 1341 can be seen in retrospect as the start of a slow recovery. It was Fossor who stood on the Maiden Bower watching the defeat of the Scots at Neville's Cross in 1346 and hailing the outcome as a joyful one for Durham. He was fortunate to survive the Black Death in 1349, and knew what was needed to raise the morale of the community. Just as an army marches on its stomach, so too does a monastery pray and work best when well fed. Fossor constructed a new Priory Kitchen which remained in service as the Deanery Kitchen until the 1930s. This octagonal beehive of space, with its complex and geometrically satisfying interlacing of stone ribs, its huge fireplaces, ovens and store cupboards still visible in its current incarnation as the bookshop, seems architecturally to transcend all ages and cultures. Detailed expenses for the building of the kitchen between 1366 and 1371 survive. From the tool account: 'For working 80 stone of iron in 23 axes for masons, and 25 puncheons, with chisels, 4 hacks, 2 picks and 19 wedges: 10s (£175); for sharpening 1800 masons' axes at 11d a hundred: 16s 6d (£288).' And when the structure was ready it had to be equipped: 'in the Flesh Larder: 2 leaden cisterns, 9 steeping tubs, one flesh axe, two dressing knives, two chopping knives, one slicing knife, one salt box, 23 dressing boards, 24 carcasses of oxen salted'. In 1373, by now nearly 90, Fossor – at the cost of 55s (£900) – had a litter made so that he could be carried to and fro in the precinct, expecting, doubtless, to see well-fed smiles on every countenance he met. How amply he merited his chantry in the cathedral, which he had set up before his death.

THE PRINCE-BISHOPS
AND THE PALATINATE

THE PURPOSE OF THE PALATINATE

'Palatine' is associated with the Latin palatium, palace. The use of palatine titles in a defined area called a palatinate was brought to England by the Normans, who had picked up the idea from the Carolingian empire. In practice, a palatinate witnessed the partial transfer of regal powers to a feudal deputy or viceroy, who was presupposed to have a special bond with the king and to be sufficiently trusted to wield an authority equivalent to his within a limited territory. The Normans created four palatinates, of Kent, Shropshire, Chester and Durham, and the Plantagenets one, of Lancaster. Kent and Shropshire were abolished within 40 years of the Conquest; Chester lasted until 1237. All

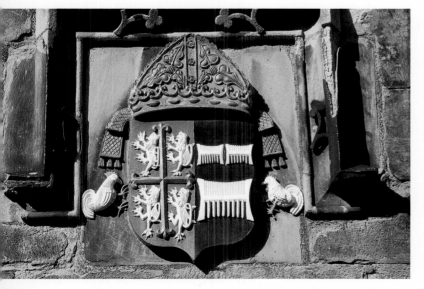

were frontier zones whose strategic importance demanded immediate and strong authority at times of crisis. The distance of Durham from London alone made a viceroy's role a necessity.

Territorially, the Durham Palatinate inherited the lands associated with the Patrimony of St Cuthbert: the area between Tyne and Tees, and the three shires in Northumberland, Norham, Bedlington and Island, gifted to Cuthbert by Ecgfrith King of Northumbria as early as 685. So a long historical memory underpinned the gradual emergence of the Durham Palatinate during the 12th century. The diocese of Durham was larger than the secular Palatinate, for its spiritual responsibilities included all Northumberland as far as the Tweed until Newcastle was created as a separate diocese in the 19th century.

The rationale for the establishment of a palatinate in the north was compelling. Centuries of harassment from further north, rising to a pitch at regular intervals in the 12th century, had made 'Scots' a term of common abuse in the district, and Durham was envisaged as a bulwark, a 'murus lapidius contra Scottos'. A second fount of violence were the reivers, the marauding clans in the dales on both sides of the vague border, especially Tynedale, Redesdale, Weardale and Teesdale, who owed allegiance to no nation and behaved as outlaws always have. It was imperative to have a promptly functioning

Left: *The coat of arms of Bishop Cuthbert Tunstall (1530–59) on the exterior wall of the castle courtyard.*

Right: *The Cathedral and Castle Gatehouse on an early spring morning, seen from the Castle battlements.*

An archbishop or bishop in medieval stained glass on the west wall of the Galilee.

judicial system in place if the north were ever to be redeemed from lawlessness. Successive kings also felt the need of a counterbalance to the barons they appointed as Wardens of the Marches, whose loyalties and conduct were equally fickle. The barons were little more than poachers turned gamekeepers, and were prone to recidivism. In contrast, a non-hereditary authority in the border region that was also the king's friend would be, it was hoped, as reliable as a rock. Yet only the Durham Palatinate was ruled by an ecclesiastic. It was as if the accumulated weight of the Cuthbert tradition had still to be acknowledged politically by kings of England as it had been by kings of Northumbria, York and Wessex. Here was an opportunity for deference to the religious and political sensibilities of a proud territory that had known independence, and a recognition that bishops of Durham still possessed political leverage as the inheritors of that tradition. Long episcopates, in the interest of stability, were the norm in Durham for centuries. It was also advantageous to the rulers of England in the south that Prince-Bishops could have no legitimate heirs or establish dynasties.

THE POWERS OF THE PRINCE-BISHOP

'Between 1066 and 1485 the Bishops of Durham desired to be as kings in their palatinate, and during most of this period they in varying degrees approximated their ideal.' 'Prince-Bishop' was a courtesy title rather than a hierarchical one: technically the bishop was a baron, though the lifestyle many of them achieved suggested a semi-regal self-esteem. The first two bishops, Walcher and William of St. Calais had combined both secular and spiritual powers as the Normans wrestled with the intractabilities the north. The ambitious Flambard had marked the territory by building his castle at Norham on the Tweed, but it was the magnificent Hugh du Puiset who consolidated the power of the Palatinate to become the first true Prince-Bishop. He was in office at the moment when the long border dispute between England and Scotland was resolved, so that the ambiguities of the northern no-man's-land were dispelled in England's favour. The reorganization of government and law under Henry II put the clear stamp of England on ancient Northumbria. Puiset took the opportunity to secure

76

charters from the king which confirmed the historical liberties of Cuthbert's see. His being Henry's cousin was probably no disadvantage. Then in 1189 he bought both the earldom of Northumberland and the crown land north of the Tees known as the wapentake of Sadberge from Richard I, who was always short of money for his Middle East adventurism. Now the Palatinate was clearly defined.

But even Puiset's championing of the power and territory of his little kingdom pales beside that of the even more imperious Antony Bek. Like Puiset, he was fortunate in his timing. One important right normally claimed by the king which was ceded to the ruler of the Palatinate was that of acquiring lands forfeit through war or treason. So in the 1290s, with the Scots in disarray, he was able to pick up Scottish estates at Penrith, Wark on the North Tyne, and Teesdale so that every route from England northwards was in Durham's control. Bek loved fighting and winning battles. He fiercely defended the liberties and privileges of the Palatinate against predatory encroachment in the 1293 Parliament, and faced down Archbishop Romeyn of York, who had excommunicated Bek for insubordination. Bek appealed to Edward I, in whose court he knew he enjoyed high favour, and secured a triumphant resolution. As Bishop of Durham he was assigned both an ecclesiastical function and a secular one as earl palatine. Only as bishop was he expected to defer to the Archbishop. Parliament upheld this formula and Romeyn was sentenced to prison for his attempted usurpation of royal authority, a punishment commuted to a fine commensurate with an archbishop's wealth. Now William of St Botolph, Bek's steward, felt entitled to crow about his lord's victory: 'There are two kings in England, namely the lord king of England wearing a crown as symbol of his regality, and the lord bishop of Durham wearing a mitre in

Durham's medieval golden glass: fragments assembled in a panel on the south wall of the Galilee.

place of a crown as symbol of his regality in the diocese of Durham.' The over-mighty subject always walks a tightrope, and in the very year of St Botolph's boast the king deprived Bek of his powers because of his alleged abuse of feudal authority in the course of disputes with the priory and with northern barons. But Bek was also a professional escapologist, and in no time persuaded Edward to act as mediator. The outcome, the Bishop's Charter of 1303, was simply a codification of Bek's powers in the spheres of justice, finance and military service. A plenitude of powers was now restored to him and his successors.

Bek lived and behaved as if he were a king. He kept a household of about 140, the equivalent of that of an earl, and when he travelled always took a cavalry escort of about the same number of knights. His arrival at the priory for the ill-fated visitation of 1300 was regal, with a large retinue of knights and clergy. When Prior Hoton objected to the secrets of the convent being so widely disseminated, Bek's rejoinder was equally regal: 'Sit down, Prior, and understand clearly that we intend that all these who are of our council shall accompany us.' But Bek was not the only king's friend to feel the draught of royal displeasure, often accompanied by temporary confiscation of powers. The perils of flying close to the sun were experienced by several Prince-Bishops. Bek's successor but one, the undeserving and luckless Louis de Beaumont, fell foul of all three factions hemming him in. While still bishop-elect and travelling to Durham for his enthronement he was kidnapped by Gilbert de Middleton, officially Warden of the Marches but unofficially an unreconstructed outlaw, and held to ransom at Morpeth. Then in 1322 he led a Durham force against the Scots, but succeeded only in provoking them to a daring raid which took them as far as the Tees. The outcome was a flea in his ear from the furious Edward II: 'It was through the negligence of your predecessor [Kellawe] that parts of your bishopric had so often been wasted by the Scots, but now we postively know that, through your default, negligence and lukewarmness, greater damage has happened and still daily happens in parts of your bishopric than in the time of your predecessor.' Edward's hopes had been sadly dashed: he had promoted Beaumont because 'he would be a wall of brass between the king and his Scottish enemies'. Weak kings, in general, bred weak viceroys; the strong bishops unsurprisingly serve strong kings: Calais with the Conqueror, Flambard with Henry I, Puiset with Henry II, Bek with Edward I, and Langley with Henry V.

PALATINATE GOVERNMENT

The administration of the Palatinate as well as its semi-independence honoured historical precedents. Before the Normans there may have been both a bishop's court and an assembly in the diocese. The assembly was perhaps an annual affair linked to St Cuthbert's feast

day in September, when barons, freemen and tenants holding land 'under St Cuthbert' met to affirm their feudal obligations. In the Palatinate, court and assembly were maintained, with the addition of an executive Council chosen by the bishop.

The rights and privileges accorded to the bishop were summed up in the formula 'quicquid rex habet extra episcopus habet intra': whatever the king possesses beyond the diocese the bishop possesses within it. He was head of the civil administration. He had authority to raise his own taxes, usually tolls and

The view of Castle and Cathedral from the railway station, described by John Ruskin as one of the wonders of the world.

customs duties, to fund his government and its defences against the Scots. He was head of the justiciary, appointed judges, heard appeals and had the power of pardon. In 1398 Walter Lewyn, using the shooting butts in Framwellgate, missed the target but hit and killed a boy sitting in the ditch next to the targets. Bishop Skirlaw pardoned Lewyn since it was an accident. The Prince-Bishop was keeper not of the king's peace but of the bishop's. He was landlord of all diocesan lands, issued charters to boroughs and licensed fairs and markets. He was entitled to all shipwrecks and treasure trove, and to royal fish. He was lord of all the forests and possessor of all the mines. All lands forfeit by traitors passed to him, and he exercised power of wardship over estates inherited by minors. He was entitled to pre-empt goods. It seems entirely apt, given such a remit, that the Great Seal of the Durham Chancery was patterned on the Great Seal of England. Both were held simultaneously by five Prince-Bishops who were also Chancellor of England: Richard Marsh, Richard de Bury,

Thomas Langley (under three successive kings), Laurence Booth and Thomas Wolsey.

The model of feudal obligation that prevailed in the king's name elsewhere in England was replaced in Durham by an episcopal alternative. So many responsibilities could only be exercised by personal and formal reliance on the landed families of the north, on whose loyalties to the Prince-Bishop law and order and military competence depended. The barons of the bishopric occupied their lands in return for military service and the bishop expected their allegiance. The Nevilles of Raby, the Balliols of Barnard Castle, the Bruces of Hart and later the Percys of Alnwick served on the bishop's council, and Ralph Neville, victor at the Battle of Neville's Cross in 1346, was the first layman to be buried in the cathedral. The Council was composed of barons, clerics and lawyers, and its duty was to administer the Palatinate, hear ecclesiastical lawsuits and protect the bishop's rights, all of high importance given that the bishops were seldom in Durham for any length of time, some absent for years on end. Little eluded the Council's punctilious supervision. In 1364 a whale was washed ashore at Seaton, and appropriated by John de Carrowe who cut it up and gave it to his friends. The Council judged it to be a royal fish and fined de Carrowe 100 marks (£23,000) for his presumption.

The bishop's regime was dependent too on the officers in his household, principally the Steward or Seneschal who was his deputy and agent, and the Sheriff, whose responsibilities included running the courts of justice and the gaols, maintaining law and order throughout the district, handling lands and possessions relinquished by felons and fugitives, and raising armed men in the event of threat. In 1400 for example, when

The Great Hall of Durham Castle, built by Bishop Bek in the late 13th century, but greatly altered later by Bishops Hatfield and Fox. It is now the dining hall of University College.

there were rumours of a French invasion in the north in support of the deposed Richard II, Henry IV sent a writ to Bishop Skirlaw to gather all the clergy in the diocese together with the numbers of armed men they were duty-bound to supply, and a great array was held on St Giles's Moor just beyond the city.

The bishop and his officers vigilantly guarded their various sources of revenue, which delivered an annual return of about £2,500 (£150,000). The annual income of the Crown at the same time was around £60,000 (£20m), and that of Winchester, the only diocese wealthier than Durham, just under £3,000 (£180,000). Income ranged from the re-sale of bishops' privileges, for example the licensing of fairs and markets, to the burgesses of boroughs; fees and tolls for each ship using the River Tyne, one-third of which, including the whole south bank, was recognized as a bishop's liberty; the seizure of hides and fleeces smuggled across Berwick Bridge, and the levying of duties on wool and wine passing through Hartlepool, the Palatinate's major port. There was also a Mint in Durham, founded in the early 12th century, which issued coinage with both the king's and bishop's head stamped upon it. It was probably a revenue-raising exercise rather than an assertion of sovereignty, and during the 15th century its production was standardized with royal mints elsewhere. By the time of the Tudors, Durham pennies bore only the image of Henry VII crowned and enthroned, and the bishop's identity was reduced to his initials stamped on the reverse side, as in other provincial mints.

The existence of a small kingdom within a greater one nurtured a predictable crop of anomalies. Though the ultimate authority in Durham was always that of the king, at whose will and pleasure the bishop retained his powers, the king's officers were not allowed to enter the diocese except when the see was vacant and the royal writ enforceable again. The

Durham Assembly and Council had no legislative powers; there was a tacit assumption that laws passed by Parliament were binding in Durham even though it had no lay representation in that parliament until the late 17th century. The absence of representation mattered less when the laity of the bishopric was exempt from royal taxation. This liberty was historical. There is no evidence that Danegeld was levied there in the 10th and 11th centuries, and the Conqueror's agents, as we have seen, met violent resistance when they tried to exact money for the king. Symeon the Chronicler recasts this liberty as a Cuthbert miracle. When William's tax collector, Ranulf, was active in Durham, Cuthbert persecuted him in dream-visions and made him ill, promising that his health would recover only when he took himself south again. He did, and it did. Durham was excluded from the Domesday survey of 1086, the basis for subsequent Norman taxation, and the survey also recorded that neither king nor earl had any 'custom' over Cuthbert's lands in Yorkshire.

It was inevitable, given the actual and reputed wealth of Durham, that kings would repeatedly try to milk it for themselves. Richard I levied a tax on portable property ('the Saladin tithe') to help fund his Crusade, but devious Puiset took the Cross and made every sign of preparing to join the adventure, thereby exempting himself from the tax. But just before departure he sought absolution from his crusading vow from the Pope and stayed at home, relishing all the more his abundant portable property. During the 15th century royal taxation was progressively extracted from the Palatinate although its only parliamentary representative was the bishop himself in the House of Lords. Such gradual encroachment on ancient liberties, however, was nothing in comparison with the treatment of Durham by the ruthlessly efficient, centralizing and unsentimental Tudors.

The Duncow: a Durham Shorthorn cow and two milkmaids, an exterior carving at the north-west corner of the Chapel of the Nine Altars. This 18th century carving refers to the legend of the discovery of 'Dunholme' as the site for the cathedral.

THE DECLINE OF THE PALATINATE

Nothing was allowed to stand in the way of the Tudor drive for the unifying and secularizing of the nation's government. Henry VIII and his principal agents Wolsey and Thomas Cromwell swiftly moved to place the governance of the north in the hands of a royal lieutenant and a Council of the North subordinate to the Privy Council. In 1525 Henry's bastard son Henry FitzRoy was created Duke of Richmond and made governor of England north of the River Trent. From 1532 a Council of the Marches took over the government in alliance with the Duke of Northumberland, the Lord Warden of the Marches. In response to the Pilgrimage of Grace of 1536, when law and order in the Palatinate broke down, the king took the opportunity to remove the bishop's judicial responsibilities. The 1536 Act of Resumption of Liberties transferred criminal jurisdiction, the appointment of judges, the keeping of

'Wedges of greenery thrust into the heart of the city': these cows may not be holy, but they are certainly blessed to be able to graze in this pasture: a view south-west from Observatory Hill in August.

the peace and the right of pardon to the Crown. The Palatine Courts of Pleas and Chancery lingered on until the 19th century, but the judicial independence of Durham had in effect been taken away. The Duke of Norfolk came north to scourge it in 1537, imposed martial law and set up a new council, with Bishop Tunstall as token President, though its remit extended to York, Westmoreland, Cumberland and Northumberland as well as Durham. Remorselessly the Palatinate was being absorbed into a united nation. Bishops Ruthall and Wolsey had made it clear that their first loyalty was to the Crown, not the Palatinate; Tunstall felt a strong allegiance to Durham but his recognition of 'realpolitik' was stronger still. He wrote to Cromwell in 1538: 'And as touchinge all other persones, of what sorte of men so ever they bee, kynne or frende or other, that shall fortune to utter their stomakke agaynst the kinges hyghness or to be accused of the same, I for my parte shall bere them lesse

favour than I wolde do to Turkes.' But even the pragmatic Tunstall proved dispensable when, during the minority of Edward VI, Protector Northumberland coveted the Palatinate for himself. Tunstall was deprived and imprisoned, his bishopric abolished and his powers seized by the Protector. The death of the young king shortly afterwards put an abrupt stop on Northumberland's rapacity. A final measure of the fading status of Prince-Bishops under the Tudors was the forfeiture of the Neville estates after the family's part in the Rising of the North in 1569. Traditionally these lands would have passed to the bishop, but when the hopeful Pilkington put in his claim, he found that the estates had already passed direct to the Crown. In a still greater humiliation, Elizabeth I, having developed a taste for northern territory, immediately confiscated a quarter of the Palatinate by Act of Parliament. The majesty of the bishop's throne had moved on.

CATHOLIC TO PURITAN 1350–1580

THE FLOURISHING OF THE MONASTERY

Medieval Durham's distress was followed by its golden age. From Bek's death in 1311 to the Black Death in 1349 had been a period of unremitting afflictions. Though Bek had been a contentious bishop he had been a staunch defender of the diocese and Palatinate, and his reward was a place in the cathedral for all time. His bones lie beneath a plain slab at the north end of the Chapel of the Nine Altars, completed and dedicated at the moment he had been appointed bishop. His successors had generally been incompetent or absent; the Scots had raided more or less at will and had had to be bought off; freak weather had brought famine and disease and then, to crown the misery, came the Black Death.

The resilience of the priory had been remarkable, but even more so was the resurgence that followed, a reaffirmation of purpose which brought both cathedral and monastery to their fullness. The grandeur of architectural ambition and its accompanying decoration raised Durham at the close of the 14th and in the early 15th century to its summit of wealth and status. It boasted an income of 5000 marks (£1m) which had entitled it to request the Pope in the 1370s to allow the Prior to display the pontifical insignia of mitre, staff and ring. It had qualified for membership of an exclusive club. Additions to and reconstructions of monastic buildings and bold enhancement of the cathedral were achieved in a period of welcome and unusual harmony between bishops and convent, and through the dedication of a

sequence of exceptional priors – Fossor, Wessington, Bell and Castell – who took the opportunity to exercise a greater share of responsibility for new construction than had the bishops. But they were supported in their initiatives by bishops who shared their vision, cared for Durham, possessed wealth and were figures of national significance wielding influence: Hatfield, Skirlaw and Langley. It was also the time when Prince-Bishops reached the peak of their importance as rulers of the Palatinate and lived in a manner commensurate with their vice-regal functions. The example of magnificence set by Puiset and Bek was sustained. Bishops had palatial residences at Durham Castle,

Above: *The head of Edward III: a carving on the north side of Bishop Hatfield's tomb.*

Right: *The 14th-century high altar screen commissioned by Prior Fossor from John Neville of Raby Castle. Carved in Caen stone by Henry Yvele in London, it originally displayed over one hundred alabaster statues of saints and martyrs.*

Far left: *The noble space of the monastic dormitory above the West Cloister, built in the first decade of the 15th century, and the only surviving complete monastic dormitory in England.*

Left: *A detail of the trusses and pegs from the great oak hammerbeam roof, the glory of the dormitory.*

Norham, Bishop Auckland and Northallerton, manors at Stockton, Darlington and Howden, a castle at Crayke near York, as well as Durham House in The Strand, their London residence where they combined national and diocesan administration. Whenever a bishop travelled he had a retinue of at least 100, and many more than that in a settled household.

This was also the period in which bishops began to look for ostentatious burial in the cathedral. Bek's grave had been plain, but Hatfield, Skirlaw and Langley all wanted chantry tombs, which they designed and had prepared before their deaths. Their willingness to donate generous sums for monastic buildings had the ulterior purpose of gaining the permission of the prior and chapter for their grand interments. In earlier centuries bishops and priors alike had been buried simply beneath the floor of the

Chapter House. The overall cost of building was met by a combination of episcopal donations, offerings left by pilgrims at Cuthbert's shrine and, as we have noted with the financing of the Chapel of the Nine Altars, the sale of indulgences throughout England. 'Peter's Pence' was a Saxon tax of one penny from each household for the Papacy, demotically known as smoke-penny or reek-penny. In 1164 Pope Alexander III decreed that the income should be used within the diocese to enhance its cathedral. Additionally, all diocesan congregations were duty-bound to visit their cathedral annually to make further donations.

The 14th century was also the period which witnessed the development of Durham's musical tradition. Bishop Richard de Bury in the 1330s promoted music: there were boys of the bishop's chapel and a clerk who was their master, and from the same decade there is the first reference to an organ, played at Easter. From at least 1345 the monastery appointed a cantor as director of music, and the first reference to the singers he directed is found in 1356–7. By the 1380s there are clerks singing polyphony and helping the monks with 'trebill song' (three-part harmony). In 1390 Prior Walworth approved a petition which read: 'Item, as much as for (enhancing) the dignity of divine worship (as for) inspiring the devotion of the people let

The spiky roofline of Prior Fossor's octagonal monastic kitchen built in the mid-14th century, seen from the central tower.

The exterior of the kitchen seen from The College.

both musical harmony and (ceremonial) be had in the choir in accordance with ancient custom. Chiefly on solemn feast days … let a suitable Cantor-Instructor who knows how to instruct the youths to sing be … at the expense of the house.' From 1414 there is continuous evidence of extensive musical education for monks and boys alike.

MONASTIC BUILDINGS

As for the buildings themselves, it was as if Fossor's noble kitchen, completed in 1371, had both restored the community's morale and provided a benchmark for the quality of subsequent projects. Just before his death Fossor commissioned a high altar screen known as the Neville Screen. John, Lord Neville of Raby paid £500 (£175,000) or 500 marks (£120,000) (the account doesn't make clear which) for an elaborate canopied screen of Caen stone bearing 107 figures of saints and martyrs carved in the Nottingham alabaster much prized for royal tombs. It was almost certainly intended as an additional monument to his father, Ralph Neville, who had died in 1368 and had been buried first at the front of the Nave and then in a chantry tomb, now lost, in the South Nave Aisle. It was designed and carved in London by Henry Yvele and then shipped in sections to Newcastle before being reassembled in Durham and consecrated in

November 1380. We learn details of its lost iconography from the author of *The Rites of Durham*, written in the 1590s, who had witnessed the desecration of the screen by the puritanical Dean Horne in the 1550s. The fashionable architect James Wyatt, brought in 250 years later for a cathedral makeover, tried to demolish what remained to use as an organ screen, but as a suspect southerner his scheme was happily resisted to leave the sinuous, delicately dancing stone tracery, shorn of all its images, to marvel at as the only surviving medieval canopied reredos in England. It was complemented in the following year, 1381, by the chantry tomb of Bishop Thomas Hatfield surmounted by its bishop's throne, now the most eye-catching of the cathedral's medieval monuments. Hatfield knew how to value Prince-Bishops: it was claimed that the throne was higher than the Papal throne in St Peter's. Hatfield's chantry was soon matched by that of his successor, Walter Skirlaw, bishop from 1388 to 1406, who constructed his own monument before his death, as Hatfield had done. The agreement of prior and chapter had been eased by his donation of £220 (£70,000) towards the cost of a new

The interior vaulting of the kitchen, now serving as the Cathedral Bookshop.

dormitory above the West Cloister, built between 1398 and 1404. It was the third dormitory, to be brought into use after the roof of its predecessor was adjudged to be beyond repair in a mason's report of 1390: 'The dormitory and infirmary are badly roofed, so that it rains continually in those places when it rains, greatly rotting and weakening the timber.' In 1398 John Middleton, mason, was contracted to build the walls, and he was replaced, for reasons not clear to us, by Peter Dryng, who spanned the walls with a daring roof. Within, each monk had 'a little chamber of wainscott verie close seuerall by them selves'. It must have seemed like a luxury hotel when they moved into it after their leaky old tumbledown. Middleton and Dryng must have scoured the county for oak trunks long and straight enough to span the 40-foot width of the hall. It is the only surviving intact monastic dormitory in the country. Its scale is unanticipated, and the visitor who climbs the day stair from the north-west angle of the cloister is stilled into wonder as the noble space stretches out before him. It is one of the very great medieval halls of England, alongside Westminster Hall and Durham Castle.

Each building project seemed to initiate the next. By contrast with the new dormitory, the Cloisters suddenly looked mean. The appreciative Skirlaw just had time before his death to donate £600 (£200,000) to the Cloister Fund, and their remodelling began around 1409 and took about ten years, the last phase coinciding with John Wessington's new Libraria above the East Cloister. He was only Chancellor when that work began, but by the time it was finished he was Prior, having been elected in 1416 to preside very properly over the dedication of both cloister and library. A monastic cloister was a place of study, and the draughts that now harry passers-by through the open window tracery that dates from a later remodelling in the 18th century had been excluded by a series of windows, some clear and some in the east cloister

Above: *Known as Prior Castell's Clock, this much reconstructed timepiece standing in the South Transept may have been derived from the first cathedral clock, which was placed on a beam above the Nave in the 14th century.*

Left: *Prior Castell built the Gatehouse, the main entrance to The College on the south side of the Cathedral, towards the close of the 15th century.*

illustrating the life and miracles of St Cuthbert, for the monks to turn their gaze to for inspiration when the biblical commentaries they were reading in their carrells failed to engage their full attention.

Wessington was prior for a reassuring and stabilizing 30 years until his resignation in 1446. His next project was to replace the rainy infirmary with a new one, completed in 1430 and demolished in the 1650s at a time when the cathedral was stripped of all leadership. Ordeal by lightning was Wessington's next test. In 1429 the wooden belfry of the stump tower said to have been built by Prior Hugh of Darlington (1258–72) was struck and set alight. Repairs seem to have been slow and perfunctory, for in 1456 it was reported that it was in urgent need of attention. It can never be affirmed, on Durham's hill-top site, that lightening never strikes the same place twice, for on Easter Day 1459 the tower was struck and set on fire again. So the last great building scheme of the cathedral was directed by Prior Richard Bell, a

Durham monk since his noviciate, who raised the funds for 'the re-edification of our steple' by efficient management of priory business and saw the tower virtually complete before his promotion to the see of Carlisle in 1478. All that remained for Thomas Castell, Prior from 1494 to 1519, to leave as his monuments were the vaulted gatehouse at the entrance to the College, still the main approach to College Green, the ambitious perpendicular tracery of the North Transept window with its long-lost glow of finest stained glass, and, by repute, the enhancement of the original 14th-century great clock, which in its much reconstructed form stands today in the South Transept.

POLITICAL INSTABILITY

The completion of Durham was the more notable because it took place under conditions of unrelenting political instability. Two great medieval bishops, Skirlaw and Langley, were deeply involved in the nation's destiny, and for much of the golden age there

Above: The 15th-century tomb of John and Matilda Neville on the south side of the Nave. The battered effigies and beheaded weepers are testimony to the periods of violence the place has witnessed.

Right: A view from the South Nave Aisle looking north-east towards the North Transept, with the damaged 15th-century tomb of Ralph and Alice Neville of Raby Castle in the foreground.

was the menace of repeated Scottish wars and raids punctuated by fragile truces. From 1406 to 1424 James I of Scotland was a prisoner of the English and released by the Treaty of Durham only after protracted negotiations. As late as the 1440s, Henry VI's choice of Robert Neville as bishop was determined by his belief that he 'may puissantly kepe (the Marches) best to the honour of God and defence of this our royaume'. In 1415 there were 115 fortifications in readiness in Northumberland alone, and though Durham city was seldom threatened, the Palatinate administration was severely tested by the collapse of morale in the East March following a near- total breakdown of law and order there. In practice Northumberland was relinquished to lawnessness until the 16th century, with 'Weregild', the Anglo-Saxon revenge code of either monetary compensation or vengeance for family members killed in a feud, the chief mode of justice. The Scots, as always, were ready to probe what they perceived as English weakness. In 1388, with Richard II's kingdom at odds with itself, they pressed south and

humiliated the English at Otterburn, when the forces mustered by the Bishop of Durham failed to show up, and for the rest there was massacre by moonlight. The long dynastic struggles between York and Lancaster presented the Scots with a harvest of opportunities and ensnared the north of England into the quicksands of national politics. Between 1399 and 1569 there were eight actual or attempted coups d'état instigated from the north by the Nevilles and the Percys; Edward IV and Richard III were both Nevilles on their mother's side, and support for Richard in the north was crucial in his usurpation of the throne in 1483, just as the desertion of his northern allies Percy and Stanley lost him battle, throne and life at Bosworth in 1485.

Walter Skirlaw, a member of the King's Council under both Richard II and Henry IV, succeeded in skirting the quicksands only to be thwarted of his principal ambition by untimely death. He was a career diplomat, often in France, and in his absences, as with other medieval bishops of Durham with duties elsewhere, a vicar-general ran the diocese in his place. Skirlaw was drawn into the plot to depose Henry of Lancaster in favour of the Earl of Mortimer in 1403, and after the defeat of the rebels at Shrewsbury he prudently withdrew to France to be out of sight, out of mind. With matching prudence and maybe foresight he began the preparation of his tomb in the cathedral at the same time. Restored to favour he had every hope of becoming Archbishop of York, a position to which the York Chapter had elected him in 1398, only for Richard II to over-rule the choice in favour of Scrope. But in 1405, in an unprecedented assertion of secular power over clerical, Henry IV had Scrope executed for his role in the rebellion. Skirlaw used his wealth and patronage to fuel his expectations, as he had at Durham, by presenting York Minster with its magnificent east window. But before the appointment was made he died at the bishop's manor at Howden.

This agonized medieval carved figure in the gallery above the crossing seems to be carrying all the weight of the lantern tower on his back.

The crossing, screen, Quire and High Altar seen from the gallery in the lantern tower.

Thomas Langley's Lancastrian loyalties were never in doubt. He had served John of Gaunt and was not only an accomplished diplomat chosen to negotiate with the Percys before the Battle of Shrewsbury but at the time of his appointment to Durham in 1406 was also Chancellor of England. Though he resigned the Chancellorship in 1407 he resumed it again from 1417 to 1424 at the wish of Henry V. For Langley, Durham was a compensation prize. He wanted York but the Pope, outraged by Scrope's execution, refused to accept the nomination. So he came to Durham for over 30 years and was a significant enough national figure to be its resolute defender. There was partial reconciliation with Rome too, for he was proposed as a cardinal in 1411. He

had authority sufficient to resist the erosion of the traditional rights of Prince-Bishops when he demanded and secured for the Palatinate the lands forfeit by the traitors Scrope and Grey. Skirlaw had allowed Henry IV to seize the lands of the Percys after 1403 in an unhappy precedent for the status of Durham. Langley founded a chantry in the Galilee in 1414 and appointed two chaplains to teach grammar and music, free to poor children, but with fees for those who could afford them. The pupils were likely to have been children from the city, for the monastery had had an almonry school since at least 1347, from which choristers and novices were recruited. The bishop generally visited his diocese twice a year and through his generous donations the Cloister was completed in 1418 and the Galilee renovated with a gift of £500 (£150,000). Towards the end of his life Langley made a rousing defence of the Durham liberties at the Parliament of 1433. Like his immediate predecessors he had prepared his monument before his death. In the restoration of the Galilee he had set his chantry tomb on the east side of the chapel before the original west doors of the church, to which his body was consigned in 1437. In his will he left money for the prior and convent to pray for his soul, and books, jewels and vestments for the Libraria and the cathedral. More than most bishops, he had deserved their prayers.

DURHAM AT THE CLOSE OF THE MIDDLE AGES

We know more about the ordering and rituals of the cathedral and monastery at Durham immediately before the Reformation than we do about any other foundation. Our principal source is *The Rites of Durham*, an anonymous account appearing in 1593, written some time after the Dissolution by someone who, though probably not a monk, was closely involved with both convent and church and possessed richly detailed powers of recall of every aspect of monastic life from the shrine to the privies. The author's tone is unashamedly nostalgic: the lost way of life he commemorates seemed to him a model of order and beauty, and his account of it is understandably idealized. His dense and heady prose is studded with breathless refrains: 'maruelously fine', 'goodly faire', sumptuous and richest', 'the rarest in all England'. Yet his rose-tinted vision recreates a more vivid impression of monastic existence than any number of modern dispassionate accounts can achieve. He has witnessed the destruction of the community he must have served, the assured order of its daily round and of the rare and precious objects assembled to embody its rituals and devotions. The pain of loss informs every paragraph. He is like a miser numbering his stolen hoard, probing

away at the raw places. *The Rites of Durham* both depicts a treasure-house and is itself one such.

The two strongest impressions conveyed by *The Rites of Durham* concern the decoration of the cathedral and the ordered life of its community. The church today is a place of plain, almost austere, light and spaciousness. But in the 1530s it must have resembled an overflowing oriental bazaar. We would scarcely have recognized it. It was very cluttered, with many screens and roods subdividing the building, dozens of small separate chapels and altars, and with lofts in the aisles. The stone walls were plastered and ornate with paintings. It was also very dark because of the dense array of stained glass. The glitter and colour of candles and jewelled images would have seemed like Christmas decorations all the year round. Religious art in all cultures has tended to occupy the whole spectrum from sublimity to kitsch, with kitsch the norm. As the author of *The Rites* verbally fondles his lost treasures and overwhelms his reader with visual and emotional excess, it is a useful corrective to reflect that what has been lost was in most instances more curious than beautiful.

A few examples must stand for the whole. The cover for St Cuthbert's Shrine could be drawn up by a rope with six silver bells attached to it so that when the cover was being raised the sweet chimes of the bells would draw to the shrine all the visitors in the cathedral. At the east side of the cover 'was painted the picture of our Saviour sitting on a Rainbowe to geive Judgement very lively to ye behoulders and on the West end of itt was ye picture of our Lady and our Saviour on her knee. And on the topp of ye Cover from end to end was most fyne carved worke cutt owte with Dragons and other beasts moste artificially wrought and ye inside was Vernished with a fyne sanguine colour that itt might be more perspicuous to ye beholders.' At the high altar the 'most sumptuous' Canopy of the Blessed Sacrament was fastened to a stone screen 'wheron did stand a pellican all of siluer uerye finely gilded giuinge hir bloud to hir younge ones'. The cloth over the pyx nearby was 'of very fine lawn all embroidered and wrought about with gold and red silk, and 4 great and round knopes of gold marvellously and cunningly wrought with great tassels of gold and red silk hanging at them.' The tone of *The Rites* often resembles that of a frenzied auctioneer working overtime to oversell his wares. The great Paschal candle constructed annually to occupy the full width of the Quire from Maundy Thursday until after Ascension Day is presented as one of the seven wonders of England. It rose to the height of the triforium vault, embellished with flying dragons as well as the evangelists, beasts and men upon horseback with bucklers, bows and shafts, knots with broad leaves from which rose seven gilded candlesticks set about with large flowers in candlestick metal. Such a medieval shrine cathedral was not very different in spirit, purpose or atmosphere from the traditional fairgrounds where people gathered to gape at curiosities, freaks and technicolour marvels. In our time people flock to secular Disneyland for parallel sensations.

Yet beneath this glittering, even flimsy surface lies an ordering of life both solemn and festive, which must have felt to those who knew it as if it had lasted and would last for ever. It was itself an image of eternity, the loss of which all on an instant the author registers as the end of all security and the start of a new formless age, all landmarks swept aside. From the three bells which rang at midnight in the new lantern when 'the monks went evermore to their matins at that hour of the night' to the two men who 'did always sweep and keep the church cleanly and did fill the holy water stones every Sunday in the morning with clean water before it came to be hallowed, and did lock in the church doors every night', we meet a way of life of reassuring predictability. The lights 'did burne continually both day and night' in the cressets in front of the high altar 'in token that the house was alwayes watchinge to god'; the bells at midnight told the clustering town that 'in the deep night all was well'.

There are rituals to accompany a monk in his death and burial in the Centry Garth, and a moving account of the daily visit by all the community to the cemetery, where they 'ther did stand all bair heade a Certain longe Space, praieng amongst the Toumbes and throwghes for there brethren soules being buried there, and when they hadd done there prayers then they did Returne to ye Cloyster, and there did studie there bookes until iii of ye clocke that they went to Evensong this was there dalie exercise'. Each night in the Dormitory there was a privy search and roll-call 'to see good order kept'; every 20th March there was Cuthbert's feast when the convent kept open house in the Frater; once a year between Martinmas and Christmas there was a banquet in the Common House, 'of figs and raisins, ale and cakes, and there of no superfluity or excess but a scholastical and moderate congratulation among themselves'. Every Maundy Thursday in the South Cloister children sat in a row on the long stone bench and each monk washed a child's feet, dried them with a towel and kissed them, giving to every child 30 pence (£35) in money and seven red herring and three loaves of bread and wafercakes. Never such innocence again. And, for air and exercise behind the Common House on a terrace above the river, a garden and a bowling alley 'for the Novices to recreate them selves when they had remedy of their master he standing by to see there good order'.

TUDOR DURHAM

In the course of the 15th century the popularity of St Cuthbert's cult began to wane. As early as 1410 sub-Prior Rypon rebuked the diocesan clergy in a sermon for their failure to join the Whitsun processions. Their dereliction was held responsible for 'the wars, pestilences and other ills' infesting the district. 'It is commonly said, Saint Cuthbert sleeps, because he shows forth no miracles, nor lends aid to his people, as formerly he was wont to do. In very truth we are the cause because we do not lend our devotions as we ought.' The last Cuthbert miracle recorded at the shrine was manifested, with exemplary timing and deference, at a visit by Princess Margaret of Scotland in 1503, and by 1514 offerings had seriously declined, from around £60 (£21,000) a year at the end of the 14th century to £10 (£2,500) by the 1530s. Pilgrimage was fading.

It was not the only straw in the wind. Successive bishops Ruthall and the great Wolsey were Tudor apparatchiks with little or no feeling for Durham. Wolsey is reputed to have begged the see from Henry VIII after a misunderstanding by which he came to believe that his income would be ten times greater than it actually was. Power- and wealth-hungry, and even disappointed in his expectations, he never visited Durham, even for an enthronement. The Cardinal's fall in 1529 left a political vacuum in the north and the king appointed the reliable Cuthbert Tunstall to fill it. He had the right name, after all. Tunstall had risen in favour by associating himself with powerful men at the right time: Warham, Archbishop of Canterbury, Wolsey and Henry himself. As a royal councillor on diplomatic missions to the continent he had become an intimate friend of Erasmus, who acknowledged Tunstall's part in the Greek New Testament he published in 1516. Tunstall was a member of the circle of distinguished humanists active in London: More, Colet, Linacre and Grocyn. Erasmus named More and Tunstall as 'the two most learned men in England, and both very dear to me'. But Tunstall lacked More's adamantine core; he was rather a political weathercock who managed to survive the political and religious tempests of the years between 1530 and 1560 only to die at the advanced age of 85, having found in the last months of his life a principle upon which he

Contrasting carved figures, formal and lifelike, in the tower gallery.

could not yield, and was for the second time in his long episcopate deprived of his see.

Tunstall reached Durham in 1530 to meet the fruits of Wolsey's neglect. He found the houses belonging to the bishopric in almost total ruin: 'I had not one house at my first coming to lie dry in.' He quickly repaired the castle, Auckland Palace and Norham, and established a reputation for charity and hospitality in the diocese. This was the easy part. A much more searching test of his mettle was supplied by Henry's marital jockeyings, his quest for supremacy of the church in England and, in Tunstall's own backyard, the Pilgrimage of Grace of 1536. He had been Henry's creature, appointed by him to the sees of London and Durham, and had predictably come round to the legality of the king's marriage to Anne Boleyn, participated in her coronation. By 1534 he was wholly the king's man, doubtless intimidated by the imprisoning of More and Fisher and by the raiding and ransacking of both his London residence and Bishop Auckland itself. In 1535 he accepted Henry's claim to be Supreme Head of the Church and championed it in Durham.

His loyalties were racked by the Pilgrimage of Grace. As bishop he was President of 'the King's Council in the North Parts', but in 1536 found that his duty to the king placed him in an uncomfortable minority on the Council, many of whose members sympathized with the aims of the Pilgrimage. Recent Acts of Parliament, especially the Act of Resumption of Liberties, had challenged the north's very identity. The transfer of authority for justice, lands and revenues to the king promised to sap its cherished independence and reduce its capacity to defend itself against the Scots. Moreover, the religious sensibilities of the north were conservative, and the organizers of the Pilgrimage selected the defence of the traditional church as their rallying point. In October news of a

The Five Wounds of Christ, depicted in stained glass by Pugin in the Galilee and in carved woodwork on the 15th-century ceiling of The Prior's Bedroom in the Deanery, an emblem of the 'old religion', became the badge of the Pilgrimage of Grace in 1536.

rising reached Tunstall at Auckland and, showing more prudence than leadership, he fled north at midnight and shut himself away for the next four months at Norham. Shortly after his ignominious retreat a force of several thousand arrived at Auckland and plundered the palace. On to Durham they streamed: they sacked the Palatinate Chancery and scattered its records, demanded and secured the Banner of St Cuthbert from the monks and marched with it to Doncaster. A centuries-old tradition of northern independence was manifesting itself for the last time. Some 30,000 'pilgrims' converged at Pontefract; faced with a popular rising on this scale, the king's representatives negotiated a peaceful outcome, with seeming agreements reached and pardons offered. But it was all a ruse. The following year the promises and pardons were revoked and 150 leaders of the Pilgrimage, including two Cistercian abbots, were put to death. Now Henry had the pretext he needed to punish the North. The Duke of Norfolk exacted a bloody vengeance, brought the great families into submission and set up a less treasonable Council. The hapless Tunstall was again compelled to preside, much against his will. One result of his weakness was the requisitioning by the king of Durham House in The Strand, for centuries the London palace of the bishops.

THE DISSOLUTION

Durham House was not all that Henry, now abetted by Thomas Cromwell, had his eye upon. Before the Pilgrimage, the king's commissioners Layton and Legh had been sent to Durham to sniff out abuses. But they could find no evidence of misconduct and reported their failure to Cromwell: 'In Durham Abbey your Injunctions can take none effect in some things, for there was never yet woman within the Abbey further than the Church, nor they (the monks) never came within the town.' But the rebellion of 1536 played into Cromwell's hands and gave him an unassailable case for the swift suppression of monasticism in the north, which could conveniently be assumed to be complicit in an event focused on its defence.

In March 1538 Cromwell's hit-men Legh, Henley and Blythman returned with a purpose. They demolished Cuthbert's shrine and appropriated all the jewels and ornaments that attended it. Next they opened the tomb, finding a wooden chest with iron bands which the goldsmith acting on their orders broke open with a forge hammer. He overdid it. 'Alas, I have broken one of his legs', he called down to the others. The saint was found, it was reported, 'lying whole, uncorrupt, with his face bare, and his beard as of a fortnight's growth'. Henley ordered him to throw the bones down. But the goldsmith said he could not get them asunder for they were held together by skin and sinews. Legh and Henley went up to check, and then ordered that the body be taken to the Revestry 'to be close and safely kept till the king's pleasure be known'. That pleasure was never communicated, and after nearly four years of the body's lingering in the air of the Revestry and decaying, Tunstall ordered a new outer coffin and asked the dean and chapter to rebury the remains at Epiphany 1542 below the site of the vandalized shrine.

Dissolution of the smaller monasteries and cells had begun in 1536 and by the end of 1537 all Durham's dependencies except Durham College had been suppressed. Cromwell's tactic was to invite 'voluntary surrender' in return for favourable treatment, including pensions. At Reading, Colchester and Glastonbury, where the abbots refused to surrender they were put to death. Prior Whitehead had little option, in the face of force majeure, but to surrender the priory on 31 December, 1539. Of the 66 monks resident at that inauspicious moment, 32 were given pensions and at least 25 were found positions in the new foundation. Prior Whitehead became Dean Whitehead, 12 of the most learned monks became canons, 12 more minor canons. There was no provision for the 100 or so monastic servants and dependents, though some would have found employment in the new foundation. Though

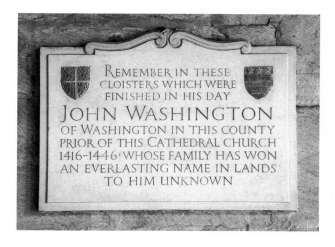

REMEMBER IN THESE CLOISTERS WHICH WERE FINISHED IN HIS DAY JOHN WASHINGTON OF WASHINGTON IN THIS COUNTY PRIOR OF THIS CATHEDRAL CHURCH 1416–1446 WHOSE FAMILY HAS WON AN EVERLASTING NAME IN LANDS TO HIM UNKNOWN

the Benedictine community and its rituals had vanished overnight, there must have remained a strong assurance of human continuity as Whitehead did his best to lead his former brethren into an uncharted land. They had to wait until May 1541 before the arrival of Letters Patent establishing Durham as a new foundation with a Dean and Chapter. And within the church, apart from the despoiled shrine which stopped the beat of Durham's medieval heart, all must have appeared almost surrealistically unchanged. The physical destruction at Durham was to arrive in the third quarter of the century, in the shape of zealous Puritans with a mission to cleanse the temple.

While Cuthbert's abused body was languishing in limbo in the revestry, his name was dropped from the cathedral's dedication by the royal letters patent of 1541. This double discourtesy had what many in the north would have felt to be predictable consequences. The next 40 years were to be a period of confusion, conflict and destruction unrivalled in Durham's long history. Extreme swings of religious policy spawned extreme reactions in the cathedral and the wider society of the north; greedy eyes were cast upon Durham's wealth and estates; Bishop Tunstall, out of favour, was first deprived of the bishopric and imprisoned, then suddenly elevated

The open tracery of the north-west cloister casts its shadows across the door to the dormitory staircase. The plaque commemorates John Washington, or Wessington, Prior from 1416 to 1446, and an ancestor of America's hero of Independence and first president.

again to a high place in the nation's affairs. He was perhaps fortunate at last to be able to die a natural death, even though under house arrest. Then a unique pairing of a puritan bishop and a puritan dean provided a free hand to destroy much of Durham's medieval inheritance.

Tunstall seems not to have been in Durham at the moment of surrender, and his view of the change is not recorded. The enlightened humanist in him may have concluded that reform of the church he served was achievable by distancing it from the corruptions of the Papacy; the politician in him was prepared to tolerate the royal supremacy. Though the dying Henry appointed him a councillor for the minority of Edward VI, he was wholly opposed to the protestant reforms pursued by Protectors Somerset and Northumberland, and his failure to cooperate made him a targeted man. The change of direction came swiftly after the king's death: in 1548 Dean Whitehead was bidden to London where he died, deprived of Durham air. With the Catholic dean removed, Somerset was able to install a new man, the iconoclast Robert Horne, who set about his task with fierce relish. He destroyed the windows in the cloister depicting the life of St Cuthbert, and a chapel with an image of the saint which stood in the cloister garth. Not one to stand and watch during the great cultural revolution, 'he did tread and break with his feet' the Corpus Christi shrine in the church of St Nicholas. Dereliction ranged widely. The close and town were depopulated, canons' residencies were abandoned, left to fall into ruin and demolished. Tunstall was helpless, preoccupied with trying to save his own skin. Under Protector Somerset he had felt free to oppose without fear the Act of Uniformity in Parliament, but the coup in 1549 by John Dudley, Earl of Warwick and soon Duke of Northumberland, removed Somerset and left Tunstall exposed to a specially nasty ruthlessness. For he was a serious obstacle both to Northumberland's Protestant zeal and his lust for the lands of the Palatinate and the Percys. The earl's glittering eye fixed on the two richest sees, Winchester and Durham. Gardiner of Winchester was deprived and imprisoned, and Tunstall was charged with misprision (failure to communicate treason), accused of alleged sympathy for a northern rebellion, and placed under house arrest in his new London home, appropriately named Coldharbour, in Thames Street. Northumberland grilled him and then wrote to Cecil: 'No doubt but the matter will touch him wonderfully, and yield to the King as good a rent (profit) as the Bp. of Winchester's is like to do, if the cards be true.' Tudor magnates were accomplished at asset-stripping, and though the language is dated the mindset is modern. During the trial of Somerset in 1551 preceding his inevitable execution, more 'evidence' against Tunstall somehow emerged, and in October 1552 Northumberland contrived to strip him of his see and imprison him, first in The Tower and then the King's Bench Prison in Southwark.

Now Northumberland could do as he pleased with the north. In March 1553 an Act of Parliament divided the Palatinate into two sees. Northumberland's aim was to promote the rampant Horne to be bishop of the reduced see of Durham, 'so may his Majesty (Edward or himself ?) receive both the castle, which hath a princely seat, and the other stately homes which the bishop had in the country.' A second see based at Newcastle would secure 'for the King' £2,000 (£450,000) a year and the best lands within the north part of his realm. But Horne refused the bait, and the Protector's scheme was thwarted by 'this peevish Dean'. So the bishopric was dissolved and in May 1553 the 'King's County Palatine' replaced the Bishop's. Northumberland granted himself for life the title of Chief Steward. He should have been more concerned about a sickly king than a peevish dean. Edward VI died in July 1553 and all Northumberland's grand

designs came crashing down, still unratified by Parliament. In August Mary Tudor entered London as queen and three days later the 79-year old Tunstall was released and sworn in before the Privy Council as Bishop of Durham. Now he was able to hunt down Horne. He charged the headstrong dean with preaching heresy in the see, having 'infected his whole diocese with new learning', and also bringing his wife into the cathedral 'where never woman came before'. Horne fled into foreign exile in October 1553, cursing 'devilish dreaming Durham', where he had left a trail of wreckage.

Tunstall was again one of the great men of the land, and instrumental in the brief Marian reaction which restored the Catholic faith. From 1555 however, he distanced himself in Durham from the vengeful burnings at the stake which followed the restoration of the heresy laws. He was 'no great bloody persecutor', and there were to be no martyrs in Durham. He refused to hold a full inquisition against one Russell, a fervent preacher, with the words 'I pray you bring not this man's blood upon my head.' He preferred to devise new statutes for the cathedral in 1555, which paid special attention to the care of the library and its records, guaranteeing the survival of Durham's rich heritage of manuscripts and printed books, and defining for the clergy of the diocese their responsibilities for 'the flock of Christ'. At the age of 83 he was still active as a diplomat in the Marches, and in 1557 rode to the frontier at Gretna, but 'he fell from weariness twice, and his men had much ado to restore him to life'.

His extraordinary career was turned upside down once more by the accession of Elizabeth in 1558. She excused him from attendance at her coronation and first parliament, but he needed to meet and counsel her in the summer of 1559 'which is the best time of the year for me to travel in, because I do not look to live long'. The Queen also needed the

An eagle misericord, the emblem of St John the Evangelist, in the Durham Light Infantry Chapel. It is believed to be the only surviving misericord from the 13th-century choir stalls.

endorsement of the last of the Henrician bishops for the sake of ecclesiastical continuity. Before he reached London, Parliament had abolished Papal supremacy, substituted English for Latin in the celebration of the Mass and imposed upon all bishops the taking of an oath of supremacy. All across London flared bonfires of religious images. Tunstall met the Queen, reproved her for meddling in religion and begged her to respect her father's will. But he was a figure from the past, and though the Council urged him to conform, he was too old to change his ways. 'Do you think that for me, who as a priest and a bishop have taught the faith for more than 40 years, it would be right, after so study, so long practice and experience, on the very brink of the grave, to accept a rule of faith from laymen my juniors?' In September he refused the oath and was deprived of his see. Elizabeth treated him considerately: he was allowed to send to Durham to dismiss his household and was given a pension. He spent his final weeks at Lambeth, under gentle house arrest with Archbishop Parker, and remained resolute to his principles. On his death in November he was buried in Lambeth church, the scene of his consecration as a bishop long before the breach with Rome.

As the aged Tunstall rode south, the Commissioners of the Northern Visitation went north in search of compliance with the new religious order. At Durham the dean and nine of the canons refused to take the oath of supremacy and found their salaries stopped. New brooms arrived: Pilkington as bishop in 1561, William Whittingham as dean in 1563. They made a formidable reforming team. Whittingham had exiled himself in Mary's reign to Frankfurt and Geneva, where he became a colleague of Calvin and demonstrated his scholarship by translating the New Testament on his own, the Old as one of a team, to produce the Geneva Bible, the first cheap and accessible bible in English. He returned to England in 1560 and served with notable courage as chaplain to the English army sent to France to champion the Huguenots in the wars of religion unleashed there. He preached in his armour, manned the walls in an attack, and was fearless during an outbreak of plague among the troops. The deanery at Durham was the reward for his services.

As a committed evangelizing puritan, Whittingham was bound to be a controversial figure at Durham, but his historical reputation as 'a great villain of the Geneva gang' is unjust. A later version of *The Rites of Durham* piles opprobrium upon him for his vandalism: 'he could not abyde any auncient monuments nor nothing that appurteyned to any godly Religiousness or monasticall life.' But the evidence we have does not suggest an indiscriminate rampage. He destroyed an image of Cuthbert that even Horne had spared; he removed some stained glass but not as much as Pilkington had hoped; he broke up the tombs of the priors, destroying the memorial brasses and carved chalices; he insensitively reused monks' gravestones to construct 'a washinge howse for women Landerers to washe in'; he ordered that two holy water stoups be 'caryed into his kitching and put unto profayne uses: and ther stoode during his liffe in which stones thei dyd stepe ther beefe and salte fysh'. His formidable French wife, having heard of the monks' claim that the Banner of St Cuthbert was indestructible, put it decisively to the test by burning it on the same kitchen fire, 'in the notable contempt and disgrace of all ancient and goodly relics'. He wanted to clear the bells out of the Galilee belfry (where they had long been in disuse), but was persuaded by Prebendary Sparke to rehang them in the central tower. He had strong views about vestments, spurning 'the Pope's attire' in favour of a black Geneva gown in which he took the air of Durham, and refusing to wear cope and surplice to celebrate communion. Carpeted for this before an ecclesiastical commission in York, he solved the problem by never celebrating again. But overall he conformed sufficiently to keep his job and support his wife and family.

But there are some notable achievements too. He loved music, preserved the cathedral organs, and was protective of the quality of music in services. He saw off the greed of local entrepreneurs who were grasping after profitable chapter-controlled leases, especially of local coal mines. And he established a decent and dignified round of services (with much preaching!) which long outlasted him. It included the severe requirements that the grammar school, song school and all the servants should resort to prayers in the church at six o'clock in the morning, and a general fast on Wednesdays and Fridays with prayers and preaching of God's word.

Men as forthright as Whittingham never lack enemies, and after the death of his accomplice Pilkington in 1576 they gathered for the kill. Barnes, the new bishop, and of a new persuasion, hoped for the cleansing of 'that Augean stable, the church of Durham, whose stink is grievous in the nose of God and of man'. Questions were asked about Whittingham's alcoholic intake, his misappropriation of chapter funds (allegedly he had made a profit of £20 (£2,500) by lowering the refectory roof and selling off the lead), and the validity of his ordination in Geneva. In May 1578 a Royal Commission arrived in Durham in expectation of removing him from the deanery. But the charges against him, 'a misliker of the English Church Service' and 'schismatick', were slight, and the enquiry was absurdly side-tracked by yet another outbreak of the ancient rivalry between York and Durham. Whittingham had denied bishop Barnes access to the Chapter House in 1577 on the grounds that his mission was in the service of the Archbishop of York. Barnes's longing for revenge was dashed when the Dean of York quarrelled with his archbishop about the validity of a Geneva ordination. Sandys, the archbishop, was reduced to playground name-calling: 'What, dost thou call me a Papist? If I be a Papist then thou art a Puritan. I am a Bishop, an Archbishop, and that is better than thine!' Whittingham travelled to London in 1579 to petition the Privy Council to terminate the hostile commission. He returned to a hero's welcome. In Durham the streets were scarcely passable for the multitude who, with doubled and trebled acclamations of joy, strove to 'exhilerate his heart after all his troubles'. But it was too late. Worn out by persecution, he took himself directly to his death-bed. The high tide of Puritan reaction in Durham had passed. Thomas Wilson, one of the Queen's secretaries who had been promised the profitable deanery back in 1563 when it was suddenly offered to Whittingham, at last acquired it, and showed his appreciation by never visiting the place.

THE RISING OF THE NORTH

Bishop Pilkington found ploughing his puritan furrow in his diocese hard work. 'The parishes be great, the people many, the wage small, priests bad and very few to be had and fewer to be hoped for.' The heart of his problem was that the religious sympathies of clergy, land owners and common people were emphatically Catholic. So great offence was given by the destruction of images, especially the targeting of images of St Cuthbert, which were integral to northern identity and history. The last statue of Cuthbert was 'defaced and broken all in pieces, to the intent that there should be no memory nor token of that holy man Saint Cuthbert'. Pilkington failed to comprehend the outrage he and Whittingham, upstart puritans from the south, were inflicting on his flock. 'Our poor Papists weep to see our churches so bare. There is nothing in them to make curtsy unto, neither saints nor yet their old little god.' He paid the price for his condescension: his house was one of the first to be sacked in the Rising of the North in 1569, when both he and Whittingham were forced to flee to the south.

The Rising was the last major collision between the very different cultures of north and south. It was the last stand of the traditional Catholic landed families, the Percys, Nevilles, Cliffords and Dacres, who, restored to influence under Mary Tudor, had since found their traditional status and authority eroded by Protestant courtiers when Elizabeth resumed her father's policy of bringing the north to heel. So the Rising grew partly from anger at the new men 'who dailie go about to overthrow and put down the ancient nobilitie of this realm', as the proclamation posted on the door of Staindrop Church worded it, and partly from eagerness to secure a Catholic succession after the Queen's death. But the common ground for all the rebels was anti-clerical. By their iconoclasm, their reclaiming of church lands previously leased out to Catholic land-owners, by their high-handed indifference to local feelings, by their conduct of services and by the very fact of their being married men, these clerical outsiders were unendurable. So the northern earls Westmorland and Northumberland who led the Rising celebrated the old Catholic Mass in Durham Cathedral on 14 November 1569 in an attempt to win popular support and present the rebellion to the people as a religious crusade. The Council of the North reported so to the Queen: 'The Earles doo not intende to obey your commandment ... they have been at Duresme with ther force in armor, to perswade the people to take ther partes, and some of ther company have thrown down the comunion table, and torne the holy bible in pieces, so as it appareth directly they intende to make religion ther grownd.' But the 'owtragiowse doinges at Duresme' led nowhere. The Earls lacked military and political strategies; Spanish reinforcements failed to arrive in Hartlepool, and the Rising was easily defeated north of Durham. The rebels were imprisoned in Durham Castle, and punishments were severe. Of the rebels, 800 were condemned to death; of these over 300 were executed by martial law, including 30 aldermen and citizens of Durham. The Neville, Percy, and Clifford families were exiled from the north, and disproportionate fines ruined the economy of the area for years to come. Pilkington, who had crept back when it was safe to do so, bleated to Cecil: 'The cuntrie is in grete mysere ... the number off offenders is so greete, that few innocent are left to trie the giltie.' Musgrove, historian of the north, makes a grim assessment of the consequences of the Rising: 'The north was never the same ... poverty was to persist and the north did not recover from the effects of the rebellion for perhaps two centuries.'

DURHAM POLITICIZED 1580–1672

LESS than 100 years separated the death of the puritan Dean Whittingham and the royalist Bishop Cosin. This short span of Durham's long history saw extreme reversals of fortune for the cathedral and its clergy. Though the north of England was peripheral in the Civil War, religious policy was inseparable from the political maelstrom that the first two Stuart monarchs were clumsily adept in provoking. Every religious dispute acquired a political weight in excess of its intrinsic insignificance, and a conflict of personalities in the Durham Chapter in the 1620s escalated into parliamentary proceedings in the 1640s. The Durham which had found itself in the vanguard of iconoclastic Puritanism in the 1560s and 1570s had to adjust to being in the vanguard of the wholly antithetical High Church Arminianism in the 1620s and 1630s. In the tormented years of the Civil War and Commonwealth, the grand organ proudly installed by Dean Hunt in the 1620s was dismembered within 20 years by raiding Scots Covenanters. Chapter revenues everywhere were confiscated by Parliament, chapters themselves subsequently abolished, and Durham Cathedral itself defiled by being reduced to a prison for several thousand Scottish prisoners who had surrendered to Cromwell. But just as 100 years before a

degree of stability and continuity in confused times had been represented by the long-lived Cuthbert Tunstall, in the 17th century the person of John Cosin embodied the spirit of Durham for nearly 50 years, and he came home after the Restoration in 1660 to devote his last energies to the renewal of the cathedral which he found, when he returned as bishop, to be little more than a hollow shell.

The north, with a traditional identity founded upon the long memory of the kingdom of Northumbria and its partial reincarnation in the Palatinate, was destined to lose its distinctiveness. The arrival of the Tudor dynasty in 1485, the Act for the Resumption of Liberties followed by the Pilgrimage of Grace in 1536, the 1569 Rising of the North, the Treaty of Berwick of 1586 which dissolved the military structures of northern society, and then the Union of the Crowns of 1603 which removed much of the north's strategic importance were all steps in the same direction, to 'the north's redundancy'. The Bishop of Durham and the traditional landed families were no longer the cocks of

Left: *John Cosin, Prebendary 1624–40, Bishop 1660–72. Portrait in oil by an unknown post-Restoration artist.*

Far left: *The length of the Chapel of the Nine Altars seen from a gallery at the south end. The raised platform on the left is the site of St Cuthbert's tomb.*

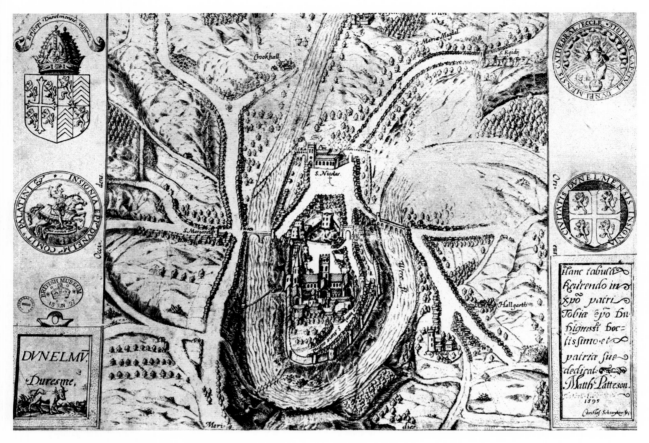

A plan of the city of Durham in 1595 by Christopher Schwytzer.

the north, and as feudal forms melted away, Durham city at last began to prosper. It gained independence of clerical control with a civic charter granted by Bishop Matthew in 1602; coal money began to flow to the gentry and tradesmen; professional men moved into the town and built their houses; the population began to rise and by the 1630s had reached 3,000. Until the end of the 16th century the Palatinate had still not been subject to general taxation, on the grounds that protection could not be provided in a frontier zone. After 1603, when the border lost its military and political importance, the northern landowners forfeited their privileged tax status. From 1610 Durham became liable to the same levels of taxation as the rest of England. But the town and county still had no representation in Parliament. Now the injustice of this anomaly was registered, and a recurrent

issue in the period covered by this chapter is the struggle between the citizenry of Durham and the bishops who had traditionally represented the district in the House of Lords, though often absent from the city and so not perceived as having sufficient knowledge or loyalty to represent the people of Durham. Bishop James found himself at odds with the citizens in 1609, grousing in a letter about 'my crabbed neighbours the townsmen of Durham, who in their pride usurp things never granted and challenge things not grantable'. On his visit in 1617 James I was petitioned about representation, and a series of bills to promote it were presented to Parliament. But James vetoed the last in 1624 on the grounds that the House of Commons was already too large – given his unhappy relations with his parliaments a Commons of any size was for him too large.

cathedral seemed impervious to sapped authority. The nave was a market with handcarts and salesmen, a promenade for more fashionable townspeople and a place of sport for urchins even during services. A renewal of purpose was sorely needed, but when it came it was to provoke still more discord.

DOBSON'S DRIE BOBBES

There is an age-old symbiotic relationship in the popular imagination as well as in reality between solemn men in gowns, whether clerical or pedagogic, and urchins. Reverend canons are caricatured by irreverent choristers, schoolteachers by the class wit. Holofernes and Sir Nathaniel need to be shadowed by a Moth. We have heard complaints from the monks that the precinct was infested in the Middle Ages by packs of troublesome boys. Not only did the cathedral present itself as a marvellously challenging playground, but the additional social frisson of taking on (or off) the toffs was irresistible in genteel times. There is an endearing, enormously enjoyable account of such sports called *Dobson's Drie Bobbes*, published anonymously in 1607 but apparently located in the 1550s and 1560s, when many of the named characters existed as historical figures in the Durham precinct. It is in essence a jest book, about a young Til Eulenspiegel by the River Wear, a form of entertainment popular in the late Middle Ages and early modern period, but the account of everyday life in and around cathedral and town reads like a documentary. It is a rich resource for local history.

George Dobson, a country boy, is given a home in Durham by his uncle Thomas Pentland, a minor canon and sacrist, thinly disguised in the fiction as Pentley. He is first sent to school in Saint Nicholas' Church, where his naivety makes him the butt of other boys' pranks, but he quickly becomes streetwise himself and learns to outsmart all his contemporaries and to outwit or

Bishop John Cosin. An elm wood sculpture by Colin Wilbourne, 1990, in the Prince Bishops' Garden (Botanic Garden).

Conflicts were common in cathedral chapters everywhere after the Reformation, as traditionalists and puritans battled for pre-eminence. Durham had known great discord in the 1570s and morale was poor. There were enemies within and without. A prebendary reflected on 'these exulcerant times when the state ecclesiastical is everywhere gainsaid, by some under colour of Reformation, by others of greediness gaping for the fall of Cathedral churches, and by all men for our contentions late among us'. Disorder in the humiliate several adults whose conduct gives him a pretext. The gang's initial high-spirited destructiveness would now merit ASBOs: 'In the winter evenings they enacted many a lewd stratagem about the shoppes in their way to the Schoole, as bursting glasen windowes, overthrowing Milke maides pailes, pulling down stalles, and crushing out the linckes which were hung foorth to give light to the Passengers in the streetes.' Dobson next becomes a chorister (there was a chorister called George Dobson between 1559 and 1568). He is installed by the Dean himself, who at his own expense provides him with a gown and surplice. Yet he is no respecter of the Dean's poultry-house, conveniently situated close to the kitchen in what is now the Memorial Garden on the south side of the Old Refectory. In order to revenge himself on Sir William the Usher he suborns a servant to give him access to the guarded poultry to steal a fine turkey, using a pair of the Usher's shoes to leave incriminating prints in the snow.

Feasting is often the objective of Dobson's scrapes. He poaches a deer from the Chapter estate at Bearpark, again implicating Sir William, who is surprised in bed with his mistress Jane by the questing Dean himself. Though hastily concealed beneath the bed, she is found in the search, 'the poor doe in a cold palsie, who for shame to be so taken, sownded in the presence of them all, and was ready to give up the ghost'. Dobson is bold enough to take on his uncle too. Delegated by the idle sacrist on cold winter mornings to do his tasks in the cathedral, such as setting up candles for early services, he is joined by his accomplice Raikebanes (another historical chorister) in the hope of gaining some candle ends. But instead Dobson traps him in the candle cupboard and locks him in for several hours. Rescued at service time, Raikebanes was 'scarcely able to crawle foorth, his ioynts were so stiffened and benummed with cold'. Sir Thomas liberally rewarded Dobson with a 'bobbe upon the mouth, insomuch as the blood followed his fist'. Dobson's revenge is to get a gang to raid his uncle's apple orchard, beating the keepers, tying Pentland himself to a tree and his sister to a wooden horse overnight; causing his real horse to be impounded because he had refused to take his nephew on a trip to the country, and adulterating the prize ale he was about to share with selected friends. Dobson draws off a quantity, topping up the barrel with water, and holds his own party at which he makes his fellow scholars 'as drunk as rats'. His parting glory was to declare a holiday and persuade all his fellow choristers of its genuineness. He was still a chorister at the age of eighteen, a telling example of changing rates of youthful maturation. His story has an entirely fictional happy ending. 'He had so well profited in Musike, and in the Latine tongue, that he was supposed fit for the University so soone as his voice changed.' He went on to Cambridge, still under the Dean's patronage, and returned later in life to Durham, as a minor canon, with a benefice, and much respected by clergy and people.

RITUAL AND MUSIC

James I visited Durham in 1617; Charles I in 1633. The contrast between the ceremonies used on these occasions is a precise measure of what had happened in the cathedral in the intervening 16 years. James 'would have all things done in plain manner without either singing or organ playing'. In 1633 Charles, on his way to his Scottish coronation, was received at the north door and entered the church beneath a silken canopy carried by eight prebendaries. The clergy wore new copes; a Te Deum was sung at a short service in the choir, followed by a formal procession to the tombs of Cuthbert and Bede. In the 16th century Durham had caught the high tide of iconoclastic Puritanism, praised in the 1580s as 'the light of the north' for its evangelizing mission in the borders. Early in the next century it caught the contrary tide known as Arminianism, the High Church

Above left: *A small part of the organ case originally placed above the cross by John Cosin, installed after the Restoration.*

Above: *An angel boss in the Cloister of unknown date, but repainted in the 20th century with the Easter and Whit acclamation 'Alleluia' written by Conrad Eden, Master of the Choristers (1930–60).*

movement inspired by Neile and William Laud, supported by Charles as Prince of Wales and Buckingham, favoured courtier to both James and Charles, and having at its spiritual heart a group of clergy associated with Durham: Neile, Hunt and Cosin. Neile became Bishop of Durham in 1617, Hunt, Dean in 1620, and Cosin, Prebendary in 1624. A dramatic transformation of Durham's ecclesiology was quickly set in train. Hunt installed a fine organ at his own expense in 1621; cornets and sackbuts soon followed to swell the accompaniment of services, and magnificent new music books were commissioned, with elaborate settings for the great feast days. Large sums were laid out on elaborate altar furniture – candlesticks, crucifixes, images – and on rich copes, first worn in 1627. The direction was unambiguous: the High

Church party desired formal services with extended rituals and music, and in Durham the leading light was the young and ambitious Cosin. He had been chaplain to Bishop Neile, acquired from him his high Anglican persuasion, and was appointed by him to be Master of Greatham Hospital and a prebendary of Durham. With the approval of Neile and Hunt he became the guardian of cathedral ritual. On one occasion he seized and tore the sleeve of Margaret Heath, one of the congregation sitting in the women's stalls on the north side of the choir and called her 'a lazy sow' for not standing for the Creed.

There were disadvantages even for some of the clergy in the welter of ritual: Prebendary Marmaduke Blakiston one day made so low a bow that his nose collided with the stone pavement and bled abundantly. ('The blood of Marmaduke' lacks the resonance of 'the blood of Christ'.) Cosin was favoured at court and was master of ceremonies at Charles I's coronation in 1626, and the following year was asked to produce a Book of Devotions for the English ladies of Charles's queen, Henrietta Maria. He was attacked by the puritan wing of the church in the punning language of contemporary polemic: 'Mr Cozens his cozening Devotions'. The rift was both doctrinal and aesthetic, but in Durham it also turned bitterly personal.

The course on which Durham had embarked was deeply repugnant to those prebendaries with puritanical sympathies who saw the achievements of the Reformation step by step reversed. They favoured a congregation-centred devotion composed of preaching, prayers and simple psalm chants in which all could join. Hunt and Cosin promoted services characterized by colour and ritual, with ambitious anthems sung by the choir. Such proceedings were clergy-centred, with the congregation reduced to an audience for the performance of the Sacrament, 'turned well near into a stage-play'; the Creed was sung, in seeming defiance of the prayer book rubric that it be said.

COSIN VERSUS SMART

Cosin's instinctive opponent in the Chapter was Peter Smart, a senior prebendary who had formerly been head master of the grammar school, and was appointed to a stall in 1609. His preference was for the simple

A musical treasure in the Cathedral Library is a set of part books, copied around 1630 but deferring to the traditions of monastic music by employing square notation. They are the most important surviving source for William Byrd's Great Service composed in the 1580s. The open book diplays the second contratenor part.

Calvinistic practices introduced by Whittingham, with their emphasis on penitence, the word of God and full congregational participation. Wholly alien to him was the attempt to elevate the spirit through dignity, ceremony and music. Throughout the 1620s he harbours his growing intolerance of 'our new fangled reformers of Durham'. Each new invention pushes up the steam pressure in his boiler. 'Our ears must attend the word of truth, not delicious tunes of musicall melody'. 'How dare they, instead of Psalmes, appoint Anthemes to be sung?' 'You think you do service enough to God and the church if you sit now and then in your stall like an idle drone, to hear piping and chanting'. The pressure always rises. His colleagues appear to him 'a mangy pack of Arminian hell hounds and spiritual fornicators'.

In such a volatile time theological disputes were readily, almost inevitably, politicized by the prevailing dialectic between King and Parliament, Royalist and Puritan. In the mid-1620s Cosin had been briefly investigated by Parliament, but was undeflected. On Candlemas Day 1628 he staged an incandescent ceremony at Durham. February 2nd was a day precious to the High Church faction because it was the date of Charles I's coronation. So Cosin was making a political statement as well as a theological one and affiliating Durham with royalism. Smart was outraged, and the birth pangs of his later notorious sermon are traceable in his reaction. 'On Candlemas Day last past Mr Cosins in reviving the Popish Ceremonie of burning candles to the honour of our Lady, busied himself from two of the clocke in the afternoone till foure, in climbing long ladders to stick up wax candles.'

The volcano finally blew at morning service on 27 July 1628. Smart preached his first sermon in the cathedral for seven years. He took a favourite, ominous text: 'I have hated them that hold of superstitious vanities'. Then he let rip with a virulence that all present were helpless to interrupt, directed

111

particularly at Cosin, 'our young Apollo, who repaireth the Quire and sets it out gaily with strange Babylonish ornaments'. He sailed into an attack on ceremonies: 'most are ridiculous. And some abominable'. He attacked candles, copes, music, 'the chaunts [chants] with Organs, Shackbutts and Cornets, which yield an hydeous noise'. He resented the displacement of ministers and communion tables by priests, sacrifices and altars. He anathematized the 'massing implements', 'an inundation of Ceremonies, crosses and Crucifixes, and Chalices, and Images, Copes and Candlesticks, and Tapers, and Basins, and a thousand such Trinckets, and that which is worst of all, guilding of Angels and garnishing of Images, and setting them up aloft'. His rhetoric grew fevered: 'The whore of Babylon's bastardly brood, doting upon their mother's beauty, that painted Harlot the Church of Rome, have laboured to restore all her robes and jewells again.' Then a final mock at his Chapter colleagues who spend their time in 'Altar decking, cope wearing, organ playing, piping and singing, crossing of cushions and kissing of clouts, of starting up and squatting down, nodding of heads, and whirling about till their noses stand eastwards'. There is no record, alas, of the lunchtime conversations in prebendal dining rooms. Dean Hunt acted promptly. At 2pm that afternoon a High Commission Court consisting of the Dean and Prebendaries Blakiston (of the bloody nose), James and Cosin was assembled in the Deanery. Smart was charged with preaching 'a seditious invective sermon, against the decent and allowed ceremonies within the

Peter Smart, Prebendary 1609–30 and 1642–49, the abrasively puritanical opponent of John Cosin. From an engraving by Wenceslas Hollar, 1642.

Church of England'. He was defiant, banned from the cathedral and his salary was suspended. He sat stubbornly on in the Chapter, however, and initiated a sequence of litigation, first at the Durham Assizes. Here his case was dismissed by the judge, who declared that he 'had been in both an eare and an eye witness that all thinges were done in decencie and in order'. The case passed to ecclesiastical courts in the provinces of both York and Canterbury, and thence to the House of Commons, once Smart had circulated a story of a dinner table conversation at which Cosin was said to have declared that the King was not the supreme head of the Church of England. But the king ordered the Attorney-General to drop the proposed prosecution of Cosin, and this gave the hostile Commons a pretext to attack Arminianism. The House set up a Committee of Religion, which was preparing to indict Cosin for high treason when Charles dissolved Parliament in 1629 and contrived to govern without it for the next eleven years.

In another civil court a Puritan judge ruled in Smart's favour but still rebuked his abrasive temper, telling him 'that his natur and disposition was to hot, to revengefull, too fierce and violent, and, according to his name, to smart'. He found 'Mr Cosin of a better temper and disposition than Mr Smart by farr'. At the ecclesiastical court in York Smart refused to recant and was 'degraded from his clerical status', excommunicated and imprisoned for non-payment of a fine of £400 (£30,000) imposed on him. For the next eleven years he brooded in jail.

Cosin's career flourished in the 1630s. He was favoured by the king and Archbishop Laud, perilous endorsements both. In 1635 he was made Master of Peterhouse, Cambridge, where he at once instituted the same liturgical practices he had promoted in the north.

Above: John Cosin loved fine wood carving – this is the font cover surmounted by an eagle.

Right: A familiar North Sea brown crab: a 17th-century misericord from the North Quire stalls.

His influence at Durham established the still active tradition of the choir singing from the tower. The dates on which the event is recorded are emphatically royalist ones: 27 March, the accession of Charles I; 5 November, the aborting of the Gunpowder Plot, and, later in the century, 29 May, the Restoration of Charles II. There is no obvious connection with the Battle of Neville's Cross which the tradition is alleged to commemorate – this had occurred nearly 300 years before and had little 17th-century resonance.

In 1640 the whirligig of time brought in its revenges. The king's blunder in seeking to impose bishops on the Scots by force led to the recall of Parliament. Smart, smouldering in a cell for a decade, petitioned both the Short and Long Parliaments for redress and was released. Cosin could read the signs, and wrote to Laud: 'These times are exceedingly bad. I doubt there will be neither any dividend nor any Church or other place left for me in that country, where all I have to live on is in the hands of the rebels (the Scots). I beseech God send us better times.' In November 1640 the tables were turned. The Long Parliament ordered that

A cheeky misericord from the South Quire stalls: a lion about to feast on a cherub's bottom.

'Dr Cousins be sent for, as a delinquent, by the Serjeant-at-Arms'. He was brought before a committee and released on bail. In January 1641 he was stripped of his ecclesiastical positions, and the House of Lords made ready to impeach him as 'the very first victim of Parliamentary vengeance'. He was labelled as one of 'an Army of Priests which doth many ways advance the design and plots of Popery'. In March 1641 articles of impeachment were published against him, though in the following weeks he defended himself with such skill that he was at last dismissed after paying bail and not summoned again. Salt had been rubbed into his wounds when Smart was put back into his former stall in Durham, though he had learned no lessons in his confinement: he tried to extract from the Chapter money he felt was owed him for the past eleven years and failed, and his demeanour at the bar of the House of Lords was so provocative that his counsel withdrew from the case, telling him that 'he was ashamed of him and could not in conscience plead for him any longer'. Smart spent part of his remaining years composing a spiteful 1,300-line Latin satire against Cosin. In the circumstances, Cosin's judgment on Smart, that 'his spleene was too big for his brayne', was a model of generous restraint.

THE CIVIL WAR AND THE COMMONWEALTH

To the divisions of doctrine, fortune and personality between Cosin and Smart was added, in the troubled years after 1642, geographical separation. Smart sat in his stall in Durham until all deans and chapters were abolished in 1649, when he retired to the country and died, probably in 1652. For Cosin it was all blackness. His wife died in childbirth in March 1642; after his harassment by the Long Parliament he prudently retreated to France in 1643. In his absence he was expelled from the Mastership of Peterhouse for sending College plate to the royal mint at York. His exile was to last for 17 years. At first he was a chaplain to Henrietta Maria in Paris, but he was dismissed and cast into poverty. Heavily dependent on the charity of other exiles, especially John Evelyn, he also suffered from protracted ill-health. He formed a bond with the Huguenots and remained a staunch Protestant in the face of Catholic overtures. 'The Atlas of the Protestant religion', Thomas Fuller christened him. He continued to write and publish from France.

Meanwhile, back in Durham the Scots occupied the town in 1640 and 1641 and began to destroy Hunt's new organ. Pipes were smuggled out at night to hide them. They also smashed the font. In 1642 all Chapter revenue was confiscated by Parliament because of its support for the king. The Scots returned in 1644, this time bringing with them an outbreak of plague. In the same year the Battle of Marston Moor near York was another disaster for the north. After the royalist defeat, the penalties imposed on Catholic and royalist families compounded the penury of the district. The next 16 years saw the diocese plunged into widespread poverty. The abolition of deans and chapters left Durham leaderless. The Captain-General of the Parliamentary Army, Oliver Cromwell, was treated to a secular banquet in July 1650 on his way to Scotland by his old friend Arthur Haselrig, now Governor of Newcastle. In September he defeated the Scots at Dunbar, and 5,000 Scottish prisoners were marched south. Many died on the journey; a large number reached Durham, where they were locked into the vacant cathedral for the winter of 1650–1. Sick, starving, they have traditionally been blamed for destruction in the cathedral, but it now seems more probable that the damage was caused by Scottish troops or Cromwell's. The medieval woodwork was destroyed, perhaps for fires, though the prisoners were given sufficient coal to keep their fires burning day and night. The Neville Chantry was demolished and its monuments defaced, as can still be vividly seen in the truncated torsos of stone on the raised tombs on the south side of the nave. The condition of the interior after a winter of such degradation must have been unspeakable. The prevailing squalor is painful to imagine. The short-term consequence was the ruination of the interior fabric and furnishings; the long-term manifested itself over 300 years later. In 1967 underfloor heating was installed and when it was turned on a dark oily film formed on the flagstones in the Choir Aisles, Chapel of the Nine Altars and the Transepts, but not in the Nave. Laboratory analysis identified it as nitro-magnesite with a little gypsum and quartz, substances not naturally present in sandstone. Hypotheses about its origins included well water used to wash the floors, residue from gas mantles, the storage of gunpowder and the decay of bodies beneath the flagstones. All were rejected in favour of the theory that the repeated soaking of the porous sandstone by up to 250,000 gallons of urine excreted by the prisoners, clustered at the west end for warmth and using the colder east end for their natural functions, had created a chemical reaction. Though a portion evaporated as ammonia, the less volatile

constituents filtered through the stone to oxidize and react with the layer of crushed magnesian limestone beneath the slabs to form magnesium nitrate. The researchers' conclusion was that 'the Scots, a tenacious race, may yet have exacted a vicarious revenge for the inhumanities which followed Dunbar'.

Church property was an asset to be used or stripped. In 1649 the Castle was confiscated and sold off to the Lord Mayor of London for £1,267.10s (£90,000). He removed the lead from the roofs for his profit. The spires on the west towers of the cathedral were also dismantled some time in the 1650s and sold on as building material. But as the stock of the church fell, that of the citizens slowly rose. Under the Commonwealth the district gained its longed-for political enfranchisement. In the absence of a bishop, Durham was allowed to send its first secular representatives to Parliament in 1653. Then in 1656 the city came close to acquiring the third university in the country when the Commonwealth Parliament granted a request from the Grand Jury of Durham for a college, to be endowed with church land, now available in plenty. But for objections from Oxford and Cambridge at the threat to their monopoly the plan might have been realized, but it was still not much more than a blueprint when the Restoration in 1660 put an end to so radical a notion for 280 years.

COSIN RESTORED

Cosin came home with the Restoration. He was at Charles II's right hand at his coronation, as he had been at his father's 34 tumultuous years before. On Advent Sunday 1660 he was consecrated Bishop of Durham in Westminster Abbey. Then after serving on the Savoy Conference, which compiled the 1662 Prayer Book, he at last arrived in his diocese in August 1661. At the crossing of the River Tees he was greeted with the traditional ceremony of the dragon's sword, or Conyers' Falchion, with which new bishops were welcomed to the see. There was a prescribed ritual with trumpets, gunfire and acclamation. At the first entry of the bishop into his diocese, the Lord of Sockburn, or his steward, meets him in the middle of the River Tees, at Nesham Ford or on Croft Bridge, and presents a faulchion to the bishop with these words: 'My Lord Bishop, I here present you with the faulchion wherewith the champion Conyers slew the worm, dragon, or fiery flying serpent, which destroyeth man, woman and child; in memory of which the King then reigning gave him the manor of Sockburn, to hold by this tenure, that upon the first entrance of every bishop into the country, this faulchion should be presented.' This odd ceremony persisted until 1774, then lapsed, but has been revived in recent times.

Cosin found Durham and the wider diocese in ruins. A disconsolate Chapter meeting on 3 November 1660 recorded the damage. 'Whereas the fabric of the Church and Chapter House is Exceeding Ruinous, the Leads much decayed, the Windows almost totally broken and noe seats in the Quire, but such as have been made since his Majestie's happy Restoration … Hospitalities, Residences etc. are impossible to observe for the present by reason of Ruines of the Deanery and Prebendarye's houses and want of furniture and other accommodation'. Three days later, after electing Cosin bishop, they felt more positive: 'Care be taken for Reparacions with all convenient speed …. And that for the present 10 trees be cutt down and brought to the College to be seasoned this winter for making Stalls and seats in the Quire next Spring.' When Cosin arrived in Durham he devoted himself to the restoration work. Now there were no Peter Smarts to oppose him as he undertook a formidable task for a man no longer young and beset by ill health. He had kidney stones, swollen legs, shortness of breath and failing eyesight. He was an addictive pipe smoker, for it seemed to relieve the pain. His accounts for 1665 include 1/9 (£6) for half a gross of

The coat of arms of Bishop Nathaniel Crewe (1674–1721) on the hopper head of a downcomer in the castle courtyard. There is both a bishop's mitre and a baron's crown because in 1697 he succeeded to the family peerage and was simultaneously a lord spiritual and temporal.

pipes and 11/- (£30) for '2 and a half lbs. of Virginia tobacco'. He was distressed particularly by the ruinous state of the cathedral he had helped to adorn, and became devoted to its restoration, much of it at his own expense. Hunt's vandalized organ was replaced by a temporary instrument one tuned in 1661, and then by a George Dallam double organ brought into use in December 1662, at a cost of £550 (£30,000). Cosin loved richly carved woodwork, and the present choir stalls, font cover, reading desk and litany desk, which bears his coat of arms, were his gifts. There was also an organ screen between nave and choir, removed in the 1847 restoration, sections of which survive in the south

The coat of arms of the Cathedral on another hopper head and down-comer. The date of 1661 makes it the work of Bishop John Cosin, who returned to Durham after the Restoration to find both Cathedral and Castle in a ruinous condition.

west side of the Green, completed in 1668 at a cost of £2,500 (£150,000) and opened in 1669, his last year in Durham, as a public library for clergy, gentry and scholars. Cosin spent £3,000 (£180,000) on books for it, and took minute interest in their welfare, stipulating a fireplace before which the books were to be rubbed once a month in winter to keep away mould. His fussy autocracy reduced Mr Davenport the Library Keeper to despair: 'My Lord hath placed his books in the new library which he hath built. But oh! What a life have I, in shifting them hither and thither! and this life I reckon I must lead till Michaelmas.' Cosin found time too to ensure that the cathedral's collection was properly catalogued and housed, the completion of a task begun 30 years earlier when he was a prebendary. In his will he provided an endowment for the new library which Dean Sudbury planned on the site of the ruined Refectory in the South Cloister.

Cosin conducted two visitations of the diocese. In 1662 he proved a severe interrogator of the clergy as he battled to restore order and decent ritual to services. His questions included: 'Do worshippers sit, lean or lay their hats upon the Communion Table?' 'Are minstrels, morris-dancers, dogs, hawks or hounds permitted to enter the church?' The Durham Chapter was continually harangued about its dilatoriness: 'Is the Communion Table or Altar recovered out of their hands that took it away? Are you about to renew the organ, and where do you intend to place it? By what other persons hath any part of the Church fabric, Altar, Font, Organ, Pulpit, doors, partitions, or stalls and seats in the Quire been destroyed? Search out and name them.'

After his second visitation of the cathedral in 1665 he had a long list of impatient complaints: the services are slack, the altar covered with coarse country cloth, the treasury out of all order, the floor of the church broken, so too the tombs of the benefactors, and the churchyard wall still not repaired. From

nave and in the Tunstall Chapel in Durham Castle. His building energies seemed inexhaustible. He restored Auckland Castle and built the chapel where he was to be buried. Durham Castle, thanks to the Scots who 'spoilt it with gunpowder' and the Lord Mayor of London's lead-stripping was ruinous too. Cosin restored the Great Hall and its stone pavement and added its exquisite stair turret. He built almshouses on the east side of Palace Green, and rebuilt Durham's Guildhall according to his highly traditional sense that the bishop was also the ruler of the city. He was all his life enthralled by books, and took his greatest pleasure in his later years in Durham from planning and building the Cosin Library on the

somewhere he found the energy to make informal progresses through the diocese, 'preaching on every Sunday in several churches', and received 'with great joy and alacrity both of the gentry and all the people'. His achievement was little less than heroic; within a decade he had reinvigorated a moribund cathedral and diocese.

The autocratic disposition inseparable from his success brought him into conflict with the citizens and gentry of the town. He was incapable of registering the sense of power and pride they had experienced through representation in Parliament in the 1650s, which the Restoration had snatched away again. In 1666 the Grand Jury of Durham petitioned the Quarter Sessions for the return of their rights. Cosin strongly objected. By his being the only representative of the district in Parliament, he argued, great expense was saved. So the people of the town had to wait upon the death of their bishop to gain what he saw as a privilege, they a right, and were enfranchised only in 1674, two years after Cosin's death. A self-interested abuse of his power over the Chapter was the appointment of Denis Granville to a prebendal stall, a position Cosin had dangled as a form of dowry for Anne, his weak-minded daughter. Granville took the bait with great expectations, and stepped into a tragi-comic saga unparalleled in Durham's history, as the following chapter relates.

Cosin's roller-coaster of a life, embodying much of the century's upheaval, came to a quiet end in his lodgings in Pall Mall in January 1672. His body was embalmed and carried north for an April funeral in the cathedral before burial at Auckland. No bishop before or since has been a greater benefactor of cathedral and city, or has suffered more for his fidelity.

Bishop Cosin's 'Black Staircase' of the early 1660s. The main structure of oak, fifty-seven feet high, stands in the angle between The Great Hall and the 12th-century castle buildings.

THE RESTORATION AND THE
EIGHTEENTH CENTURY 1660–1830

DEAN GRANVILLE AND BISHOP CREWE

The Restoration brought little peace to Durham. For the next 40 years personal, political and religious divisions, local and national, continually disrupted the Christian purposes of cathedral and diocese. A staunchly Anglican dean backed the losing side in the constitutional upheaval of 1688 and had to flee to Catholic France; a bishop who was supposed loyal to his ousted monarch proved to be a shameful turncoat.

In his eagerness to provide for his daughter, John Cosin surrendered his judgement and paid dearly for it in personal disquiet. Denis Granville, a younger brother of the Earl of Bath, had attached himself to Cosin at the Restoration. After only one year in holy orders, he married Anne Cosin on the promise of a generous dowry, partially provided when Cosin instantly appointed him a prebendary and Archdeacon of Durham in 1662. But Granville was an incurable spendthrift, and when the scale of his debts became known to Cosin, the promised dowry was placed in the care of trustees. Granville felt cheated, and from that moment until Cosin's death in 1672 there was to be no peace between them, though to Cosin's credit he continued to do what he could to improve his son-in-law's prospects.

Detracting from all Cosin's achievements in restoring the ravaged cathedral and diocese was the bitter knowledge that he had selected a profligate and troublesome son-in-law as a rod for his own back. Granville was a champion of indiscretion. His words and deeds always came to the notice of those from whom he most wished to conceal them. A reference to

Above: *Denis Granville, Prebendary and Archdeacon 1662–84, Dean 1684–89, who encountered troubles domestic, financial and political throughout his career in Durham. From an engraving by G.F. Edelinck, after Beaupoille, 1693.*

Right: *In the early Romantic period artists flocked to Durham to work. This watercolour is by J.S. Cotman, 1805. British Museum.*

'squeezing' money out of his father-in-law reached Cosin's ears. He wrote to Granville: 'your intencion to squeeze me will not depart out of my mind', and he returned to it obsessively in his remaining years. Next, Cosin found out that Granville had been trying to borrow large sums from his relations, and remonstrated again: '(this) is grievous to me to heare, and as I wonder what you do in lavishing away so much money, and for aught I know paying no debts.'

It had been a common practice for many centuries for the monarchy not only to interfere with the distribution of church appointments but also to support exploitation of the positions gained. Granville was a royal chaplain, and so secured royal permission to be absent from Durham from 1666 to 1668 (but keeping his salary). It was a trick Granville was to use regularly to escape from his creditors, but this time it was also to evade the censures of his father-in-law. It was a foolish tactic: both Cosin and creditors were angered by his flight, and his troubles were compounded when Granville next petitioned Charles II about Cosin's withholding the dowry. The king wrote to the bishop in protest, so Cosin, in Granville's absence, appointed him to the rich living of Sedgefield and to Durham's 'golden stall', the 11th, with a variable but relatively high income from the estates associated with it. It proved of no avail. The more Granville ran from his creditors, the more he spent. Not the least issue between the ill-matched relatives and colleagues was Cosin's inability to acknowledge his daughter's impaired condition. By 1670 Mrs Granville was suffering episodes of distraction or mild insanity, so her husband took her away south but then abandoned her to chase up a Doctorate of Divinity in Oxford. Cosin was beside himself: 'I thinke he studyes all ways he can (and nothing els) how to grieve and vex both his wife and all her friends.' His continuing absence from Durham is a further vexation: 'The man is still gadding at Oxford, and I doubt borrowing of money there also.' Indeed. Leaving large debts in Oxford Granville took refuge in France for a couple of years, and only felt it safe to return to Durham after Cosin's death in 1672 provided him with both financial and emotional relief.

This easing of his circumstances was very temporary. His creditors were waiting in Durham when he showed up there in 1674. He was subjected to what was probably the greatest public humiliation suffered by any member of the post-Reformation Chapter when, on July 8th, after he had conducted the funeral of a Captain Foster, three bailiffs appeared and 'in an odious manner arrested me in the very cloysters of the Cathedrall in my hood and surplice, immediately after Divine Service, in the presence of two hundred gentry'. He was carried off to prison, and had to petition the king again to establish that the officers had exceeded their rights. But he was one of fortune's fools. In December, while making merry in Dr Brevint's house in the College, he had another shock: 'Whiles we were fooling last night, too much indeed for ye tyme (a time of Danger), and ye day (a day of Devotion) it pleased God the wind Blew downe Misses chamber, ye Roof crushing ye very Bed flat on ye floor.' He thanked God for his deliverance and resolved once more to amend.

A new bishop arrived in 1675. Nathaniel Crewe, Cosin's successor, was in high favour at the Stuart court and had officiated at the marriage of James Duke of York to Mary of Modena. Durham was his reward. Beyond the royal family he was not highly esteemed. 'The spawn of a puritan turned papist', Bishop Compton called him. Bishop Burnet was less flattering: 'An ignorant, worthless, vain and abject man, without any one good quality.' With or without such recommendations, he was to hold the see, against all the odds, for 47 years.

Crewe, like most Princes Palatine, loved his grandeur. His intimacy at court disposed him to think

Nathaniel Crewe, Bishop 1674–1721. From an engraving by F. Place 1699.

himself royal too. He entered his diocese with a cavalcade and, as Lord Lieutenant, called a muster of all the local train bands in August 1675, at the head of which he rode into Durham, attended by many of the local gentry. He was reliving the glory of such Prince-Bishops as Antony Bek. Pepys recorded after a visit to Durham that the bishop lived 'more like a prince of this than a preacher of the other world'. In 1676 he made a grand visitation of his diocese. In the cathedral the names of Chapter members were called out in turn. Dean Sudbury responded and then sat down. 'Mr Dean', said Crewe, 'your posture does not become you.' 'Your predecessor, my Lord, always bade us sit down.' 'Yes, when I bid you sit down, sit down.' For his first three years on his throne, however, he was spared the petty quarrels which Granville's character habitually provoked because he had again secured

royal permission to be absent, released from his duties of residence 'on royal service', but with full salary.

For all his transparent faults, Granville, like the Micawber he so often resembles, displayed endearing strengths of character as well. One of these was his absolute honesty about himself. Before going abroad in 1676 he looked into the mirror and wrote: 'My prodigality hath been one of my most notorious sins whereby I have offended God; and that I believe hath been the fruit of my vainglory which is a branch of pride, and pride the proper spawn of the devil.' Resolving, in the strength of his dear Jesus, to mortify his pride and conquer his prodigality, he glimpses a golden future when 'my vainglory will die, my debts will be paid, my head will be composed, and my heart in better frame and I shall become a Christian indeed'. But the wish was never to be father to the deed; all his life, where money was concerned, he remained 'a poor helpless dove among hawks ready to be devoured'.

In December 1679 Granville returned to Durham repentant and with a renewed sense of purpose. He began to display another strength of character, a persistence in doing battle with his fellow clergy to achieve the higher standards of worship and pastoral vocation he aspired to despite his own questionable example. As Archdeacon he was critical of the slackness of many diocesan clergy, who changed the times of services at short notice or set them aside completely, 'sometimes upon no better account than that they and their people may go to a horse-race or some such idle sport and divertisement'. He waged a passionate campaign for the provision of a weekly sacrament nationwide in cathedrals, collegiate churches and colleges, a service widely neglected. 'I will make a filthy bustle before I die among the Clergy of the nation, as contemptible a mushrump and silly ignoramus as some do make me.' He lost the fight with his own chapter, but not for ever.

Trying another tack he compiled a long list of irregularities in services and in the management of the precinct which needed rectifying. He saw slackness everywhere. The cathedral was a general thoroughfare for the carriage of goods; youths played rowdily in the cloisters on Sundays; animals were allowed to wander in and out of the church; women hung their washing out in the churchyard. The choir was a disgrace. Men and boys wore surplices so nasty and dirty they gave much offence; the choristers and sometimes the men staring, gazing, and laughing, indecently lolling, and sometimes scandalously sleeping, 'not only during sermon but also service'. Before the sermon the congregation would rudely crowd up to the lectern, jostling and punching one another for position. In 1681 he sent boys to the correction house for Sunday play in the cloisters, 'which I had pardoned upon their submission, if I had not found they had been guilty of playing at cards upon the Communion Table'. Not even the clergy were exempt from misbehaviour. Francis Blakiston, minor canon, gave 'notorious and insolent offence in striking Richardson our Porter, and felling him with his staffe in the very midst of the Quire'. Summoned before the Chapter, he was compelled to confess his fault publicly during service. Slowly Granville's determination to dignify the character of worship at Durham began to take effect. Somehow, despite his contretemps with Cosin, his long absences and his provocative character, he succeeded in restoring to worship in Durham the High Anglican tradition which Cosin represented. Celia Fiennes, visiting in the 1690s, recorded that she saw several fine embroidered copes ... one above the rest was so richly embroidered with whole description of Christ's nativity, life, death and ascension: this is put on the Dean's shoulders at the administration of the Lord's Supper ... here is the only place they use such things in England, and several more ceremonies and rites retained from the times of popery.'

The carved wooden ceiling in the Prior's Bedroom in the Deanery, under which James VI of Scotland slept on his way to assume the throne of England in 1603.

But however patchy his personal and professional record appears to us, it met with a predictable reward given the influence of his family at court. In 1684 Denis Granville was made Dean of Durham. Ten years earlier, with Dean Sudbury thought to be on his death-bed, Lord Bath, Granville's brother, began to move at court in an effort to secure the succession for Denis. As if in defiance of the unthinkable, Sudbury recovered to complete 22 years as dean. This time round there was comic intrigue. Crewe wanted to see his nephew Dr Montagu in the Deanery, and hoped to distract Granville with the lucrative Mastership of Sherburn Hospital. Sancroft, Archbishop of Canterbury from 1677 to 1690, also tried to block Granville, who 'was not worthy of the least stall in Durham Church'. Hearing of Sancroft's view, Crewe at once performed a volte-face and backed Granville. He 'would rather choose a gentleman than a silly fellow who knew nothing but books'. Sancroft was virtually speechless: 'I beshrew thee!' Granville now toadied to his archbishop: 'I do confess to God and your Grace that it is my great sin that I am so much and so long in debt ... but I have not spent my money in lewdness or debauchery. For God's sake, my Lord,

The Resurrection, a 15th-century wall painting in the Deanery discovered only in 1974. It was painted on the north wall of what was originally the Prior's chapel.

forgive what is past and do not despair of me. I am four and twenty years older than when your Grace first knew me.' In the end none of this posturing counted. The Granvilles were in favour at court, and Charles II backed Denis, approving the appointment as soon as news of Sudbury's death reached London in December 1684. For once Granville was in luck, for within two months the king was dead and the Bath influence at court evaporated. Granville was installed dean by proxy in December 1684. Now as dean he had the huge income of £2,300 (£140,000). But his debts were greater still, amounting to over £6,000 (£360,000) at the time of his promotion, and not diminishing despite his regular lists of resolutions. After a prudent spell at court he arrived in Durham in the autumn of 1685 and proved full of initiative. He won his fight with the Chapter for a weekly sacrament, saw to the provision of 'proper' altar furniture and revived the practice of sermons in Advent and Lent. He also began to establish a theological seminary linked to the cathedral. But his character was its own minefield and he was involved in many contentions. He quarrelled with the Mayor and Corporation over their failure to attend services. He was at odds with many of his own Chapter. Private letters

with unflattering remarks about Crewe were intercepted and read to the bishop, so there was more grovelling to do, both to Crewe and to Sancroft. He readily acquiesced in Crewe's appointment of Sir George Wheler, Granville's nephew by marriage, to the wealthy second stall. And he was widely suspected of seeking to bring back the Mass. 'I have had a very hard game to play these 20 years in maintaining the exact order which Bishop Cosin set on foot here' was his belated tribute to his oppressive father-in-law.

THE CRISIS IN CHURCH AND STATE

But a much harder game to play was just around the corner. In the 1680s the Restoration Church of England was assailed from two sides, by popular nonconformity and a resurgent Catholicism confident that, backed by the monarchy, its time had come. Religious tensions again fuelled a political ferment in which Durham's leading clergy were caught up. The outcome, the 'Glorious Revolution' of 1688 and 1689, was to be glorious for neither the bishop of Durham nor the dean, but in wholly different ways.

From the mid-1670s there were regular skirmishes and affrays involving Presbyterians and Covenanters who had found refuge in a sympathetic Northumberland. Even though the corporation of Newcastle was loyally Anglican, the town was a centre for 'seditious meetings', where large conventicles of armed men were determined to assert their preferred form of religious worship, by force if necessary. There was nothing new in Durham's history about provocation offered by Tynesiders: for centuries they had been as a thorn in the flesh. From Bishop Walcher's murder in Gateshead in 1080 through running disputes about River Tyne revenues and the boundary line on the Tyne Bridge, riversiders equalled trouble. Ambitious entrepreneurs in the prosperous town cast covetous eyes on Gateshead, which belonged to the Palatinate, and even tried to annex it during the Episcopal vacancy of 1559. The blue marble 'Cuthbert stones' marking the northern limit of Palatinate authority one-third of the way across the bridge were regularly dug up by men of Newcastle and shifted south. And up to 1674, when Durham city was still disenfranchised, the electors of Newcastle had got into the habit of electing Durham gentry to Parliament to annoy the bishop. The laws against meetings of nonconformists were deeply resented in the diocese, and the mood in the 1670s and 1680s was seditious. Strict orders for the suppression of the meetings were issued, but for pragmatic reasons not always obeyed. The court-pleasing Crewe, however, charged with searching for and seizing weapons, was assiduous in his devotion to the cause.

The tide of dissent was popular and seditious; that of Rome was of the establishment, and led to constitutional crisis. In 1679 Crewe had provided on a lavish entertainment for James Duke of York and his wife in Durham Castle. He greeted his royal guests on the steps of the Great Hall and James gave him a public kiss as a token of special favour. Crewe was reckoned to be one of his 'twelve disciples'. The widespread hysteria surrounding the Popish Plot which came to a head in 1681 threw suspicion on James and his disciple: rumours spread that Crewe was to be impeached for his role. Another national furore over the Exclusion Bills of 1679 and 1680 showed to which mast Crewe had nailed his colours. Charles II observed to him that Mr Parkhurst, Crewe's steward and a member for Durham, had voted for the bill. 'Sire, I'll turn him off tomorrow,' Crewe replied.

James II's authority quickly crumbled in the second half of 1688. Crewe, who was also Dean of the Chapel Royal, was at court in preference to Durham, and approved James's scheme for general religious toleration, the Declarations of Indulgence of 1687 and 1688 which were the cloak for a Catholic monarchy. The order that it was to be read in churches was ill-received across the country, and seven bishops were imprisoned for their refusal to do so. But in Durham, Granville's character and background left him no choice but to obey a royal command: 'I can be contented to die for, but will never rebell or resist my lawfull Prince, to save the religion of the Church of England.' He alone of the Durham Chapter read the Declaration in the Cathedral. The rest were opposed. Prebendary Morton changed the words of the suffrages from 'O Lord save the King' to 'O Lord save the people'. He and Prebendary Grey had a heated discussion with Crewe in the castle when both refused to read the Declaration. Tempers broke. Crewe told Grey that age had pushed him into dotage and that he had forgotten all his learning. Grey retorted that he had forgotten more learning than his lordship had ever possessed. Crewe led them to the gate where the porter opened only the narrow wicket. 'Sirrah', called Crewe, 'why don't you open the great gates?' 'No', said Grey, 'we'll leave the broad way to your lordship; the strait way will serve us.' Crewe is said to have suspended 30 clergy for refusing to read the Declaration, and lost respect and authority in the diocese for so doing.

In September rumours of an invasion by William of Orange swept the country. Granville called a Chapter meeting to present his colleagues with their duty 'to assist the King in his present exigency with their purses as well as their prayers'. He collected £700 (£42,000) for his Majesty's service and sent off a loyal address, but only from himself, for no-one else would sign it. 'I do from the bottom of my soul, abhor and detest this treacherous and unnaturall invasion of the Prince of Orange.' Granville's habitual misfortune accompanied this gesture on its way south, for it was intercepted at York and fell into 'enemy hands'. In November William landed at Torbay and marched on London, joined by

The Cathedral, the River Wear and towpath, and South Street, from the Castle battlements, seen across the Fellows Garden in early May.

Granville's brother Lord Bath. On 5 December Lord Lumley 'took' Durham for William (there was little opposition, but for the Dean himself), and read his declaration at the castle to an audience of leading gentry. Granville, who was preaching an Advent sermon at the time, refused to hand over the horses and weapons Lumley's troopers demanded and was placed under house arrest in his own deanery. He was allowed to preach in the cathedral on the following Sunday, a loyal sermon scorning 'that horrid rebellion'. But James had already fled the country and Granville prepared to follow suit. 'I did resolve accordingly to hasten into France, to share with my Sovereign in his misfortunes.'

His own comic misfortunes attended him in his extremity. A rabble apprehended him in the Borders as a popish priest. They heaved him out of bed, stole his money and horses and sent him back to Carlisle for interrogation. Soon released as harmless, he stayed in Carlisle for some days incognito to avert suspicion, then made a dash for Edinburgh, where he found a ship to take him to Honfleur in March 1689. Apart from one risky return to England, typically to get money, that

was the last of his native land. He wrote to Sancroft: 'I am resolved to retain, live and die in those honest notions and principles of the Church of England which (I) sucked in almost with my milk.' He joined James at the court in exile in St Germain, where he was given a small annuity and the compensatory title of Archbishop of York in exile, though he soon fell from favour because of his refusal to convert to Rome. He retained his Durham salary for a time, but had difficulty securing it, especially after war broke out between France and England. He had abandoned his sad wife, who now became the target of his many thwarted creditors, was made penniless and homeless as a result and mercifully died in 1691. In 1698 Granville left St Germain for a rural life at Corbeil-sur-Seine where he became a passionate angler, an appropriate metaphor for his whole life. He discovered, or thought he did, a French ancestry descended from the Earls of Corbeil and even called himself Corbeil in his last years. Micawber-like to the end, he wrote hopefully to a friend: 'I have some irons in the fire, and I need money to blow the forge.' James

II died in 1701 and Granville, isolated and poor, suffering from ague, gout and mental muddle followed his master in April 1703. His funeral expenses were paid by James's widow, Mary of Modena.

Granville, however absurd he sometimes appeared, was at least steadfast to his principles. Crewe's conduct was craven and contemptible. First he escaped to Holland for some months, to lie low and avoid the new Coronation. His dismissal or resignation was generally expected. But to equally general amazement he returned to London in July 1689 just in time to swear the oath of allegiance to the new order, the refusal of which deprived Granville of his position. The Dean-in-exile wrote sadly that 'I was told that I was well-enough served in that my bishop had left me in the lurch.' Crewe was exempted from the Act of Indemnity as a mark of royal displeasure, but still made a rare appearance in the House of Lords both to make a theatrical apology and to be one of only two bishops to support the parliamentary resolution in favour of the succession. As a Vicar of Bray he was unequalled, and fully merited the bitter comments made about him by his contemporaries. 'Oh falseness! He that ran with the humour of King James now forsakes him to cringe to the Prince of Orange in hopes to keep his bishopric,' recorded Anthony Wood. And Clarendon underscored his betrayal: 'The Bishop of Durham, who had been at the House but twice before, came today to give his vote against the King who had raised him.'

He returned to Durham, loathed by the Whig establishment, to find himself replaced as Lord Lieutenant by Lumley. Apart from the vacant deanery, Durham had been little affected by the change. A mob had destroyed the chapel of the Catholic Mission in Old Elvet and some Catholic houses were ransacked and torched. The Quaker community suffered too, but only in the ignorant belief that they were Jesuits. Our age should not be too quick to scoff: in the 21st century paediatricians in Britain have had their consulting rooms trashed by mobs who seemed to believe that child abusers put brass plates on their doors.

Relations between Crewe and Thomas Comber, the new dean, a genuine supporter of the Revolution, were icy. The dean lost no time in fingering Crewe to the authorities as a closet Jacobite. In retaliation, Crewe refused to contribute a penny to Comber's efforts to improve the organ and bells in the cathedral, and took refuge in other delights. First, at the age of 58, a belated marriage, and then in 1697 the satisfaction, on succeeding to the family title, of finding himself the first man in English history to hold both a spiritual and a lay peerage. The year 1699 saw the death of the hostile Comber, and Crewe was at last able to slip into the Deanery his patient nephew, John Montagu, Master of Trinity, Cambridge: 'A harmless man, if he has meat and clothes and ease he concerns himself little more with the affairs of the world.' Death carried off his first wife in the same year, but undeterred he remarried, to a woman 40 years younger than himself, Dorothy Forster, whose family seat was Bamburgh Castle. The Forster estates and fortunes were in disarray so Crewe not only efficiently set them to rights, but subsequently bequeathed them for charitable purposes. 'His posthumous munificence', records the DNB, ' has done much to outweigh a discreditable career.' As the years passed, he wintered in the south but still conducted visitations and confirmations as late as 1716. He officiated at the Coronation of George I, managing to suppress his Jacobite yearnings, lost his second wife, who died of anxiety about her family's implication in the Jacobite rising of 1715, but survived to complete 50 years as a bishop and die, himself a slice of history, in September 1721.

THE EIGHTEENTH CENTURY

E.F. Benson called the 18th century 'the siesta century' for churchmen. Though Dean Comber was briefly alarmed by the seditious after-shocks of the Glorious Revolution, when papists were carrying arms, the late King's health drunk openly on the streets and there was, he thought, a threat of general defection, 'encouraged, or at least connived at by our great B' (Crewe), Durham quickly slid into a historical and social backwater, where there was not too much news but too little. There were no larger-than-life characters such as Granville to muddy the waters and make news. Pluralism and its natural partner absenteeism were the norm. Plum jobs were usually held simultaneously by socially well-connected prebendaries, while the bulk of the clergy from lower orders were anchored in their parishes on tiny stipends, sometimes as little as £30 (£1,800) a year. In Durham, deans and prebendaries were rarely present except when required for their period of residence. The town perceived them just as rent gatherers. Without leadership the minor canons who remained were often lazy and the laity disaffected. Across the diocese the minor clergy neglected preaching and catechizing in favour of secular pastimes; Communion was rarely celebrated and festival days ignored. For the superior clergy the power of patronage was all: rich livings and generous leases were generally distributed to relatives and friends. From contemporary letters and journals it is apparent that intrigue for preferments and position consumed more time, interest and energy than clerical duties. The bishopric was described in 1750 as 'a place of ease for men of family and fashion'. But it must be said in defence of the church establishment that its members were conducting themselves with total propriety according to the criteria of the time, and we should not be too hasty in judging them by more recent standards. The leisure their lives afforded was expected to be devoted to scholarship, and some bishops, deans and prebendaries of Durham in this period – Chandler, Basire, Comber, Sharp – all produced theological works regarded as important in their day. Joseph Butler, a prebendary who held the rich living of Stanhope, used the opportunity to produce *The Analogy of Religion*, published in 1736, an eloquent and comprehensive review of the arguments in defence of Christian belief which is still regarded as a classic.

From the Reformation up to the reforms of the Church Commissioners three hundred years later, the principal occupation of deans and chapters was conservation of their estates. In Durham the retreat of 'interesting times' left full opportunity for entrepreneurship. Once Comber was sure that sedition had died down he took up 130 acres in Bearpark, 'fenced them well and planted 1,500 Oakes and 500 Ashes there for the good of posterity'. He was less successful in the pursuit of his own good: he sank a coal pit in the same estate and found very good coal, but the operator let him down, sales proved bad, and after two years he had it filled in again for a loss of at least £60 (£3,600). Bishop Crewe's farming leases were applied to felling rather than planting trees. The Bishop could cut down and carry away the wood on all his farms without making any compensation. He could also make ways through any of his tenants' grounds, not excepting their houses and gardens, and 'without a penny damages'. Bishop Talbot fell out with the Dean and Chapter over mining leases. He won by replacing several elderly prebendaries, who conveniently died in a clutch, with his friends in order to procure a majority vote in the Chapter for his transactions.

The material preoccupations of the Durham clergy encompassed, naturally enough, their accommodation. Slowly the run-down prebendal houses were restored to a condition fit for gracious living, though everyone coming into the Deanery found much to complain about. Comber in 1692 thought the north side rooms 'mean and in great decay', so had them pulled down for twenty yards in length and built two long rooms with two good chambers above, with a large staircase, 'which

The Cathedral as seen from the Gatehouse roof.

cost me at least £300 (£18,000) besides furnishing and adorning'. Still not good enough, though, for the patrician Dean Spencer Cowper in 1746, who recorded that some rooms (are) so dark and dismal you cannot see your hand in them. All wretchedly furnished, and dirty, most so bad it deserves an apology to lay a footman in them.' Interest in the fabric, however, was limited to the domestic. Little or no attention was paid to the condition of the cathedral itself, a neglect which was to have serious consequences before the end of the century, and the attitude of the Chapter to their cultural heritage would now be regarded as criminal. Two pages from a Gospel manuscript in the library were cut out and given to Samuel Pepys as a memento of his visit in May 1682, 'a present to me from my most honoured and reverend friends, the dean and chapter of Durham'; the excisions remain in the Pepys Library at Magdalene College Cambridge. And when Prebendary Dobson's wife or nursemaid took his child to play in the Library on wet days, some of the letters from Puiset's 12th-century Bible were cut out for the sprog's amusement.

A sequence of bishops conducted themselves arrogantly, or egregiously, or both. There was still a Court of Chancery in Durham over which bishops were entitled to preside in person. Crewe delighted in doing so, but commented on one occasion 'that John Doe and Richard Roe were very litigious persons and accordingly summoned them to appear before him to be censured', thereby exposing his complete ignorance of the law he was so keen to administer. Bishop Talbot had his son returned as member of Parliament for Durham; Bishops Chandler and Trevor both secured the see through the influence of the Duke of Newcastle. The first complained to his patron about the swarm of 'projectors' in the town seeking to deprive him of his privileges (i.e. income); the second, indebted for his promotion to a man who had overborne the opposition of George II, simply rolled over: 'Your desires will always have the force of commands with me.' It was Durham and the nation's great loss that the only bishop of real distinction in the period, Joseph Butler, lived for only two years after his appointment in 1750. He was also the only senior Durham churchman of his age noted for the austerity of his life.

Austerity was not much known in the College. After Cosin's death the duties of dean and prebendaries when in residence were social rather than spiritual. The requirement of providing hospitality was enshrined in the 1555 Statutes, extending the practice of monastic charity to the new foundation. Residence was defined as a period of 21 consecutive days declared in advance so that there was no duplication. Within this period a prebendary was required 'to keep more sumptuous entertainment than they are wont at other periods of the year, giving meat to the choir and inviting the citizens or strangers'. An additional income was assigned to fund such hospitality: £40.1.3 (£8,000) for a dean, £8.4.9 (£1,600) for a canon. The allowance was increased in 1624 and again in 1675, when it became £50 (£3,000) for a canon and £100 (£6,000) for a dean. The opportunity for excess was curbed by a Chapter rule of 1662 that no canon in residence was to invite more than six guests a day, except on one day a week. The penalty, a £5 deduction from salary, was given appropriately to the poor. Even so, the scale of entertainment burgeoned. Over three weeks in residence in 1687 Dean Granville entertained the bedesmen, the prebendaries, the petty canons, ecclesiastical officers, the singing men, Justices of the Peace, the bell ringers, the country gentry, tradesmen, poor widows, tenants, shopkeepers and workmen, the master and scholars of Durham School and the organist and choristers. George Wheler, holder of one of the wealthier stalls, took a utopian view of the socializing, which may be accurate: 'each prebendary entertains with great liberality the poor and rich neighbours and strangers with generous welcome,

Christian freedom, modest deportment, good and plentiful cheer, moderate eating and sober drinking. They give God thanks, read a chapter in the midst between the courses, during which all reverently uncover their heads: and after grace again, there is seldom more drunk than the Poculum Charitatis, or the Love Cup, and the King's good health, and then every one to his home, business and studies'.

Between that assessment and what Spencer Cowper, Dean from 1746 to 1774, called 'the age of gustle', the truth might lie. Cowper's letters to his brother are weary with repletion: '1747. Residence ended yesterday, and with it gusling.' '1749. Gussling is now over, and here ends our Annals.' His residence is 'my Carnival', 'the season of cram'. *The Newcastle Courant* in 1751 reported after one such deanery excess: 'Mr Thomas Norris, who kept the Red Lion Inn in Durham, died suddenly of an epoplectick fit after dining with the Dean at his residence'. John Thacker, the College cook, who toured the prebendal houses to prepare the feasts, published his *Cathedral Cookery* in 1758, with appropriate month by month recipes, all heavily weighted with meat. His recommended dishes included Hashed Duck, A Pupton of Lobsters, Whitings broiled Lord Exeter's way, Roast Weetears, Lumber Pye and Salmagundy. The bill of fare for Dr Sterne's first dinner for the Prebendaries listed 26 substantial courses, among them Sturgeon, Stew'd Oysters, Ruffs and reserv'd Wildfowls, A Leveret and Haunch of Venison.

It is wholly to be expected, in consequence, that one of the favourite topics in correspondence is the state of the clerical body. At Christmas 1698 Dean Comber was 'extream ill, but relieved by bleeding at the Emerods, yet the difficulties troubled me long after'. In 1699 he had to write from London to confute 'a rascally letter' that he was already dead. The rascal showed prescience, however. Later in the year Comber, back in Durham,

wrote to his bookseller in St Paul's Churchyard apologizing for not replying: 'The hypochondriac was so violent, I could not sit to any businesse …. Of late I begin to recruit a little with drinking Asses milk.' But to no avail: he was dead within the month. Spencer Cowper notes a 'hysteric disorder', requiring a 'course of stinks', leading to much eructation. Other remedies tried were spa water, tar water, hartshorn, assa foetida, and, for a fit of the cholic, fasting and slip-slop.

Cowper, with his long tenure of the Deanery, is a fair representative of the superior clergy of his age. He had no particular gifts as pastor, preacher or theologian, but he endeavoured to lead a dutiful life. He abhorred 'enthusiasm', and spent only the minimum time at Durham each year, generally three months from September to early December, for one month of which he would be 'in residence'. He dreads the return journey north at the end of each summer, and is heartily relieved when his duties are over: 'Residence ends today, so that trouble is over for one year.' He found the town on his first visit in 1746 'nasty, the streets narrow and wretchedly paved, and the houses dirty and black, as if they had no inhabitants but colliers'. He was greeted by 'a concourse of fools old and young'. The Cathedral displeased him. It had so little beauty in it that it is no improvement to the prospect. The inside is very clumsy. 'The Great Isle is filled with heavy massy pillars out of all proportion.' A feast for 43 of the gentry is spoiled because the ladies' hoops were too large. There are a few concerts, but fewer marriages: 'Marriages are very rare, for both male and female here seemed already advanced to that Angelic State where they neither marry nor are given in marriage. I beleive there is not such a stock of Old Maids to be seen in any Town of the same size in England.' He visited Newcastle once, but found it so filthy and dirty he had no desire to go again. So little human interest does he find that his letters south are filled with dogs and horses. Year after year he apologized for the absence of news from 'our little horseshoe which the Wear surrounds'. 'This is not a place for news. I will not pretend to send you any news from this place. News from this place is next to exporting it from the Highlands. Durham is a dull place. Nothing passes through this deserted town but Scotch peers, Scotch members and Scotch pedlars.'

Then out of the blue he has a piece of news, of the kind a modern tabloid editor would swap a week's lunches at The Ivy for. It deserves recounting at some length: 'No doubt you have heard of a mad clergyman in this country who has circumcised a child he was to christen. It is very true, his name is Cook, he was curate of Alnwick, and the child was brought to him to christen a month ago, but instead of that after talking very madly he shoved the parents out of the room, and circumcised it with a penknife, of which it soon after died. Upon this feat Dr Sharpe, his Archdeacon, suspended him, but he willing to do something still more extraordinary, got Dr Sharpe to permit him to preach a farewell sermon. This indulgence was strange considering what had passed, but the Doctor gave it, not imagining anything could happen from it, but our circumciser the next Sunday, having preached a great deal of mad stuff upon the present national union of Jew and Christian, walked down to the font, and in the face of his congregation, not one of which was inclined to interrupt the operation, cut off his own preputum, and became an Israelite indeed! Loss of blood made him faint, and he was soon after put under confinement, where he still is. A few days before this he had a fancy to go to sea a-horseback, being certain his faith in Christ would carry him safe over to Holland. Numbers being on the shore, both he and his horse were got out safe and sound, and nothing happened worth mentioning, except his answer to some who endeavoured to convince him of his folly from the event. "No", says he, "you mistake the thing quite. Had I been on foot my faith would have carried me over safely, but my horse having none his want of it might have cost us both our lives."'

'IMPROVEMENTS'

Over the centuries the fabric of the cathedral had been gradually sinking into neglect, and the solution chosen for was curiously similar to the treatment applied to Mr Cook's unhappy member. From the Reformation onwards there is no record of significant attention to the fabric of Durham except for the occasional renewal of lead roofing. There had been many alterations to the windows and their glass, for reasons both of fashion and necessity. Medieval priors changed the fenestration both to leave their mark and to keep up with changing architectural tastes and skills. It is necessary to remind ourselves that the valuation of antiquities just because of their age was in its early stages. The Society of Antiquaries had only been incorporated in 1751, and it required the shift of sensibility broadly associated with European romanticism to disseminate its convictions more widely in the culture of the day. The renovation of the cathedral between 1777 and 1810 occurred on the cusp of this change. Much was lost – vandalized, in the modern view – but, crucially, much more might have vanished but for strenuous public protest, especially from the antiquarian John Carter who wrote a series of influential articles for *The Gentleman's Magazine*. He is one of the saviours of the Galilee Chapel.

It is understandable that the priority of successive Deans and Chapters was the furnishing and glazing of the interior rather than its stone fabric. Puritan deans in the 16th century attacked the medieval glass; more still was knocked out during the ravages of the 1650s, a time when much of the furniture was also burned to provide warmth in winter. Next, Sudbury's new library and the prebendal houses required the attention of the masons. In the 1760s the Cloisters were remodelled, and then the great flood of 1771 swept away Prebends Bridge and George Nicholson, the College Architect, had to build a replacement between 1772 and 1775.

'As if Picasso had turned his hand to glass jigsaws': fragments of medieval glass assembled in panels in the Galilee.

At last in 1777 Dean Digby asked John Wooler, a Newcastle surveyor and engineer, for a report on the fabric. He was assisted in his survey by Nicholson, who knew the building well. Wooler completed his work in nine days in November 1777 and his findings were sweeping. He urged an extensive scheme of rebuilding and renewal. There was a 'rent' in the Nave vault to be filled; the north and south gables of the Chapel of the Nine Altars needed reconstruction; the North Porch was to lose its upper storey (the room occupied by the gatemen who received sanctuary seekers). But his most extraordinary recommendation concerned the external stonework, in places much eroded by centuries of Durham weather. It was 'to chip or pare off the outsides to the depth of one, two or three inches … to bring the upright of the wall to a tolerable even or streight surface.' At the same time rainwater pipes were to be affixed, presumably for the first time. Christopher Downs, the present architect, has pointed out the folly of this stratagem. Not only was much of the original decorative detail hacked away, but also good stonework which had acquired a patina of resistance to the elements was trimmed back to expose its more vulnerable interior. Wooler's estimate was that 40 men working for eight years could accomplish the work at a total cost of £9,000 (£480,000). From 1778 the chisellers were at it, removing an estimated 1000 tons of stone from the east, west and north sides of the building. Masons also added pinnacles to the west towers, turrets above the north transept and little spires at the north end of the Chapel of the Nine Altars. The North Porch was also largely rebuilt. The resident architects overseeing the work were Nicholson, who was also Clerk of the Works until his death in 1793, and his successor George Morpeth.

A second wave of vandalism rolled in when Earl Cornwallis, the Dean, and Shute Barrington, the Bishop, summoned from the south the architect James Wyatt, whose work Barrington had known at Salisbury, 'to give a Plan on the future Repairs and Improvements'. He arrived in 1794 and made further proposals. His proposed 'improvements' included the demolition of the Galilee Chapel, the removal of Cosin's 17th-century organ screen and the 14th-century Neville Screen, the demolition of the 12th-century Chapter House, which he judged to be beyond repair, and, in compensation, the erection of a spire on the central tower. The indictment for this programme must be divided between neglectful Deans and Chapters of the earlier 18th century, the indifference of the 1795 Chapter to its heritage, and the vanity and presumption of fashionable architects. In November 1795 the Chapter ordered the demolition of the Chapter House and its replacement by a 'Chapter

Room'. Morpeth simply had the keystones knocked out so that the vaulting came crashing down to the floor beneath which the earliest bishops and priors were buried. In 1796 preparations were made for the destruction of the Galilee, and the lead stripped from its roof to await the sledge-hammers. Morpeth was a busy man, fortunately. He removed the original steep-pitched oak roof of the Nave and replaced it with the present roof, with a pitch ten feet lower. He was also active in executing Wyatt's plans for new tracery in windows of the Chapel of the Nine Altars. Partly as a consequence of 18th-century inertia there was still a quantity of medieval glass in place, in the Choir, Transepts, Galilee and Chapel of the Nine Altars. But in the late 1770s a gale had blown in the east window in the latter chapel, and the fragments of its glass lay about openly in baskets for souvenir hunters to help themselves. The alterations to the tracery all along the east wall of the chapel led to the loss of almost all the remaining medieval glass. Some of it was 'recycled' by people of the town, as the local historian Surtees recorded: 'About twenty-five years ago, great repair of the cathedral was made, and every house in the neighbourhood bears testimony to the wreck of the smaller decorations suffered by the church in that repair.' The removal and purloining of old glass continued, despite the protests of antiquaries, for much of the 19th century. The fragments that were left have been displayed in surreal panels in the Galilee, as if Picasso had turned his hand to glass jigsaws.

It is almost a Cuthbert miracle that the progress of Wyatt's 'improvements' was slow. John Carter's sad and indignant reports in *The Gentleman's Magazine* in December 1801 and January 1802 after a visit to Durham were influential in rousing opposition, and Cornwallis and his Chapter were induced to rescind their order for the Galilee's removal. He excoriated the new work in the North Porch as 'one of the most barbarous commixtures of Saxon and Pointed arch features pilfered from our antient buildings, when under a derangement of the improving mania, that I ever beheld'. The state of the Galilee was still more reprehensible, the roof without covering, the floor strewn with heaps of coals and all kinds of building materials, the North aisle partitioned off into offices and the oratory converted into a closet for occasional retirement. Then he turned his fire on the hapless Wyatt: 'He who should have been most forward to set aside the premeditated blow then hovering over these walls, who has seated himself as prime imitator and preserver of our antient architectural glories, to come these ailes among and tread where Durham's benefactors lie interred, when, after turning askance his eyes on this and that, to give his orders thus: 'All this must come down, I want a walk here!' Wyatt in consequence is held up as the chief villain in the desecration of Durham. In fairness it should be pointed out that he appeared only half way through the process, and that the ultimate decisions were taken by the Chapter. The cathedral's ordeal was not quite done. In 1806 William Atkinson began facing the tower with a newly invented mortar rendering which covered the stone surface. It was quickly abandoned when the bland effect became clear, and it was eventually removed in the 1860s by George Gilbert Scott in the course of the next renovation.

INVESTIGATING SAINT CUTHBERT

One more episode of vandalism remained in this phase of culpable custiodianship of Durham Cathedral. It came at the hands of one who should have known better, James Raine, an otherwise distinguished local historian and antiquary, and the Chapter Librarian. In May 1827 he decided to examine the remains of St Cuthbert for the first time since the reburial in 1542. What followed seems to have lacked objectivity and rigour, and was apparently motivated by sectarian prejudice. The investigation did not receive the approval of the full Chapter, who were divided in their views. Sub Dean Darnell wrote to Raine: 'I wish no evil may befall you for having been engaged in this wicked spoliation of the dead.' Raine found three coffins. The first inner coffin, that of the 1104 translation, was covered in hide. It held a jumbled pile of bones, including some of children, listed in earlier inventories as 'the bones of the Innocents'. The innermost coffin was of richly carved wood, its lid set with two iron rings. Within it were the skull of King Oswald and Cuthbert's skeleton shrouded in silk or linen, resting on five robes, one of which was embroidered with waves, fruit and flowers, solan geese, eider ducks and porpoises. Found also were an ivory comb and silver altar, both recorded in 1104; a stole with gold woven into the fabric; a maniple, girdle and gold bracelets which may have been the gifts bestowed by Athelstan in 934. There was also a gold cross decorated with garnets, and fine threads of gold wire which had originally fixed a coif to the saint's head. It was these that Elfred Westhou the sacrist had held in a flame for his 11th-century conjuring trick, designed to prove that Cuthbert's hair was as imperishable as his body. Raine next noted the skeleton. The bones were intact but disjointed, unsurprisingly after the body's manhandling by Henry VIII's commissioners. The right arm was fixed in an upright position as if in benediction. There was no earth nor any evidence of decomposed flesh.

Cuthbert was reinterred the same evening in a new coffin, and the treasures removed to the Chapter Library. The care of these was off-hand. Some were later mislaid, purloined or given away. A small linen bag was 'lost in Darnell's house'. Mr Gilly took a tooth, and several pieces of the vestments were distributed to his friends. Raine himself gave pieces of cloth to one of his illustrators. A piece of the stole found a home at Ushaw College, a piece of silver in the British Museum, and over 6,000 fragments of wood were stored in the Triforium.

Raine concluded his account of the exhumation with the argument that the tradition of the uncorrupted body was a fraud perpetrated to establish sainthood and maintain the subsequent status of the cult. This was the conclusion that perfectly suited his agenda. In 1827 sectarian feelings were running high in Durham as a result of the passing of the Catholic Emancipation Act. A new Catholic church in the town, St Cuthbert's, was to be dedicated on 31 May. So Raine, by opening the tomb a fortnight before, had a strident Anglican purpose: to disprove two traditions, one the miracle of Cuthbert's preservation, the other that his body had been substituted by the last monks before the commissioners' visit in 1538 and had been in the clandestine care of Catholics ever since. The testimonies of the other eye-witnesses to the event do not entirely match Raine's, and at the very least confirm that the investigation was seriously compromised by haste and muddle.

In religion, as in politics, the practices of the 18th century held fast for nearly three decades of the 19th, resistant to the political, economic and social transformations sweeping over Europe. Places such as Durham were first targeted ideologically, sometimes vindictively, by Whig dissenters. Then a popular clamour for reform swelled towards the end of the 1820s. Catholic Emancipation was one of the first fruits of that clamour, and unsettled the Anglican hierarchy. An obdurate bench of bishops in the House of Lords thought they could stem the reformist tide. The consequence was that they and their church would be swept off their rock of ages, and the inequities and self-indulgences of a complacent Anglicanism would themselves be reformed away.

Assize Sunday service in the Quire, 1835. An oil painting by Edmund Hastings now hanging in the Durham Dormitory.

REFORM AND BEYOND 1830–1970

THE REFORM MOVEMENT

There was no more indefensible target of the reformist spirit than the ecclesiastical hierarchy of Durham between 1800 and 1830. Their wealth was fabulous. The estates of the Benedictines with which Henry VIII had endowed the cathedral, particularly on Tyneside and in Weardale, were yielding galloping returns in industrial times from the mining of coal and lead. Chapter income doubled in those 30 years. In addition to the salaries ear-marked for particular prebendal stalls, excess profits were pooled and distributed as dividends to each prebendary. By 1830 the annual dividend had exceeded £2,000 (£60,000). Four prebendaries had higher incomes than most of the deans in the land. Brougham, later the Whig Lord Chancellor, characterized the church in Durham as being 'endowed with a splendour and a power unknown in monkish times and Papish countries'.

Resentment of such wealth was magnified by the perception that it was unearned. These clerics enjoyed generous terms of employment. Each prebendary was required to be in residence for only three months a year; the obligation to preach a sermon was rare; there were no pastoral duties, and the services were conducted by eight minor canons who also held local livings. No wonder that Archdeacon Thorp in his

The Stella Maris window by Leonard Evetts in the north-west corner of the Galilee. It was the gift of the American Friends of Durham to commemorate nine hundred years since the foundation of the present Cathedral on the site in 993. Stella Maris, star of the sea, was the name given to the Virgin by Bede. The left hand light contains the letters AM for the Virgin, the right the Chi-ro sign for Christ.

response to the reforms proposed by the Ecclesiastical Commissioners described the canons in 1835 as 'a most useful and meritorious class of incumbent'. There were generous hospitality allowances for those in residence, and the 18th-century habit of giving and receiving dinners persisted in presenting itself as a duty more essential than attendance at services. A still more outrageous privilege, in the judgement of reformers, was the practice of pluralism, which was more the rule than the exception for the higher ranks of the clergy. In 1829 the dean and two prebendaries were also diocesan bishops elsewhere in the country; all the minor canons and ten of the 12 prebendaries held other livings, and nearly half of all incumbents in the diocese were pluralists. A brief roll-call highlights the abuse. Earl Cornwallis, Dean from 1794 to 1824, who came within a whisker of sanctioning the demolition of the Galilee Chapel, was also Bishop of Lichfield for the same 30 years, and was absent from Durham after 1816, returning only to die in the Deanery; Jenkinson, his successor, was also Bishop of St Davids. The extreme example of clerical exploitation was Francis Egerton, Earl of Bridgewater, who held the fourth stall at Durham from 1786 to 1829, and also two Shropshire livings which he never visited. From 1802 he was non-resident at Durham, preferring the Rue St Honoré in Paris, where he collected manuscripts, fathered a brood of illegitimate children, filled his garden with rabbits which he shot and his house with dogs dressed in human attire. He appeared once in Durham in 27 years.

The choristers in determined mood in the East Cloister on their way to music practice in the Song School.

The radical-tempered *Durham Chronicle* waged an outspoken campaign against the outrages on the hilltop. 'How long was this corruption to be tolerated?' If the rich pluralists were purged, the sums saved could be given to 'the meritorious clerical labourers', and the Church might 'once more lift up her head'. Even Van Mildert, arriving as bishop in 1826 in the midst of the storm, agreed with the perception that some clergy were 'wallowing in wealth … at best but honourable lumber who have been turned over to spiritual pursuits from inability to succeed in more arduous professions'. And he was no reformer, as will be seen.

Among the higher clergy, Van Mildert's awareness of the problem of public perception was unrepresentative. Many believed that the conditions they enjoyed were part of the fabric of society. Some who egregiously entered public debate on behalf of the status quo to attack social and political reform exposed themselves to further opprobrium which they failed to comprehend. The ferment that followed the Peterloo Massacre of 1819 induced the privileged prebendary Phillpotts, Rector of Stanhope, where he was non-resident but received £4,500 (£135,000) a year from the London Lead Company, to engage in an ill-advised public joust with 'Radical Jack', John Lambton, MP for Durham and son-in-law of Earl Grey. Phillpotts attacked both Lambton and Grey for provoking the populace to sedition. The extravagance of his language and sentiments roused Grey to characterize the entire Chapter at Durham as savages: 'What was to be thought of professed followers of Christ shooting forth their poisoned arrows into the world, ignorant and careless where they might hit, so that their malignity was justified?' The Chapter poured fat into the fire in 1821 when it refused to toll the bells on the death of the widely popular estranged wife of George IV, Queen

The Cathedral, the river and old mill house and its weir: a stormy sunset in August.

Caroline. *The Durham Chronicle*, 'speaking for the people', now let fly: such conduct renders the very name of our established clergy odious till it stinks in the nostrils', and deprives them of all pastoral influence and respect, unsupported by the people. The ecclesiastical system was 'at war with the spirit of the age', and its representatives were reviled as 'the beetles who crawl about amidst holes and crevices'. Confronted by such lese-majesty, the Chapter issued a writ for libel against the editor, J.A. Williams. The case was heard at the assizes in Durham in August 1822, with the notable Brougham, who had taken Lambton's side in the earlier dispute with Phillpotts, appearing for the defence in a trial which had turned into a highly politicized cause celebre. It was, Brougham declared, 'the most pitiful folly for the Clergy to think of retaining their power, privileges and enormous wealth, without allowing free vents for complaints against the establishment and delinquency in its members'. Williams was convicted of libel, but any mud that stuck adhered firmly to the physiognomies of the Chapter. Besides, the issue of clerical corruption had been placed by the case on the national agenda, to remain there for

the best part of 20 years until the reformist tide reached it. 'We said they had "no prop in the attachment and veneration of the people"', wrote Williams, 'and as if they were eager to give a proof of the truth of that remark, they apply to a court of law to supply one.'

In 1826 Shute Barrington, Bishop of Durham for 35 years, died at the impressive age of 92. He had held three bishoprics in his time, but had had no pastoral experience. To have been brother to a Chancellor of the Exchequer was no disadvantage. By his longevity he had extended into the age of reform the perfect model of the unreformed superior cleric, dutiful, fixed in a tradition, and seemingly impervious to social cause except for his commitment to the change of education in the diocese. The death of an old-style Prince-Bishop suspended the workings of the Palatinate administration, especially the operation of the law, so in such volatile times a quick succession was desirable. William Van Mildert seemed to be a new man, the son of a failed gin distiller of Dutch origin. He had begun his career as a humble curate, and was thought of in the diocese as an upstart. His ten years as bishop capture perfectly the tension between reaction and reform which his conduct exhibited in exact balance. He was a man on the very cusp of the matter of his time.

Van Mildert inherited the tradition of lavish hospitality associated with the Palatinate and the see. In the week of the Durham Assizes he entertained 200 guests at the Castle over three days and 300 at Bishop Auckland over four days. But nothing equalled the scale of the grand banquet given at the Castle in honour of the Duke of Wellington in October 1827. The occasion was effectively an endorsement of the old order, masked by Wellington's heroic popularity. His younger brother, the Hon. Gerald Wellesley, who had just been appointed to a stall at Durham, was also Rector of Bishopwearmouth, carrying the astonishing salary of £3,000 (£90,000), Rector of St Luke's Chelsea, Vicar of Thetfield and royal chaplain at both Hampton Court and St James. The appointment, and the milieu it represented, had provoked derision and indignation among reformers.

In Gerald's wake came the great brother Arthur. There was a civic welcome. Bands played 'See the

Conquering Hero Comes'. Bells rang, cannon roared and the people cheered. Addresses were delivered at the Town Hall and then townsmen drew the duke's open carriage uphill to the Castle. A perfunctory visit to the cathedral preceded the banquet. The choir sang 'Non Nobis Domine' and the toasts followed. Van Mildert toasted Wellington, offering 'that humble tribute of veneration and gratitude, which is due from everyone who knows how to value the blessings of our admirable Constitution in Church and State'. It was a highly politicized event, the last of its kind in the city. The hall was decorated with pink ribbons and banners, the local Tory electoral colour. Van Mildert eulogized another guest, Sir Walter Scott, who was staying in the district. Scott's thanks were emphatic: 'I must ever consider it one of the proudest moments of my life, that I am praised by the Bishop of Durham, in his own hall, when he was entertaining the Duke of Wellington.'

Within two years, however, Wellington, now Prime Minister, had to set aside his reactionary instincts and promote the Catholic Emancipation Act, which the pragmatic soldier in him understood was necessary in order to avert civil war in Ireland. The enfranchising of dissenters by the repeal of the Test and Corporation Acts and of Catholics by the 1829 Emancipation Act deeply unsettled the Anglican church, accustomed as it was to the unthreatening complacency of establishment. Like most of his Episcopal colleagues Van Mildert opposed Catholic Emancipation, but to no avail. The erosion of the confidence of the church in Durham was hastened by the accession to government in 1830 of a Whig administration led by Earl Grey, whose cabinet included those proven opponents of the status quo in the cathedral, Brougham and Lambton, now Lord Durham. The Durham Chapter had good reason to believe itself a prime target. Grey in the House of Lords referred specifically to Durham as the possessor of 'an accumulation of church property which did not operate for the useful purposes of religion'. Durham's defences were not strengthened by the nominal

Durham in 1843: a drawing by R.W. Billings from 'Illustrations of the Cathedral Church in Durham'.

presence there of the egregious Phillpotts, who had improbably been appointed Bishop of Exeter in 1830 by the outgoing Tory administration, reputedly as a reward for his falling into line over Catholic Emancipation. But Exeter was a poor diocese, unfitted to support his 14 children, and, being a relation by marriage of Lord Eldon, he looked to retain the lucrative parish of Stanhope. The incoming Whig government refused him, so he opted for a stall at Durham and obtained permission for non-residence. The case for reform was strengthened.

The beleagured bishops, including Van Mildert, now opposed Grey's Reform Bill. Van Mildert condemned it as the mark of a restless disposition which 'fostered atheism, infidelity, dissent and discord, attacked institutions merely because they were ancient, and sought to set subjects above their rulers'. When he voted (by proxy) with 21 other bishops against the bill, his effigy was burned at the gates of his palace at Auckland and he daily expected an attack on his person. Violent abuse of the clergy was tumultuously acclaimed at public meetings in dissident Newcastle. He also voted against the second reading, but faced with Grey's agreement with the king to appoint sufficient peers to secure its passage in the Lords, he abstained, like most other bishops, at the final reckoning. But it was too late; their conduct had exposed the Church of England to attack, and hundreds of articles, tracts and proposals poured out, lambasting the unpopular bishops and advancing reforms. Cathedrals, 'the fortresses of sloth and ignorance', were particularly held up to ridicule. Church reform nationally and the final abolition of the Palatinate locally were the inexorable consequences of the bishops' political intransigence.

While the reactionary Van Mildert was fighting the Reform Bill, the enlightened Van Mildert was striving to redress decades of neglect and indifference within his diocese. In his view, time was short to save the Church of England, which was in danger of being marginalized by social change to which it had failed to adapt, and by the prevailing reformist spirit targeting it. Van Mildert believed that the church could only retain respect by acting in ways that won the approval of the laity. He worked indefatigably to restore a central role for his church in a rapidly changing and expanding diocese. His priorities were a higher calibre of parish clergy, adequately accommodated and paid, and a sufficiency of churches to meet local needs. He directed the building of 14 new churches in his ten years as bishop, contributing generously from his own pocket, convinced that the creation of new parishes in industrial towns was necessary to restrict the growth of Methodism among factory labourers. In the cathedral itself a first effort was made to reach out to the masses: a 'popular' Sunday service in the Galilee was held after Evensong from 1828. Not until 1837 was the nave made accessible to visitors, though only until noon. In 1841 the hours were extended and the east end included in the concession.

Van Mildert also offered himself as a champion of the Durham miners. The special relationship between cathedral and mining villages, still commemorated in the annual Miners' Day Service, was rooted in the early 1830s. The Colliers' United Association of Durham and Northumberland was founded in 1830, an embryonic trade union seeking to prevent exploitation of mine workers. A bitter series of disputes and strikes followed in 1831 and 1832, and the mood of the locality was inflammable. Whigs had the major share of colliery ownership, and united with the local Tory gentry in a move to suppress industrial dissent. The owners put pressure on Grey's government to promote their agents as magistrates in order to weight court decisions in their favour. Lord Chancellor Brougham pressed Van Mildert, who as Prince-Bishop had the appointment of magistrates in his power, to act as the owners desired. To his great credit he refused, and launched an outspoken attack on Brougham over his conduct. It was the last noble act by a ruler of the Palatinate: on Van Mildert's death in 1836 the vestigial temporal powers of a prince-bishop, including the appointment of the magistracy, were returned to the Crown.

THE FOUNDING OF DURHAM UNIVERSITY

Van Mildert's greatest service was not to the miners but to education. This was an issue upon which he was largely in tune with the spirit of his time. The Society for the Encouragement of Parochial Schools had been founded in Durham in 1811, and in the 1820s 27 new elementary schools had opened in mining villages. The educational movement was powerful nationally: in 1828 University College London opened as a non-denominational university in 'godless Gower Street'. The threat of a comparable radical foundation in Newcastle precipitated the speediest conception, parturition and delivery of a university in the history of higher education. The creation of Durham University owes everything to Van Mildert's energy, vision, determination, financial acumen and political skills.

Early in 1831 at a meeting of the Literary and Philosophical Society in Newcastle, Thomas Greenhow proposed the establishment of a university in the city, naturally non-denominational in accord with its distinguished record of dissent. The idea at once attracted the support of Earl Grey but was perceived at Durham as another secular threat. Archdeacon Charles Thorp, agitated by Newcastle's enterprise, wrote to Van Mildert proposing a university in Durham: 'it would give to the Dean and Chapter strength of character and usefulness, preserve the Revenues to the church and to the north, and prevent the establishment of a very doubtful Academical institution which is now taking root in N'Castle.' Hardly the noblest of sentiments, but at a time of both deep unpopularity and the likelihood of reform, the Church had to combine altruism with self-preservation. The redirection of some of Durham's wealth into a university would be an excellent piece of public relations and ensure continued control of the income. Van Mildert leapt at Thorp's idea, and during the summer of 1831 plans were finalized and put to the Chapter. In September they won unanimous approval.

Van Mildert had asked Thorp for 'a producible shape, so as to anticipate, not only any mongrel attempt at Newcastle, but any fierce attack upon Church Dignities from the House of Commons as soon as the Reform Bill is disposed of'. He saw the university as both 'a peace-offering to the public' and 'for its own sake'. Dean Jenkinson's approval was exclusively pragmatic. He saw 'the necessity of adopting some measure which shall extend the utility of our Collegiate body, and give the public an interest in its preservation'. The Chapter agreed to reserve three prebendal stalls for academic posts and to endow the university with income from its estates in South Shields. It also opted for a full-scale institution rather than a theological college, with professorships in Divinity, Classics, Mathematics and Natural Philosophy. But it was to remain an Anglican foundation, financed by the church, so that, as at Oxford and Cambridge, a degree would entitle a student to take holy orders should he wish to. Thorp was named as Warden, with the Dean and Chapter as the Directing Body and the Bishop as Visitor. The only objection was from Phillpotts, who declared that there were more than enough educated men already, and that the addition of more would merely make them discontented with their lot.

By October 1831 Earl Grey's support had been won and a Parliamentary Bill was in preparation. The leverage Van Mildert had exercised on the Durham Chapter was now transferred to Westminster. The government wished the university to be non-denominational. Van Mildert refused; the funds were, after all, Anglican. But he was prepared to accept the Cambridge compromise: students of any religious persuasion might matriculate and study, but to gain a degree they must subscribe to the Thirty-Nine Articles. There would also be a required daily church service for all students. The Durham University Act received the royal assent in July 1832, the same year as the Reform

William Van Mildert, portrait in the throne room at Auckland Castle, by Sir Thomas Lawrence.

Act, to which the idea of the university owed its inception as a defensive counterbalance. On 28 October 1833 the university opened, with five divinity students, 19 students of the 'foundation' and 18 other students. Newcastle had been out-manoeuvred, chiefly as a result of Van Mildert's total commitment of energy and vision 'to make the public partners in our income'. Worn out by his efforts he sank into a prolonged incapacitating illness and died in February 1836. His grand funeral procession was sabotaged by stormy weather, and he was buried not at Auckland, as he had desired, but within the altar rails of the cathedral. From the year of his death morning prayers for the new university were held every day in the Galilee Chapel and on Sundays there was a university matins with seats reserved for academics, staff and students in the choir and north transept.

Van Mildert was perhaps fortunate in the timing of his death. He did not live to see the encroachment of ecclesiastical reform, which he had opposed, and which even his grand conception of the university could not

Above: *Restoration of the interior by George Gilbert Scott in the 19th century included the replacement of Cosin's 17th-century wooden organ screen by a delicate stone reredos, and the addition of a pulpit decorated with marble mosaics.*

Right: *Richly decorated 19th-century organ pipes on the north side of the Quire.*

withstand. Grey had convened the Church Revenues Commission in 1832, which was also endorsed by his successors Peel and Melbourne. The results of its deliberations were the Ecclesiastical Commissioners Act of 1836 and the Cathedrals Act of 1840. The number of prebendaries and minor canons was reduced, their periods of required residence extended and their incomes equalized. No more 'golden stalls'. Prebendaries were henceforward rechristened canons, two of whom at Durham were to hold professorships in the university. The dean's income was fixed at £3,000, and a canon's at £1,000. These salaries still saw Durham at the top of the league table: all other deans, except at Westminster and St Pauls, received £1,000, and all other canons £500. In draft form these proposals were greeted at Durham as a deep affront. The Chapter objected that the proposals 'must go far to destroy the influence and usefulness of cathedral establishments, and to render them unfit to accomplish the objects for which they are to be preserved'. Prebendary Smith had a still more consuming anxiety. If canonical houses were alienated, 'this would be productive of great inconvenience to the members of the Chapter, and might lead to the introduction of very objectionable inhabitants'. His argument failed to sway Parliament.

VICTORIAN DURHAM: WADDINGTON AND LAKE

The Chapter reshaped by Act of Parliament now needed stability and settlement. Victorian Durham was fortunate in that the two deans who led the cathedral to within sight of the 20th century – George Waddington and William Charles Lake – were energetic and devoted men of very different temperaments who between them renewed a moribund cathedral and rescued a university suddenly ailing in its infancy.

Waddington was a new broom with an old handle. In some respects he harked back to an earlier era. He maintained a gourmet's bachelor life in the Deanery, embodied the dining culture inherited from the previous century and even bottled a Deanery Ale. A visitor in 1861 found that 'his chief topic of conversation was his sherry of 1815, for which he gave £12 (£380) a dozen'. He did not observe fast days. He had a pronounced taste for noisy and showy music, especially organ versions of the operatic music of Haydn and Mozart. But he was also a man of high intellect and moral stature, who descended on both cathedral and town like a benign genie. There was much to him. He had had a romantic youth exploring the higher reaches of the Nile in highly dangerous times; he had been in Greece during the War of Independence and was a distinguished scholar of the

George Waddington, Dean 1840–69. An oil portrait commissioned by the canons in 1850 which hangs above the entrance to the Cathedral Library Waddington established in the Dormitory after the prebendal house inserted into it was removed in 1848.

Orthodox Church, a founder member of the Athenaeum Club and an admirer of Byron. He was entirely fearless, and caused a great stir in the town by backing the radical John Bright in the 1843 hustings, dominated by the issue of the Corn Laws, 'to win, if he might, for the poor of England the priceless privilege of untaxed bread'. The *Durham Advertiser* was appalled. 'Can these be called faithful soldiers of the church, who admit an enemy into the very citadel?' Waddington, unmoved, invited Bright to share in the deanery's cornucopia. As a single man he chose to marry the town, where he became greatly beloved. He was a generous supporter of Durham's hospitals and infirmary, all of which he funded from his

own pocket. Rarely did he miss a governors' meeting. He championed Mechanics' Institutes and the cause of education generally: 'In the storehouse of retribution there is no curse that stings so deeply as the degradation of a child.' He was an ever-popular visitor to Durham's fairs, including, reputedly, jousts in the boxing booths. After his contribution to the election of Bright he was on future polling days escorted by a cheering crowd from the gate of the College down to the count in the Market Place. The affection the town had for him was finely displayed at his funeral in July 1869. On a fine summer's day every citizen of Durham seemed to be there, many weeping in the streets, and 6,000 mourners packed into the cathedral for the service.

On his arrival in 1840 Waddington found both morale and spirituality in the cathedral at a low ebb, and for nearly 30 years strove tirelessly, often at his own expense, to turn things round. He was a compulsive improver and left no part of the precinct untouched. His devotion to the fabric was more successful than his influence on services, the style of which he left Dean Lake to redress. Congregations were thin – barely a dozen at a Sunday matins – and the presentation of services shoddy. Though he appointed a good musician, J.B. Dykes, as Precentor in 1849, at a generous salary of £340 (£14,000), in 1854 Dykes admitted that he was only able to hold a choir practice 'by begging it as a personal favour'. But Waddington did succeed in making the building more accessible, opening up the internal spaces. In 1847 he persuaded the Chapter to remove Cosin's 17th-century organ screen, which separated the Choir from the Nave, by promising to pay the cost of its restoration if after a trial period the Chapter wanted it. As a piece of work it was judged as 'boldly and not unskilfully carved, but after designs wholly inappropriate to a place of worship'.

This success led him on. He restored 'Norman' style windows to the north and south sides of the Nave, moved Cosin's canopied font from the middle of the Nave to the west end, rearranged the layout of the Choir and reglazed many windows. The Nave and Choir he had refloored; heating and lighting were installed, and then there were renovations to the Neville Screen, the

Chapter House, the bells and belfry, the churchyard, Prebends' Bridge. He ensured that the Library and Museum were properly endowed, and extended them over a six-year period from 1848. In that year Canon Wellesley died. He was the last occupant of the prebendal house which had been crazily inserted into the south end of the monastic dormitory. On his death Waddington was free to demolish the intruding structure and had the imagination to restore the room to its original dimensions. He fashioned a close bond with Durham School and many of his best addresses were delivered to the boys. A different but characteristic address was directed at a scamp he caught imitating his distinctive waddling gait in the College. 'Hand him up on the church front', he ordered, and the urchin was led off to the masons' yard to have his head, complete with straw hat, carved for a corbel. His authority as a churchman is precisely captured in one of the series of Durham Sketches in a local journal: 'You perceive that Dr W., after he has preached a quarter of an hour (and he seldom exceeded that) is a clear-headed, unaffected person, a gentleman and a scholar. You perceive that he is no Puseyite; nor is he of the other Calvanistic (sic) extreme, full of death, darkness, misery and woe. You perceive that Dr W. is a divine who will do his utmost to serve you.' Strength of personality matched with power of intellect and expression made him one of the most formidable of Victorian deans. A man of substance in every sense, his huge portrait and leonine bust greet visitors at the doorway of the Library he nurtured. He was buried in the churchyard alongside the path to the North Porch, where all who enter the building may salute him.

Dean Lake could not have been more of a contrast in personality. He appeared shy and aloof, though younger members of his congregation found him highly approachable when he held court in the College after services, wearing his distinctive black velvet skull cap. He was at his best with children, often riding out with them on horseback, and offering hosts of little prizes for the progress of those in his circle. He could be less sensitive with colleagues. On one occasion he rebuked Minor Canon Greenwell, a devoted

The arrival of the railway in Durham in 1846 transformed the economy of local coal mines and brought in large numbers of visitors for the first time. The view north-west from the Cathedral tower is dominated by the great viaduct that spans the west side of the city centre.

fisherman, for joining a service in thick laced boots. Greenwell sought comfort from Archdeacon Bland, who gave it after a fashion. Lake, he declared, was 'possessed by three imps: he is impervious, he is impetuous, and he is impertinent'. Bland's response was a measure of the Chapter's resistance to the changes Lake was pursuing. His energetic tenure of the deanery witnessed transformations of cathedral services, of the fabric, and of the prosperity of the university. On all these fronts he had an uphill task. Lake found worship slack, and the cathedral failing to reach a wider society. The choir would arrive in their places in a hurry and still fastening their surplices. Lake noted that 'the services were so neglected that the nave in the afternoon was filled with persons who strolled about in the aisles merely to hear the anthem'. He had to fight his Chapter to change the assumption that the cathedral was primarily for sightseers, with worship coming second. Steadily he restored decorum, asking the choir to robe in the vestry and join a formal procession. The Eucharist had been relegated to a marginal role in the order of services, and Lake made it the very centre of worship, an act which won him accusations of Puseyism.

The fabric, despite Waddington's attentions, was still suffering the legacy of James Wyatt. The pillars were covered in plaster, and the whole church had only three stained glass windows. In 1870 Lake launched a huge renovation programme directed by George Gilbert Scott. The choir and east end were closed and services shifted to the nave. Plaster and whitewash were stripped from the stonework, and the present marble and alabaster screen constructed. The windows in the Chapel of the Nine Altars were filled with stained glass. Lake also salvaged as much as he could of the violated Chapter House. Throughout the work he was often in contention with his Chapter and at war with Bishop Baring, who opposed the restoration. But on St Luke's Day 1876 there was a triumphant service of rededication attended by several thousand people, though not Baring, who absented himself in a sulk.

Waddington and Lake were both beset by problems with their fledgling university. In the early

years numbers had grown steadily to around 150, but then fell in the 1860s to as few as 50. The new railway system was now able to convey ambitious young men to Oxford and Cambridge, and Archdeacon Thorp, the Warden, was possessive and fixed in his ways. A Royal Commission was appointed in 1862 to address the crisis. Charles Thorp refused to appear before it, preferring to resign. The humiliation killed him; he was dead within four months. The Chapter increased its endowment to extend the academic range and attract more students. Waddington opted to succeed Thorp as Warden in his 70th year and with his usual energy began the invigoration. But the credit for the full revival of the place is Lake's. He succeeded Waddington as Warden and involved himself fully, making it his practice to interview every student at the end of every term with a welcome blend of kindness and humour. From 1881 onwards he fought to gain approval for the admission of women students, but the move was sadly resisted until 1896, when Lake had been dead for two years. More valuable still was his scheme for establishing a School of Science at Newcastle. Single-handedly he garnered support from the leading businessmen of the area, notably Lord Armstrong and Joseph Cowen, the proprietor of the *Newcastle Chronicle*. The success of his college would have exceeded even Lake's hopes. Founded in 1871, by 1900 numbers had risen to 500, and the young Newcastle University, still under Durham's wing, was flourishing.

Some of the Chapter, however, persisted in looking backwards. In 1899, at the desire of Canon Greenwell (he of the thick laced boots), Cuthbert's tomb was reopened. He wanted an anatomist and a Catholic priest present, one to make an inventory of the bones, the other to attest to his flock to the saint's condition. He also hoped to recover objects reinterred by Raine in 1827. They found that Raine's new coffin had already collapsed and its contents had fallen to the

Above: *The 67th Durham Miners' Gala, 22 July 1950. The spectacular annual parade, founded in 1871, has been interrupted only by war and major strikes.*

Right: *The processional banner of the Haswell Lodge Branch of the Durham Miners' Association, 1893. The banner has hung in the South Transept since 1990, and embodies the bond between cathedral and miners, established in 1896, which still continues, despite the closure of the pits, with an annual service on Gala Day.*

bottom of the chamber to mingle with more bones and decaying wood. There were enough bones for one complete skeleton and around 180 surplus bones, including three lower jaws, 20 ribs, 35 foot bones and seven left shins. It was thought doubtful by the anatomist that a complete 'Cuthbert skeleton' could have been assembled. It would have been a taxing jigsaw. Victorian curiosity was satisfied but little gained, except the villification Greenwell incurred from the Newcastle Society of Antiquaries.

DURHAM AND THE MINERS

In the course of the 19th century the city of Durham doubled in size, from 8,000 to 16,000 inhabitants. In the same period the appearance and character of the diocese was transformed. The age of coal and its close relation, heavy engineering, particularly shipbuilding on the Tyne and Wear, had created challenging new conditions for the exercise of Christian ministry, principle and moral leadership. Though the full range of cathedral and diocesan life continued, it is industrial relations which claim the foreground, particularly between 1870 and 1940, and it is industrial relations

that measure the characters of the bishops and deans who held office in those years. The 20th century at Durham is framed by the enthronement of two bishops, no strangers to controversy, at moments when the diocese was convulsed by labour unrest – Hensley Henson in 1920 and David Jenkins in 1984. The roles they chose to play and the public response to them are classic case studies in the difficulties of Christian leadership in modern times. Both brought Durham to national prominence.

The bond between Durham and the miners grew strong in the 19th century. Forty years after the formation of the first miners' association and Van Mildert's resistance to loading the law courts against them, the first 'Big Meeting' or Miners' Gala was held at Wharton Park in Durham in August 1871. The next year it moved to the Racecourse, and developed into the greatest single event in the socialist calendar, addressed by all the leading figures in the Labour Movement. It was the big day out for all the local mining communities, who marched or flocked into Durham in their hundreds of thousands. It was described as 'the greatest unorganized ceremony in the

Brooke Foss Westcott, Bishop 1889–1901. He invited the miners to the cathedral for an annual service on Gala Day, a practice which continues today.

world', combining seriousness of political purpose and community affirmation with the pageantry and atmosphere of a medieval festival, with fancy dress, lines of people dancing in the streets and all the allowed excesses of carnival. Its very heart was the procession of the mining communities behind their elaborate iconographic banners held aloft on poles, some each year draped in black as a mark of fatality or disaster in the year gone by.

The church in Durham and the miners were thrown together at the Big Meeting. On Bishop Lightfoot's first arrival in the city in 1879, a miner eyed his stocky frame and commented 'they spiled a grand pitman when they made yon man a bishop'. His successor, Brooke Foss Westcott, earned the soubriquet 'The Miners' Bishop' when, during the strike of 1892, he summoned the contending parties on a Saturday to Auckland Palace, put the moral case for a peaceful solution and then went from group to group to try to secure peace. It was a gesture which acquired the power of myth in the district, and in 1896 he invited the miners to a service in the cathedral that brought the formal proceedings of Gala Day to a close.

His last appearance as bishop was his sermon at the Miners' Service in 1901. He presented the love of Christ as the model of their conduct: 'Try by its divine standard the thoroughness of your labour and the purity of your recreation, and the Durham which we love will soon answer to the heavenly pattern.' A week later the elderly scholar who had become so popular at all levels in his diocese was dead. His successor, Handley Moule, a saintly and innocent evangelical, was enthroned in 1901. He was the first bicycling bishop, though his progress through the Durham streets was often perilous. He was also the first bishop to use a car, a 1908 Austin in which his chauffeur drove Moule for 100,000 miles before the bishop's death in 1920. His simplicity and directness gave him an easy rapport with children, with whom he used to play hockey while wearing his Episcopal gaiters. The same qualities recommended him to labourers and their families. In 1908 the West Stanley pit disaster took the lives of 168 men and boys. Moule left Convocation to go to the pithead, where he addressed survivors and the bereaved and visited their homes. He followed up with a letter to the people of the town, recalling the scenes of brave and patient grief in the houses he visited, and 'the solemn Sabbath evening, the crowded church, the soul-moving hymns' which will 'all be with me while life, and thought, and being last'. He wrote a hymn for the miners:

> Thou with the miner in the dark
> Dost down the shaft descend;
> Then, while he plies his venturous work,
> Art with him as his Friend.

Like Westcott, he tried to mediate in a dispute in the Jarrow shipyards in 1910. He argued that the employer had to depend on fidelity to contract, but also that collective bargaining was essential to protect the artisan. 'That is his right, most certainly. And the

Herbert Hensley Henson, Dean 1912–18, Bishop 1920–39, pencil drawing by Aidan Savage.

employer must just as carefully as the workman remember that right and heartily respect it.' Like Westcott before him and Henson after him, he found that advocacy of the reasonable middle ground at a time of bitter polarization, however justifiable morally, was ineffective in securing reconciliation, and was readily interpreted by both sides as betrayal. There is an endearing glimpse of a boyish old bishop near the end of the Great War. At a confirmation in Hartlepool in March 1918 an air-raid warning sounded. After the service, while the rectory party was at supper, there was a second warning and explosions nearby. The rector ran to the front door, Moule close behind him. 'I would not have missed this,' he cried, 'it is sharing danger with your people.'

Moule was joined in Durham in 1912 by a clerical bird of a very different, and rare, feather, when Herbert Hensley Henson became dean. He came to Durham from a canonry at Westminster with a reputation as a powerful preacher, before which he had given exemplary service in the deprived parish of Barking. He was not from an establishment stable. From a humble background he had been accepted at Oxford on charitable terms but not admitted to any college. From this marginal existence he had won a fellowship to All Souls at the age of 21. His intellectual gifts were matched by clarity of thought and power of expression; the experience of adversity, his own and that of his parishioners had forged in him a core of steel and the courage of his principles; as an outsider he also possessed an often felicitous, sometimes acerbic, sometimes misunderstood wit. By being true to himself he was bound also to controversy. His long life, nearly 30 years of which were devoted to Durham, embodies one of the most distinguished clerical careers of modern times.

He accepted the deanery of Durham in October 1912. His journal was apprehensive. He feared the dissipation of his purpose 'on a multitude of petty concerns, responding with too facile good nature to the requests of fussy folk … who gather about all men in gaiters and smother the aspirations of even self-respecting ecclesiastics in muffs and shawls'. He had foresight here: the academic ambitions he hoped to further by connection with the university were never realized. Moule wrote to congratulate him on his appointment but with the clumsiness of many saintly men added that in his view Archdeacon Watkins should have had the deanery. Even before Henson arrived Watkins had written to the local newspapers to announce that the new dean proposed to turn the medieval Great Kitchen, regarded as the chief glory of the Deanery, into a tourist centre. Henson could be forgiven for feeling he was entering a deranged community. Of his predecessors, he observed that of none of them was heard anything religious. Dean Kitchen, his immediate predecessor, 'baffled by the chapter in some effort of nepotism, sulked in such wise that he would no more attend the daily services'. And, not content with absenting himself, having seen a few students misbehaving, he had banned students entirely from the cathedral.

Henson's unease lingered. He had noted gifts as a preacher but felt that Durham, in comparison with Westminster Abbey where a sermon was the talk of the town, was a marginal pulpit with small congregations. And the practical pastoral ministry which he had relished at Barking was absent from Durham. His life was dominated by invitations to deliver addresses instead, which, happily, he was good at and enjoyed. Controversy attached itself to his name almost at once. At a time of suffragette agitation in 1913 there were vague threats to the cathedral because Henson was opposed to votes for women. He held the traditional view of the social role of women appropriate to a man born in 1863. He feared that political life would be debased by the 'frenzied females' who would bring too much emotionalism into it. Then came the war, of which he was a patriotic supporter, stressing the 'moral obligation to resist Germany in her career of cynical and violent aggression'. He enlisted as a recruiting sergeant, regretted that the priesthood was exempt from service, and supported conscription in 1916. But another facet of his character courted hostility. He was contemptuous of the rise of sentimental and popular superstitions that accompanied the course of the war, such as the Angel of Mons, which he dismissed as 'Episcopal prayer-wheels'. He was also critical of the wave of anti-German feeling which demanded reprisals. He insisted on the distinction between the German government and the German people, and made himself unpopular by sermons in which he praised the excellence of German culture and society. He also expressed public sympathy for conscientious objectors. He earned the label 'the brewers' friend' by arguing against the teetotal movement which became linked with the war effort. His stance brought him into conflict with Moule, a lifelong abstainer, whom he took issue with in a letter to *The Times*. Henson disliked bandwagons, and argued powerfully against this one: 'Total abstinence is no part of morality and certainly has no support either in the teaching of Christ, or in the practice of the Christian Church. To offer total abstinence as a cure for national drunkenness is as reasonable as to offer celibacy as a cure for national impurity'. He thought it foolish to strive for a sudden revolution in the nation's habits at a time when the conflict was already demanding so much of the people. By 1917 he had garnered 'a rich harvest of superfluous resentments'. Among his opponents he could number feminists, total abstainers, sabbatarians, fundamentalists, spiritualists, ritualizers of varying degrees of absurdity, faith-healers, fire-raisers seeking reprisals against the Germans and the inexorable patriots who refused to distinguish between conscientious Pacifists and mere shirkers. His reward for this brouhaha was for Lloyd George, a fellow outsider, to offer him the see of Hereford. The outrage generated in parts of the Anglican church by the appointment, following as it did some carefully qualified remarks about miracles and the virgin birth, was echoed closely over 60 years later on the appointment of David Jenkins to the see of Durham. Henson had come to love Durham, and was cast down at his departure: 'the laments of the Durham people make me feel a beast. Even the choir boys look at me with an et-tu-Brute expression in their eyes which is very trying.' But within three years he was back in Durham as Moule's successor, to face with the people the ordeal of the decline of the coal industry and the General Strike.

Henson returned as bishop in 1920 to a sea of local troubles. The demand for coal, and coal prices had been falling for some years; now the oil beginning to flow from the Middle East spelled the onset of the protracted death throes of the British coal industry. As an economic necessity the coal owners felt they had no choice but to

Snow on the roofs of Durham's terraced houses: a photograph taken from a train crossing the viaduct in January.

reduce wages and extend working hours. In 1921 there was a lock-out of miners in the course of a dispute. Henson was invited to address a miners' meeting in West Hartlepool, where he argued against the use of the strike as a bargaining tool. He also opposed the campaign for a minimum wage because it invited shirking. In the heat of the time he was misunderstood and thought to have said that all miners were shirkers. His car needed police protection when he left. Jeered and booed by miners at Ferryhill, this diminutive man halted the car and stood up in it to address them: 'Is there ca'canny [shirking] in the pit?'. Silence. He went on to emphasize the importance of coal for the survival of the poor across the land. Hecklers told him to sell his ring and give the proceeds to the poor. He replied that it was a gift from Durham friends which he wore for love of them. 'Now gentlemen, I am not unemployed as unfortunately you are. I have much to do, and I must therefore bid you goodnight.' He raised his hat to them and was allowed to leave, having earned at least a grudging respect. But the damage done clung to him. *The Miners Campaign Special* pointed out that to talk of 'immoral strikes' which would lead to 'economic confusion and

lamentable social embitterment was a bit rich from a man with a salary of £7000 when many miners did not even earn £100.

But it was moral principle, not Tory principle, that seemed to place him in the owners' camp. He attacked capitalism throughout his life for its inherent injustice and its exploitation of labour. Capitalism unchecked became a tyranny and so, in his opinion, it must eventually be dethroned. But the same moral convictions made him an opponent of strikes, which involved the breaking of contracts, bullying and intimidation of others by pickets, and, given the prospects for the coal industry, all with no hope of better conditions. His arguments were clear, highly authoritative in their own terms, but offered no practical solution when passions were inflamed. 'Christian morality cannot possibly make terms with any system which does involve violence to the rights of man ... "To do evil that good may come" is a procedure which carries the promise of failure, for it involves such a progressive debasement of the well-intentioned evil-doer, that when at length the victory has been gained, it is not the good end which was originally designed, but something evil enough to suit the demoralized victors.' He was compared unfavourably, and unfairly, with Westcott. Henson did not, could not intervene, because in 30 years political and economic conditions had changed. Miners now had Labour members of Parliament to represent their interests, and by the 1920s there was dole for the unemployed, which had not been available in the 1890s.

The Durham church's response to the labour issue was comically entangled in the mismatch of bishop and dean. The contrast was physical, moral and intellectual. Dean Welldon was a vast man, six feet five inches tall and with a 63 inch waistline. Henson's pet name for him was 'the rhinobottomus', a word invented by the young Princess Elizabeth, now H.M. The Queen, to describe her favourite animal in the zoo. He had a tiny voice, was given to volcanic explosions of laughter, and was perceived by Henson as an intellectual lightweight. He was a kind and affable man who enjoyed much popularity because of his common touch. He was always ready with homely advice and saw himself as an agony uncle, never without a consoling platitude. He was good at dealing with disasters. He was also fervently puritanical. 'I have been called to fight the trinity of evils by which the working people are demoralised – lust, gambling and drink.' Like Moule in Durham before him, he was an advocate of the Temperance Movement and so not on easy terms with 'the Liquor Bishop' whom he attacked in a speech at the Miners' Gala of 1924. Asked at a railwaymens' meeting at Stockton 'Who is worth more to the country, a dean or an engine-driver?', he seized the moment: 'A dean, if only because the engine-driver would take people from Stockton to Newcastle, but a dean would take them from Stockton to Heaven.' Silence was not his forte. An elderly lady meeting him on a train passed judgement: 'Dean, I tell you what it is, you spout too much.'

In 1925, with industrial strife intensifying, Henson published a piece in the *Evening Standard* at the time of the Big Meeting. He wrote that strikes were economically self-defeating and were morally compromised by the violence they engendered. He proposed that secret ballots should be required to legitimise strike action and prevent intimidation. Simultaneously Welldon was critical of the unions in a speech at Bishop Auckland. Between them they had pushed some miners beyond endurance. Joshua Ritson, a Sunderland pit checkweighman now MP for Durham, drew attention to the money that bishops of Durham earned from royalties on coal. The 1925 Gala on 25th July was addressed by Ramsay Macdonald, who hinted that Henson had failed the miners. Among the slogans carried in the procession appeared 'To Hell with Bishops and Deans' and 'We Want a Living Wage!'. The unmistakeable Welldon arrived at the Racecourse to address a temperance meeting. As he was about to ascend the platform the cry went up 'Here's the bishop', followed by a chorus of 'Hoy 'im i'the river.' Crowds surged round him and forced him towards the bank. A miner with a long cane dislodged his tall hat; his umbrella was seized; he was struck on the head and kicked. The huge figure vanished under the throng, but at the river's edge was rescued just in time by the police with the help of a motor launch. He was taken home to a glass of lemonade brought to him on a silver tray. 'Manny' Shinwell supported the action; Henson was totally unsympathetic to him, though he might have been grateful. 'He has given abundant provocation by his incessant and untimely talking, and his folly in appearing at the demonstration was gross.'

May 1926 saw the General Strike. Henson opposed it because it was a tactic that hurt the innocent. But he felt helpless, and unhappy about his own apparent prosperity in contrast with the privations of the poor and out of work. 'My heart with the men, my head with the masters.' His relief was to occupy himself raising funds and distributing charity to unemployed families. In May he was set to preach against the strike in Monkwearmouth. But in the church before the sermon he was felled by pain: it was peritonitis. There followed a dramatic drive to hospital in Newcastle along roads blocked with trees felled by pickets. He refused a police escort; the car was stoned. But maybe he was safer than if he had preached.

Lucky to survive, he was out of action for the months ahead. His frustration at the failure of reason and the polarization of attitudes was acute: 'What do you wish from the Bishop of Durham? That he should not concern himself with the interests of the miners? Or, that he should become the mere echo of their opinions, true or false? I hold rather that they can claim from me the faithful use of such intelligence and knowledge as I possess, and such counsel as expresses my genuine convictions. So much I will always try to give them; but flattery of their class prejudice, or an unintelligent echoing of their party-cries, they will never get from me.' He was deeply wounded when George Lansbury declared that the miners hated Henson, and again when he was caricatured in *John Bull* as a Dives indifferent to the poor at his gate. His relations with individual miners were always easy and unaffected. Though he opposed dole, he did so because of his conviction that charity necessarily demoralized its recipients into dependency. His preferred solutions were new employment or emigration. These 'good and honest workers … are the finest human material in the world, and we seem to acquiesce in their debasement. There is a Nemesis in such folly.' His remedies were more to the point than that suggested by Lord Dunglass, later the Earl of Home and Conservative Prime Minister, who proposed that unemployed miners be transported south as domestic servants.

Belatedly, in 1934 the National Government introduced a Special Areas Bill, naming local commissioners with wide powers of economic alleviation. Henson strongly approved and took a leading role in its operations. It was an untimely moment for Durham Castle to choose to threaten to slide into the river, but Henson, leading the appeal for funds to save it, was adept in linking the rescue work with local unemployment, retraining of labour and the area's future prosperity.

Henson had great gifts as a pastoral bishop. Over time his rigour of mind, directness of expression and sometimes wounding wit were forgiven by the recognition of his devotion to the diocese, his courage and his practical compassion. He set and exacted high standards from his clergy, and attracted and trained many accomplished young men with a vocation to the ministry. His favourite activities were confirmations and preaching. He was both inspirational and thoughtful. He led Good Friday processions of many thousands through Sunderland, Gateshead and Hartlepool. On festival days in the cathedral he took time to go round the choir, shaking each chorister's hand and giving him a shilling. He was the kind of preacher who 'made people want to clap in church'. He was habitually generous towards clergy in trouble or debt, relieving them from 'a fund at the bishop's disposal', a euphemism for his own pocket. But he could also be severe and paternalistic. He inspected the fiancées of bachelor clergy who contemplated marriage. At a service at Pelton, discovering obscene scribblings in the hymn book in his stall, he took it up into the pulpit and scolded the congregation for the moral condition of the parish. His pet hate was coughing in church. He would pause in his sermon and wait for silence. If it did not follow he would ask the choir boy or member of the congregation to leave. One such victimized figure passed Henson's chauffeur on the way out and spluttered, 'I hope that bishop dies of whooping cough.'

He was not happy in his 'deserted and derelict' palace at Auckland, which he described as 'a lonely boulder, deposited on some plain and which has no affinity with its present surroundings'. It was a desperately cold home, even after the arrival of electricity in 1924. Visitors had to be given shawls to help them survive dinner and chapel services. He resisted the telephone and his secretaries were

Cyril Alington, Dean 1933–51. A drawing by Francis Dodd in the Deanery (1937).

compelled to spend uncomfortable hours in the nearest public call-box. But he welcomed the invasion of his park by the poor in search of coal from surface seams, timber and fencing for their fires, for it gave him the chance to sit and talk with them in an always welcoming and courteous manner. Not for him the reaction of Bishop Moule who, seeing local lads playing football in his park on a Sunday, had halted his carriage and ordered his butler to confiscate the ball. At Durham Henson settled for a fragile truce with the luckless Welldon. But in 1932 the dean collapsed at a service and his huge frame could not be raised up. For a while he took to a bath chair, in which his stillness was so great that he was sometimes mistaken for a monument. But he could not continue and was succeeded in 1933 by Cyril Alington with whom Henson was on much happier terms until his own retirement in 1939. The idea of Welldon still hung over him, however. In the memoirs he compiled after retirement he was acerbic about him: 'He united a

heavy frame and blustering manner, which suggested a truly virile personality, and a sentimental sensitiveness which would have been hardly pardonable in a schoolgirl! And he was found, in the experience of colleagues, to be radically untrustworthy, not deliberately or consciously, but because he could never resist the appeal of the gallery. He would never fail to sacrifice a friend to a cheer.'

Such treatment of a bête-noire is uncharacteristic of most of his diocesan correspondence, which is generally finely discriminating, sympathetic and gently humorous, even in dealing with such intractable topics as a vicar who had become Master of the Beagles, the poor physique of the clergy, a request from a group of nudists to be given the Eucharist, and the dilemma caused by an unavoidable social encounter with von Ribbentrop. In 1943, in retirement in Suffolk, he became an 'octogeranium' (gleefully quoting a former dean's gardener). A year before his death he recounted with delight a comic episode in the cathedral when an equally aged friend, Bishop Headlam, foolishly railed against Durham University in a sermon to a congregation which included university members. But in a fit of coughing he 'evicted his false teeth with some violence. However, he just managed by a very creditable effort to catch the errant treasure', and 'indulged in the difficult and gradual process of replacing them in his jaws'. The only thing lacking to complete the spectacle, Henson suggested, was for a Durham schoolboy to have interjected 'Oh well played, sir'. Henson's eyesight failed and he had a serious heart attack. Knowing he was near the end he wrote in character to Dean Alington about his will: 'I propose to direct that my carcass shall be cremated, and if so, I wonder whether you and the Canons, and of course the Bishop, would think it improper or unseemly if the ashes were deposited in some corner of Durham Cathedral, where they might be comparatively

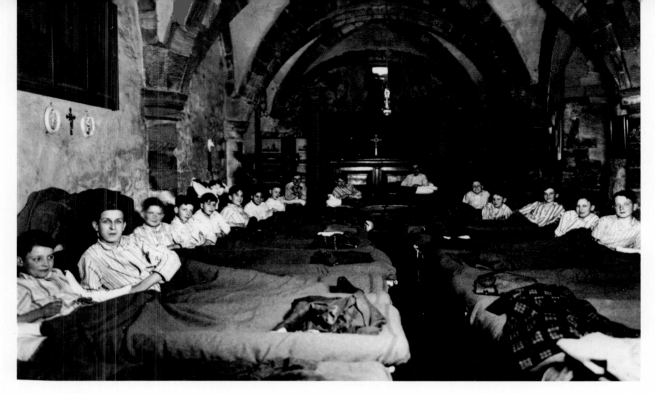

In the Second World War the choristers slept in the Undercroft of the Deanery, considered a safe shelter in the event of a bombing raid.

inoffensive.' In February 1947 the Miners' Memorial was dedicated in the south aisle of the nave in the presence of Tommy Daniels and Harry Inglis from Bearpark Colliery, who had come direct from the coalface with unwashed faces. Within the year, in a fine conjunction, Henson's ashes were laid in the Chapel of the Nine Altars, alongside the grave of Antony Bek, and beneath an equally simple slab. Alington's verse on Henson's death do as much as six lines can to sum up his spirit:

> He waged, as led by some peculiar star
> With power and prejudice a truceless war.
> While craven souls the big battalions seek,
> He pledged his sword to service of the weak,
> And, self-consistent to a long life's end,
> Forgave no folly and forgot no friend.

ALINGTON AND THE SECOND WORLD WAR

Cyril Alington came to Durham as dean after 25 years as headmaster of Shrewsbury and then Eton, and seemed to run the cathedral community as if he were still headmaster. With his tenure of office we enter living memories. The story from now on is enriched by personal recollections, but it follows that impressions and anecdotes of an inevitably selective or subjective character have greater prominence than the potentially unsafe ground of general judgements.

Alington was an old-style patrician figure with the genuinely democratic manner that real patricians sometimes possess. Wartime choristers recall the wonderful Christmas parties he used to give for them. Each boy had a letter pinned on his back at the beginning and together they spelled out a Latin tag which had to be unscrambled before the bunfight. But he was quick to help them decipher it. He gave extra Latin lessons to boys of Durham School. He was a competent amateur poet, a hymn writer and a lover of cricket. Alec Douglas-Home, his son-in-law, reported that Alington could never process up the nave without wondering whether it would take spin. He was a compulsive chewer of daisies, perhaps because of their pain-reducing effect upon his limp. Junior choristers were on a rota in the daisy season to pick them freshly in the College and leave them on a ledge by his front door. The choristers also exercised his two dogs, one called Mu, a gift from the Mothers' Union, the other Pu, for more obvious reasons.

He had a god-like way in the cathedral and his chapter must have felt like junior masters. He had a casual way with medieval vestments, which he wore in preference to an overcoat, but tended to fling them over chairbacks when he disrobed. He introduced the purple cassocks that the choir still wears. He also commissioned the canopy hanging above St Cuthbert's tomb. On his arrival in 1933 he had the sense and foresight to found 'The Friends of Durham Cathedral'. Alington led the community through the war years. Clergy and staff were greatly reduced in numbers, and all had to take turns as fire-watchers. Palace Green was filled by a huge water tank in case the worst happened; the College reverted to its medieval character of a farmyard, and the choristers were woken by duck and chicken alarm clocks. They had to carry gas masks as they went to and fro to services, and slept at night for safety in the undercroft of the Deanery, which Henson had turned into a chapel. 'It never entered my head', Henson wrote from Suffolk, 'that the chapel would be tenanted by so goodly and valiant a company. Give my love to the boys and tell them that they are fortunate in living in the most glorious episode of English History.' Here, supervised by a naval headmaster, they lived much as the sailors below decks in a man o'war. They also made full use of the otherwise empty deanery, with its many tunnels and mysterious staircase as an adventure playground. Conrad Eden, Master of the Choristers, was in India for the duration of the war; John Humphrey King, the Precentor, was five years in a German POW camp; Alington himself suffered the death of his son, in Italy in 1943; he is commemorated by a memorial window at the west end of the South Nave Aisle. So there was a special intensity about the hastily devised service of thanksgiving for the end of hostilities in Europe in May 1945, and again in 1947 when Alington preached in German to a congregation of returning German prisoners of war on the subject of reconciliation.

Alington was married to an even more patrician wife, Hester, born a Lyttleton, 'with a voice like Paul Robeson'. When she commanded all Durham heard, and all Durham obeyed. Towards the end of the war plans were announced for the building of a power station on the Wear, within sight of the cathedral. The story goes – and myth can reflect truths other than the literal – that she wrote to her brother Oliver, a member of the War Cabinet, and the scheme was quietly shelved.

The Durham war effort was joined in 1940 by the unlikely figure of Michael Ramsey as Canon and Professor of Divinity. Although only 35, he already

looked venerable, with a massive bald dome and hedgerow eyebrows. Physically clumsy, he was not good in processions, and a serious hazard on a bicycle and as a fire-watcher. Some thought him a lunatic. But his innocent integrity endeared him to the Chapter and the University. 'He is nice,' judged Hester Alington in a letter. 'But he has no small talk. He can talk about the Atonement. But, whether unfortunately or not, that is not the subject which is usually uppermost in our minds.' Ramsey was married in the Galilee Chapel in April 1942, and, after a short absence at Cambridge, returned to be enthroned as bishop in 1952. In 1955 the ageless figure led a barefoot pilgrimage of three thousand across the sands to Lindisfarne, and in his address told the pilgrims that this was their true home. Durham was probably his true home, but for all too short a time. In 1956 he was translated to the archbishopric of York. Durham's last glimpse of their bishop was of a man weeping with grief in the station waiting room leaving a place he loved. He returned to Durham to live for a short time after his retirement as Archbishop of Canterbury.

THE CHORISTER SCHOOL

Of Alington's post-war contributions, the most significant and, for a noted headmaster, most appropriate was placing Durham's Chorister School on secure foundations. It had had a chequered history over the centuries. A monastic almonry school had existed since at least the 1340s, and the first singing boys were recruited from it. As early as 1390 Prior Walworth approved a request from the monks and appointed a Cantor to teach singing to both monks and boys. The Sacrist's account roll for 1414–15 has an entry for 'five surplices for the boys assisting at private masses'. *The Rites of Durham* recorded that before the Reformation six boys were instructed in the Schoolroom, at the south end of the Chapel of the Nine Altars. The statutes of 1555 prescribe ten choristers of the new foundation. The fun and frolics of George Dobson and James Raikebanes suggest that, however ill-disciplined, the choristers contributed regularly to worship on Sundays and feast days after the Reformation. After the hiatus of the Civil War and Commonwealth, there had to be a new start under the music-loving John Cosin. The song school was established in a room along the West Cloister, where it remained for over two hundred years. From then until the arrival of Dean Lake in 1869 there was little formality about the choir's contribution and no processing. Members of the choir not in their places by the end of the first psalm were fined one farthing. Two Masters of the Choristers, James Heseltine and Thomas Ebdon, spanned the century from 1711 to 1811, but their musical initiatives were undermined by the indifference of the Chapter, which was inclined to grant long periods of absence to choir members.

By the beginning of the 19th century it seemed that reform was needed: choristers are charged with stealing lead, and one is killed in a fall from the roof. No-one seems to accept responsibility for them. Nobody except for Maria Hackett, an energetic and spirited lady who devoted her long life to improving the condition of choristers across England. In *The Gentleman's Magazine* of 1818 she wrote of the Durham choristers: 'Their antient and well-endowed school has greatly declined; and the singing boys receive a mere charity school education and wear a corresponding dress'. She achieved for the choristers in *The Gentleman's Magazine* what John Carter had achieved shortly before for the Galilee Chapel. Unwelcome publicity stung the Chapter into action and some reforms were adopted: an increase in pay for choristers, a larger apprentice fee when a boy's voice broke and he had to leave the choir, and the stirrings of an academic education. Reading and writing were taught by lay clerk Thomas Brown. Miss Hackett continued to bombard the Chapter with enquiries. She was told there were ten choristers, who attended service twice a day, at 10 and 4. They were provided with two suits of clothes a year, and were paid a salary of £9 (£275). From 8am till 10am they were taught music by the organist in the Song School. A master taught reading, writing and arithmetic 'at such hours as do not interfere with the organist'. 'There is no provision for them afterwards, though such of them as have behaved well are not neglected by the Chapter.' It sounds as if

their expectations were not great, though they were examined every quarter by an apothecary.

The improver Waddington sought a report on the choristers in 1847. The proposal for a boarding house which it recommended was rejected by the boys' parents. So up to the 1890s the Song School in the Cloister functioned as a day school, as it had since the 1660s. But a more serious academic education began to be offered, together with preferential promotion to the grammar school for the able boys. For a few years there was a sequence of temporary homes, which included the servants' hall beneath the Deanery, the dining room of one of the canon's houses, where ladies living above complained of the noise. So back they were sent to the Deanery cellar where, in an escapade worthy of Dobson, they smuggled in some sticks of dynamite which they had 'found' on Prebends Bridge. All but one were confiscated, but the escapee was put into the boiler with a shovelful of coke and exploded. It is fortunate that the Deanery was built like a fortress. Expelled to the Minor Canons' Vestry, at length they were found a decent home in 3 The College, with Minor Canon Dolphin as headmaster. On his appointment he undertook to marry at once in order to secure a capable housekeeper. Now that there was space, boarding for choristers became available. In 1906 the school moved into 4 and 5 The College. Here in 1948 its future, its financial security and the quality of its education were underpinned by an expansion to include non-choristers. It had become a preparatory school of 36 pupils, with boarding space available both for the choristers and for other pupils who wished to board. In 1953, when St Mary's College vacated buildings at the west end of The College the school moved into the characterful range of houses it still occupies, perched on the cliff above the river, from which neither young Anthony Blair nor young Rowan Atkinson, contemporaries in the 1960s, were flung, or flung one another, to the nation's enduring benefit.

The choristers leaving the Chorister School for early morning music practice, wearing their cloaks and 'boards' even in the height of a hot summer in July 2006.

DURHAM PRESENT AND FUTURE

THERE is no constant except change. The modern insight of ancient Heraclitus is the motto for all times, especially the present. Adapting to change seems to have become a continuous rite of passage for individuals and organizations. It is a hurdle, or series of unending hurdles, which some leap eagerly, others when driven, and from which some simply turn away. In the Anglican Church, clergy and congregations have had little choice but to recognize that they are a minority in a largely secular society. The purpose of the church and those who serve it has had to be questioned, redefined, reinterpreted in order that the church continues to be a living organization and an active component of society at large. Cathedrals and parish churches great and small have faced more challenges and witnessed more change between 1970 and the present than in any comparable period in their history, including even the English Reformation. The story of Durham concludes with an account of its management of that change, its adaptation to social and cultural conditions unimaginable even in the years following the Second World War, during which a society grateful for survival turned back for a while to the security of pre-war assumptions.

The early decades of the 19th century had brought about the transition from an 'ancient' to a 'modern' style of cathedral life, and the last decades of the 20th century witnessed a process as least as far-reaching. Central to this process was the shift of generations. John Wild, dean from 1951 to 1973, was born in the year of Queen Victoria's death, and like most men of comparable

Above: *John Wild, Dean 1951–73, photographed on Prebends Bridge in 1954.*

Right: *Evensong is celebrated each day in the Quire, with the rest of the cathedral hushed and darkened. It is seen here from the bishop's throne over the Hatfield tomb.*

position in the church, belonged to a favoured class and received a favoured education. They were already elderly when the norms that had governed social conduct in their lifetime began to dissolve. Michael Turnbull, later Bishop of Durham, has a memory from the 1950s when he was a student, of Dean Wild, dressed in full-rig gaiters

walking his whippets early in the morning. He doesn't say whether the whippets too were in gaiters, but the notion is appealing. Those who recall the cathedral in the 1950s and 1960s remember it as being on the stuffy side, a kind of private club for 'nice' people, largely isolated from the town and indeed from other congregations, Anglican, Catholic and Nonconformist. There were particular seats in the Choir which women members of the congregation were not allowed to occupy. It sounded like a last echo of Barchester.

When Wild's generation retired either side of 1970 it was replaced by a generation born after the First World War, tempered by political, social and economic instability, many of whom had known war service between 1939 and 1945. Inevitably they were a different, more adaptable breed of men. In Durham the change was particularly emphatic. Eric Heaton arrived as dean, registered at once how forbidding the cathedral was for many visitors, and imaginatively transformed a dusty junk room off the south-west corner of the Cloister which, curiously, contained the skeleton of a whale, perhaps Jonah's, and doubled up as a place of assembly for the choir before services, into an inviting, well-lit, comfortable undercroft refectory and bookshop. Even this effort of welcome, christened 'Heaton's Eatin', was received in some quarters with misanthropic disapproval. 'What next?', cavilled a local journal, 'Bingo in the Nave ?' But Heaton had announced himself as the first modern dean. At the same time Ian Ramsey was enthroned as the first modern bishop. He hailed from a very ordinary Lancashire background, was short of stature, plump and vigorous. He didn't at all match the 'nice' people's idea of a bishop but won the hearts of the young, who cherished him as their 'Diddy Bishop'. He was a friend of the working man, defended the existence of the nightclubs of the north-east and gave an acclaimed address at the 1971 Miners' Gala in which he praised their long fight for justice and urged

During and after the Palm Sunday procession in the Cloisters, April 2006

negotiation and partnership between management and labour as the civilized way forward. He was equally in his element at the annual choristers' party, where he was himself the starter, handicapper and judge of all the competitions. His strength and his weakness was his compulsive sociability. He could not say no, whether to dominoes in a working men's club, to the dance floor at the local journalists' annual knees-up, or to the presidencies of scores of institutions and organizations which for him were always active roles, not token ones. He made a point of shaking hands with every member of the congregation after every service he participated in.

He died at the age of only 57, in a television studio, of overwork, a modern episcopate cruelly terminated by modern pressures. Michael Ramsey, in his address at Ian's memorial service, said of him 'I have known other men who had something of Ian's winning warmth of heart, and others who had Ian's liveliness of mind; but I have never known one in whom the warm heart and the lively mind were so completely of one piece.'

The media and some sections of the Anglican church were far more fussed than most people in Durham by the appointment of David Jenkins, Professor of Theology at Leeds, as bishop in 1984. He was named in March, and the following month, in an Easter debate on television, 'Jesus, the Evidence', spoke of miracles and the virgin birth as expressions of faith rather than exact dogmas. This was a view that liberal theologians from the mid-19th century onwards had advanced, and one strikingly similar to the interpretation of Hensley Henson nearly 70 years earlier which had dogged his appointment as Bishop of Hereford. But Jenkins's remarks gave rise to a furore in the media and he was christened 'the unbelieving bishop'. From that point on he was vulnerable to the 'headline and snippet' brigade of media misrepresentation or misunderstanding. A phrase in a later discussion, 'a conjuring trick with bones', was taken to be his view of the Resurrection, whereas he had very clearly said that that was not what the Resurrection was about. 'The Bishop of Blasphemy' became a marked man and knew it. Though he was not always as careful as might have been advisable, he took deliberate risks throughout his active career, some of which he has acknowledged in retrospect to have been unwise, but all of which he entered into knowingly and with a clearly thought-out purpose.

His notoriety was swelled by the melodrama surrounding his consecration in York Minster in July 1984. The public protests during the service paled before the 'lightning strike', or more probably electrical mishap which set the minster roof on fire two days later. Only too readily claimed by traditionalists as 'an act of God', they failed to explain why God was two days late and struck down the building rather than the bishop. In September he was enthroned at Durham. The last and increasingly bitter miners' strike was under way, and miners and their families had already turned to him for help and advice, particularly about what they saw as the manifest brutality of the police. His legendary enthronement sermon, 'On the Cost of Hope', sprang directly from the ugliness of the confrontation at the pits. Like Henson before him he spoke of the cost of hope as the readiness for compromise. There must be no 'victory' for either side, but a speedy settlement which recognized the pain of the suffering communities. He rebuked the Government for its apparent determination to defeat the miners, and its seeming indifference to poverty and powerlessness. Both sides must withdraw from the absolutist positions, both Mr Scargill and Mr MacGregor (Chairman of the Coal Board). But in describing MacGregor as 'an elderly imported American' he loaded the scales unfairly, especially since Macgregor was a Scot, and some in the congregation felt that he had over-reached himself, as Jenkins readily conceded later. At the end of the sermon the congregation applauded; Jenkins, deeply moved, struck his hand several times on the pulpit edge to control his emotion, but was reported as having conducted the applause.

Jenkins was inevitably at the fulcrum of divisions in the church. He categorized them as the 'certainty-wallahs', the 'liberals' and the 'quiet life' parties. His disagreement with the certainty-wallahs was that their assumption that the word of God was complete, literal and unchanging forced the church to look always backwards and to be always on the defensive. As for the quiet-lifers, he thought a bishop had more important things to do than utter unctuous platitudes. So he was certain to exacerbate division, as he was also certain to stimulate those able to listen to him. Durham was an animated diocese during his episcopate, and his use of the pulpit to air social and political controversies ensured that the question of the church's mission could not be ducked. The clarity and eloquence of his arguments in Synod against its prevarications on the issues of sexuality and the ordination of women gave forward-thinking members of the Anglican church reasons for gratitude and hope.

Following the lead set by Eric Heaton, succeeding deans – Peter Baelz, John Arnold, Michael Sadgrove – and their Chapters have led Durham Cathedral in what seems to most contemporary eyes to be a sustainedly enlightened direction. Fifty years from now history may judge; the task here is to record.

A significant change in the cathedral's constitution arose from legislation. The Care of Cathedrals' Measure of 1990 and the Cathedrals' Measure of 1999, which followed the recommendations of the Cathedrals' Commission of 1992–6, radically altered the ways in which cathedrals were governed. Additional members, two-thirds laymen and women, were added to the Chapter; a Cathedral Council was established to assist the Chapter in accounting to the wider community for its stewardship, and the College of Canons was enlarged to include lay members both local and national. The aim was to fortify the second element in the definition of the cathedral as 'the seat of the Bishop and a centre of worship and mission'. A new constitution and new statutes took effect in Durham in 2001, their broad aim to widen public understanding and support for the work of the cathedral and to assist in its task of accounting for itself beyond the confines of the College. What was at first viewed suspiciously as another burden of bureaucracy has already proved its worth. The mission of the cathedral has been buttressed by committed, sympathetic and sometimes expert lay advice. Another bulwark has been the support of the Friends of Durham Cathedral. Presciently founded by Cyril Alington in 1933, the organization, with more than 3,000 members, has proved a prodigious raiser of funds for the cathedral's needs. Recent contributions that catch the eye include £100,000 for lighting in 1991–2, £130,000 towards the exhibition of Treasures in 1994–6, £180,000 for a new sound system in 2001–5, and, in 2005–6, over £200,000 for Nave choir stalls, improving disabled access, repairs to the Refectory roof and a donation towards a memorial window for Michael Ramsey. With Friends like these, charging for admission can be postponed, though perhaps not indefinitely.

The character of activity within the cathedral has been transformed. Common Worship has been introduced, in tandem with the Book of Common Prayer, and the number of special services has multiplied. Laymen and women are prominent in services. There is a sense of a community coming together in worship. From the late 1980s the prevailing liturgy has been influenced by the Catholic Revival movement. Incense is used on appropriate occasions; votive candles burn at the east end of the Nave, a simple feature expressing the idea of continuous spiritual life and drawing visitors into their orbit; there are more processions involving the congregation, particularly suitable for a pilgrimage church. Dean Baelz began the continuing process of enriching the building and softening its severity by commissioning works of art. Sculptures of the Annunciation by Josef Pyrz and of the Deposition by Fenwick Lawson, new windows by Leonard Evett and Joseph Nuttgens, altars and icons of St Hild and St Margaret in the Chapel of the Nine Altars by Edith Reyntiens and Paula Rego – all remind worshippers and visitors that Durham is not a place fixed in the past. The cathedral is used increasingly for concerts and for exhibitions in the Galilee Chapel and the Monks' Dormitory; it has an artist in residence; notable instances of its readiness to open itself to the new have been Bill Viola's video installation 'The Messenger', a liturgical performance of Duke Ellington's Jazz Mass, and the commissioning of John Taverner's *Icon of St Cuthbert*.

In 1983 Durham was named a World Heritage Site. Visitors pour in in ever-increasing numbers. The cathedral receives getting on for three-quarters of a million visitors a year, an average of two thousand a day. The challenge for deans and chapters is to give them a fitting welcome without sacrificing the sense of sacred space which has to remain at the heart. The building itself naturally acquiesces in that aim. Its uncluttered spaces and huge volume are adept at softening the simultaneous presence of hundreds. The notice board outside the North Porch entrance is unusually warm: 'We hope you will feel very welcome here'. One Muslim visitor obviously felt at home, and was observed unrolling his prayer mat in the Galilee Chapel. But all visitors receive the red carpet treatment. Successive deans and chapters have passionately resisted charging for admission. A discreet and professional team of stewards is on hand, greeting everyone with a smile, but they are not obtrusive or assertive. Those anxious about bringing in push-chairs are reassured. The provision for visitors must be the best in the land. There is an award-winning Refectory, and opposite it the Durham Treasury, an Aladdin's cave of marvels renewed with the help of a Millennium grant. There is an Education Centre to make school parties feel at home, and an Undercroft display beamed at the interests of children. Another kind of treasure-house is the bookshop recently developed in the great medieval kitchen where, after threading tight and twisting passages, the visitor arrives with a gasp of wonder in the huge vaulted 14th-century

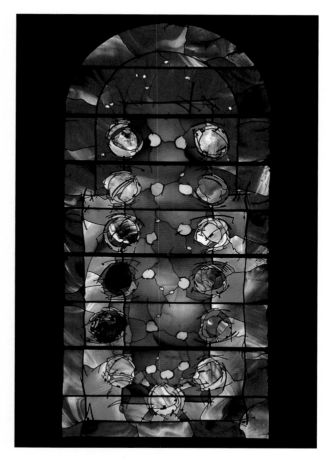

'Daily Bread': a window at the west end of the North Nave Aisle by Mark Angus, 1984, presented by the staff of Marks and Spencer on the occasion of the firm's centenary.

beehive. There is the Tower to climb. And for those in need of support there are both chaplains and lay 'listeners' quietly on hand for the distressed.

Durham Cathedral reaches out both to its myriad visitors and, after a period of dissociation when it was perceived locally as self-sufficient and stand-offish, to the town, the university, other Christian congregations and the surrounding district. In 2005, 464 years after the cathedral's dedication to St Cuthbert was dropped from its legal title by the Tudor statutes, the saint was restored to it. The dedication is once again to Christ, the Blessed Virgin Mary and St Cuthbert. It is much more than simply an historical affirmation. Cuthbert and the monks of Lindisfarne were the evangelizers of the north. They had a mission. So too does Durham Cathedral 1400 years on. Mission continuing. The cathedral is alive, and has work to do.

ACKNOWLEDGEMENTS

Many people in Durham have given generously of their time and knowledge to make this book possible. I would like to express my particular gratitude to Joan Williams, Catherine Turner and Jill Ivy from the Chapter Library for their ever cheerful welcome and support. Jill Ivy has acted as Durham Picture Editor and her unrivalled knowledge of local illustrations has greatly enhanced the finished work. Alan Piper, Patrick Mussett, Margaret Harvey and Anne Orde have been my 'academic angels' overseeing the evolution of the text and gently correcting my follies. Bill Apedaile, Lilian Groves and Brian Crosby of the Friends Office, each a genius loci, have advised and supported beyond all reasonable expectation. Alan Oyston and George Worthington gave me the story of Cyril Alington and the war years. Christopher Downs and Norman Emery, Cathedral Architect and Cathedral Archeologist, took me on memorable journeys of discovery which enabled me to feel a bond with the cathedral and precinct. Bob Matthews, Clerk of the Works, and the team of Vergers have been generous of spirit and generous with their time in providing every possible practical assistance, and Anne Heywood, Chapter Steward, has taken the project to her heart and made the impossible possible for the taking of photographs. Richard and Odile Fong have been welcoming hosts in Durham. In Durham Castle Shona Miller, the Bursar, the Gatekeepers and Paul Raymond have given enthusiastic support. Beyond Durham I have appreciated the help of Geoffrey Moorhouse and Richard Sharp for their comments on individual chapters. But the chiefest thanks are due to Michael Sadgrove, Dean of Durham, who with patience, courtesy, good humour and wisdom has been the 'onlie begetter' of the book.

A word of appreciation has been earned by Leofric and Godiva in Durham, Sophie and Otto in Callaly who in their distinctive ways gave this project their imprimatur.

BIBLIOGRAPHY

General history of Durham
This Sumptuous Church, C.J. Stranks, SPCK, 1973; *Durham Cathedral: A Celebration*, D. Pockock (ed.), City of Durham Trust, 1993; *Durham Cathedral*, D. Shipley, Tauris Parke, 1990; *Durham: 1000 Years of History*, M. Roberts, Tempus, 1994; *Durham City*, K. Proud, Phillimore, 1992; *Seven Sages of Durham*, G.W. Kitchen, Fisher Unwin, 1911; *Durham*, Martin Dufferwiel, Mainstream, 1996; *The North of England*, F. Musgrove, Basil Blackwell, 1990; *Conflict and Disaster at Durham*, (Published transcripts of Friends' Lectures), 2003

Lindisfarne and the Foundation of Durham 618–1138
Anglo-Norman Durham, Rollason, Harvey, Prestwich (eds), Boydell, 1994; *Symeon of Durham*, Rollason (ed.), Oxford Medieval Texts; *Lindisfarne*, Magnus Magnusson, Oriel Press 1984; *St Cuthbert and the Normans*, W.M. Aird, Boydell, 1998; *The Norman Conquest of the North*, W. Kapelle, Croom Helm, 1979; *St Cuthbert: His Cult and Community to 1200*, Bonner, Rollason, Stancliffe, Boydell, 1989

Medieval Durham 1138–1539
Church and Society in the Medieval North of England, R.B. Dobson, Hambledon, 1996; *Hugh du Puiset*, G.V. Scammell, Cambridge, 1952; *Durham Priory*, R.B. Dobson, Cambridge, 1973; *Thomas Langley and the Bishopric of Durham 1406–37*, R.L. Storey, SPCK, 1961; *North of the Tees*, H.S.Offler, Variorum, 1996; *A History of Antony Bek*, C.M. Fraser, Oxford, 1957; *The Rites of Durham (Surtees Soc)*, Fowler (ed.), 1902; *Lordship and the Urban Community 1250–1540*, M. Bonney, Cambridge, 1990; *The County Palatine of Durham*, G.T. Lapsley, Longman Green, 1900; *The Battle of Neville's Cross*, ed. Rollason/Prestwich, Shaun Tyas, 1998; *Thomas Langley*, I.C. Sharman, Dovecote-Renaissance, 1999; *St Cuthbert: His Life and Cult in Medieval Durham*, D. Marner, British Library, 2000

The Reformation and the 17th century 1540–1672
A Life of John Cosin, P.H. Osmond, Mowbrays, 1913; *Cuthbert Tunstal*, C. Sturge, Longman, 1938; *The Last Principality 1494–1660*, Marcombe (ed.); *John Cosin*, M. Johnson (ed.), Durham Turnstone Ventures, 1997; *Life of Walter Skirlaw*, G. Jarrett, Highgate, 2004; *The Rising in the North*, C. Sharp (ed.), Shotton 1975; *The Anglicanism of John Cosin*,G. Cuming, Dean and Chapter of Durham, 1975; *Close Encounters*, D. Marcombe and C.S. Knighton (eds), Sherwood Press, 1991

The Long 18th century 1672–1830
St Cuthbert: with an Account of the State in which his remains were found, J. Raine, 1828; *Cathedral Cookery*, J. Thacker, Durham University Library, 1985; *North Country Life in the Eighteenth Century*, E. Hughes, OUP, 1969; *Memorials of Dean Comber*, C.E. Whiting (ed.), Surtees Society, 1941–2; *Letters of Dean Spencer Cowper*, E. Hughes (ed.), Surtees Society, 1950

Durham since 1830
The Last of the Prince-Bishops, E.A. Varley, Cambridge, 1992; *The Durham Miners 1919–1960*, W. R. Garside, Allen and Unwin, 1971; *Hensley Henson*, Owen Chadwick, Canterbury Press, 1983; *Memorials of Dean Lake*, K.Lake (ed.), Arnold, 1901; *Michael Ramsey*, Owen Chadwick, Oxford, 1990; *Lightfoot of Durham*, G.R. Eden and F.C. Macdonald (eds), Cambridge 1932; *Bishop A.T.P. Williams*, C.H.G. Hopkins, Mayhew-McCrimmon, 1975; *Memories*, C.H.G. Hopkins, D. Brown 1989; *Bishop Handley Moule*, Harford and Macdonald, Hodder and Stoughton, 1922; *Come On, Choristers*, Brian Crosby, 1999; *The Deans 2004*, T. Beeson, SCM Press, 2004; *The Calling of a Cuckoo*, D. Jenkins, Continuum, 2002; *Ian Ramsey*, D.L. Edwards, OUP, 1973; *Retrospect of an Unimportant Life*, Hensley Henson, OUP, 1942; *Barchester: English Cathedral Life in the 19th Century*, P. Barratt, SPCK, 1993; *Leaders of the Church of England 1828–1944*, D.L. Edwards, OUP, 1971; *George Waddington*, A. Klottrup, Dean and Chapter of Durham, 1990; *The Founding of the University of Durham*, Alan Heesom, Dean and Chapter of Durham, 1982; *Hensley Henson and the Durham Miners*, O. Chadwick, Dean and Chapter of Durham, 1983; *Masters and Servants*, H. Beynon and T. Austrim Rivers, Oram, 1994; *Durham Miners' Gala*, M. Richardson, Breedon Books, 2001; *Letters of H.H. Henson*, E.F.Braley (ed), SPCK, 1950

TIMELINES

RULERS IN ENGLAND ————————

Early Rulers
580–616	Ethelbert, King of Kent
d.638	Edwin, King of Northumbria
d.642	Oswald, King of Northumbria
670–87	Ecgfrith, King of Northumbria
757–94	Offa, King of Mercia
688–728	Ina, King of the West Saxons

Anglo-Saxon Kings of England
802–39	Egbert
839–58	Ethelwulf
871–99	Alfred the Great
899–924	Edward the Elder
924–39	Athelstan
939–46	Edmund I
946–55	Eadred
955–9	Eadwig
959–75	Edgar
899–924	Edward the Martyr
978–1016	Ethelred
1016–35	Cnut, the Dane
1037–40	Harold I
1040–2	Hardicnut, King of Denmark and England
1042–66	Edward the Confessor
1066	Harold II

House of Normandy
1066–87	William I
1087–1100	William II
1100–35	Henry I
1135–54	Stephen

House of Plantagenet
1154–89	Henry II
1189–99	Richard I
1199–1216	John
1216–72	Henry III
1272–1307	Edward I
1307–27	Edward II
1327–77	Edward III
1377–99	Richard II

House of Lancaster
1399–1413	Henry IV
1413–22	Henry V
1422–61	Henry VI

House of York
1461–83	Edward IV
1483	Edward V
1483–85	Richard III

House of Tudor
1485–1509	Henry VII
1509–47	Henry VIII
1547–53	Edward VI
1553–58	Mary I
1558–03	Elizabeth I

House of Stuart
1603–25	James I (and VI of Scotland)
1625–49	Charles I
1649–53	Commonwealth/ protectorate
1653–58	Protectorate of Oliver Cromwell
1658–59	Protectorate of Richard Cromwell

House of Stuart restored
1660–85	Charles II
1685–88	James II
1689–94	William and Mary (jointly)

House of Orange
1694–1702	William III (sole ruler)
1702–14	Anne

House of Hanover
1714–27	George I
1727–60	George II
1760–20	George III
1820–30	George IV
1830–37	William IV
1837–1901	Victoria

House of Saxe-Coburg
1901–10	Edward VII

House of Windsor
1910–36	George V
1936	Edward VIII
1936–52	George VI
1952–	Elizabeth II

RULERS IN SCOTLAND ————————
1056–93	Malcolm III
1107–24	Alexander I
1124–53	David I
1165–1214	William (the Lion)
1214–49	Alexander II
1249–85	Alexander III
1290–1314	John de Baliol
1299–1328	Robert I
1328–71	David II
1371–89	Robert II
1390–1406	Robert III
1424–37	James I
1513–42	James V
1542–87	Mary, Queen of Scots

BISHOPS OF DURHAM ————————
955	Aldhun
1020	Eadmund
1041	Eadred
1042	Aethelric
1056	Aethelwin
1071	Walcher
1081	William of St. Calais
1099	Ranulf Flambard
1133	Geoffrey Rufus
1143	William of St. Barbe
1153	Hugh du Puiset
1197	Philip of Poitou
1217	Richard Marsh
1229	Richard le Poore
1241	Nicolas Farnham
1249	Walter Kirkham
1260	Robert Stichill
1274	Robert of Holy Island
1284	Antony Bek
1311	Richard Kellaw
1318	Louis de Beaumont
1333	Richard Bury
1345	Thomas Hatfield
1382	John Fordham
1388	Walter Skirlaw
1406	Thomas Langley
1437	Robert Neville
1457	Laurence Booth
1476	William Dudley
1484	John Sherwood
1494	Richard Fox
1502	William Senhouse
1507	Christopher Bainbridge
1509	Thomas Ruthall
1523	Thomas Wolsey
1530	Cuthbert Tunstall
1561	James Pilkington
1577	Richard Barnes
1589	Matthew Hutton
1595	Tobias Matthew
1606	William James
1617	Richard Neile
1628	George Monteigne
1628	John Howson
1632	Thomas Morton
1660	John Cosin
1674	Nathaniel Crewe
1722	William Talbot
1730	Edward Chandler
1750	Joseph Butler
1752	Richard Trevor
1771	John Egerton
1787	Thomas Thurlow
1791	Shute Barrington
1826	William Van Mildert
1836	Edward Maltby
1856	Charles Longley
1860	Henry Villiers
1861	Charles Baring
1879	Joseph Lightfoot
1889	Brooke Foss Westcott
1901	Handley Moule
1920	Herbert Hensley Henson
1939	Alwyn Williams
1952	Michael Ramsey
1956	Maurice Harland
1966	Ian Ramsey
1973	John Hapgood
1984	David Jenkins
1993	Michael Turnbull
2003	Thomas Wright

PRIORS OF DURHAM ————————
1083	Aldwin
1087	Turgot
1109	Algar
1137	Roger
1149	Lawrence
1154	Absolom
1158	Thomas
1163	German
1188	Bertram
1209	William
1214	Ralph Kernet
1233	Thomas of Melsonby
1244	Bertram of Middleton
1258	Hugh of Darlington
1272	Richard of Claxton
1285	Hugh of Darlington
1289	Richard of Hoton
1308	William of Tanfield
1314	Geoffrey of Burdon
1322	William of Cowton
1341	John Fossor
1374	Robert of Berrington
1391	John of Hemmingburgh
1416	John Wessington
1446	William of Ebchester
1456	John Burnaby
1464	Richard Bell
1478	Robert of Ebchester
1484	John of Auckland
1494	ThomasCastell
1524	Hugh Whitehead

DEANS OF DURHAM ————————
1541	Hugh Whitehead
1551	Robert Horne
1553	Thomas Watson
1557	Thomas Robertson
1560	Ralph Skinner
1563	William Whittingham
1580	Thomas Wilson
1583	Tobias Matthew
1596	William James
1606	Adam Newton
1620	Richard Hunt
1639	Walter Balcanquall
1645	William Fuller
1660	John Barwick
1662	John Sudbury
!684	Denis Granville
1691	Thomas Comber
1699	John Montague
1728	Henry Bland
1746	Spencer Cowper
1774	Thomas Dampier
1777	William Digby
1788	John Hinchcliff
1794	James Cornwallis
1824	Charles Hall
1827	John Jenkinson
1840	George Waddington
1869	William Lake
1894	George Kitchin
1912	Herbert Hensley Henson
1918	James Welldon
1933	Cyril Alington
1951	John Wild
1974	Eric Heaton
1980	Peter Baelz
1989	John Arnold
2002	Michael Sadgrove

DURHAM CHRONOLOGY

627 Baptism of Edwin, King of Northumbria, by Paulinus at York

634 Battle of Heavenfield, near Hexham. Oswald restores Christianity to Northumbria.

635 Arrival of Aidan from Iona. Foundation of community on Lindisfarne.

642 Death of Oswald in battle against the Mercians at Oswestry.

651 Death of Aidan at Bamburgh

664 Synod of Whitby

c.665 Cuthbert arrives at Lindisfarne from Melrose

678 Cuthbert becomes a hermit on Inner farne

685 Cuthbert consecrated Bishop of Lindisfarne

687 Death of Cuthbert on Inner Farne

698 Discovery of Cuthbert's uncorrupted body by the monks of Lindisfarne

793 First Viking raid on Lindisfarne

875 Lindisfarne abandoned

875–883 Community of St. Cuthbert on the move across the north of England and southern Scotland

883 Community settles at Chester le Street

934 Athelstan of Wessex a pilgrim to Cuthbert's shrine

995 Cuthbert community moves to Durham

998 Consecration of the Ecclesia Major on the Durham peninsula

1022 Elfred Westhou obtains relics of Bede from Jarrow

1069 Slaughter in Durham of Robert Cumin and his Norman troops

1070 The Harrying of the North by William the Conqueror

1072 William flees from Durham in a fever; beginning of construction of Durham Castle

1075 Bishop Walcher begins construction of a monastery

1080 Murder of Bishop Walcher by Nothumbrians at Gateshead

1083 Bishop William of St. Calais establishes Benedictine monastery

1093 Foundations of Durham Cathedral laid

1096 Death of St. Calais

1104 Translation of St. Cuthbert's coffin to shrine in the new cathedral

1120 Cenotaph church built on Lindisfarne

1121 Bishop Flambard builds Norham castle on the Tweed

1128 Death of Flambard

1133 Cathedral complete but for west towers

1135–40 Bishop Geoffrey Rufus builds Chapter House

1141–43 William Cumin attempts to seize Durham for Scotland

1153 Hugh du Puiset Bishop

1170 Murder of Thomas Becket at Canterbury

1172 First St. Godric miracle reported at Finchale

1189 Consecration of the Galilee Chapel

1229 Le Convenit attempts to settle disputes between bishop and monastery

1242–1280 Construction of the Chapel of the Nine Altars

1283 Antony Bek Bishop

1314 Battle of Bannockburn. Scots defeat English and raid the north repeatedly

1315 Robert Bruce takes Durham

1346 Battle of Neville's Cross. Scots defeated near Durham

1349 The Black Death reaches Durham and about two thirds of the monks perish

1366–71 Building of the Great Kitchen

1380 Bishop Hatfield founds Durham College Oxford; consecration of the Neville Screen

1381 Hatfield tomb and Bishops' Throne

1388 Battle of Otterburn. Scots defeat English

1398–1404 New Dormitory constructed

c.1409–19 Remodelling of Cloister

1414–18 Wessington's Library built

1459–80 Present Tower constructed

1536 Pilgrimage of Grace; Act of Resumption of Liberties prunes powers of the Prince-Bishops

1538 Henry VIII's commissioners demolish Cuthbert's shrine

1539 Dissolution of the priory at Durham

1541 Letters patent create Durham as a new foundation cathedral with Dean and Chapter

1552 Bishop Tunstall deprived of his see

1553 Death of Edward VI; accession of Mary Tudor; Tunstall reinstated as bishop

1559 Death of Tunstall

1569 The Rising of the North

1603 Union of the Crowns reduces strategic importance of the north

1607 Dobson's Drie Bobbes published

1617 Visit of James I

1628 Peter Smart's inflammatory sermon

1629 Smart fined and imprisoned

1633 Visit of Charles I

1640 Cosin appears before a commitee of the Long Parliament; Smart reinstated

1640 Scots occupy Durham and vandalise the cathedral

1641 Cosin deprived of his church positions

1643 Cosin takes refuge in France

1649 Deans and Chapters abolished by Parliament; Durham Castle confiscated and sold

1650–51 Scots prisoners incarcerated in cathedral over the winter

1660 Restoration of Charles II

1661 Cosin returns to Durham as bishop

1661–69 Cosin's restorations and new buildings

1672 Death of Cosin

1674 Arrest of Prebendary Granville in the Cloister for debt

1675 Nathaniel Crewe Bishop

1682 Visit of Samuel Pepys to Durham

1684 Denis Granville Dean

1688–9 'The Glorious Revolution'

1689 Granville flees to France

1721 Death of Bishop Crewe

1756 Mr Cook's antics in Alnwick

1777 John Wooler surveys the cathedral fabric

1778–86 Chiselling off the exterior stonework

1794 James Wyatt's scheme for improvements

1795 Partial demolition of 12th century Chapter House

1802 Order for demolition of Galilee Chapel withdrawn

1822 Chapter libel case against the Durham Chronicle

1826 Van Mildert bishop

1827 James Raine opens Cuthbert's tomb; Van Mildert's dinner for the Duke of Wellington

1829 Catholic Emancipation Act

1833 Founding of Durham University by Dean and Chapter

1840 Cathedrals Act

1870 Restoration of cathedral by George Gilbert Scott

1871 First Durham Miners' Gala

1896 Bishop Westcott invites miners to a cathedral service to conclude Gala Day

1906 Choristers begin to board in The College

1925 Dean Weldon escapes a ducking

1926 The General Strike

1933 Dean Alington founds Friends of Durham Cathedral

1947 Dedication of the Miners' Memorial

1948 Expansion of the Chorister School to include non-choristers

1953 Chorister School established in present home

1983 Durham named a World Heritage Site

1990 Care of Cathedrals Measure

1999 Cathedrals Measure

2001 New statutes for cathedral

2005 St. Cuthbert restored to Cathedral's dedication

LIST OF SUBSCRIBERS

Francis John Adams
Peter Adi
M.A. Akin
Mrs Leonie Allday
Mr I.T. and Mrs M.P. Allen
Helen and Michael Altringham
American Friends of Durham Cathedral
Mrs Betty Anderson
Helen and David Anderson
Martha Anderson
Simon John Anderson
Patricia R. Andrew
Dr William Walker Apedaile
Dr David Appleyard
J.H. and E. Armes
M.S.G. Armstrong
Frances Arnold
Matthew Arnold
Jean Arthur
John and Rowena Ashworth
Catherine Atkinson
Miss Eileen M. Atkinson
Jane and Alan Atkinson
R.W.J. Austin
Mr and Mrs John Ayton
Margaret Baggs
Mrs Marion N. Bagley
Rosalind Bainbridge
Ruth Bamberger
Mr Paul Bamlett
Wilfred and June Banks
Mrs Elaine Barbour
W.D.C. Barham
Mrs A.P. Barker
The Lord Barnard
Angela Barnes
Raymond W. Barnes
Mrs Margaret H. Barton
Jo and Kit Bartram
Professor and Mrs Gordon Batho
Marian S. Baynes
The late Reginald Ernest Bayston
Joan Beardsworth
Lorna Isabel Bebbington
Eleanor Bell
Professor Jeanne E. Bell
Dr Graeme Bennet
Miss Joan Bernard
Geoffrey Berriman
Mrs K.M.D. Beswick
David and Rosalind Beveridge
Miss Elizabeth N. Bewick
D. Bickerdike
M.I. Birch
Gloria Blackett
Mark Blacklock
Wilmer T. Bloy
Dr David Boardman
Geraldine Boardman MSc
Mr and Mrs J. Bolam
Chris and Tina Bond
Mr and Mrs F.J.P. Bone
John and Wendy Boult
Marion K. Boville

Mr and Mrs A. Bowman
Dr Michael Bowman
Dr Nicholas Boyall
Dr Michael Boyd
Sonia Boys-Stones
M. Jacqueline Bradley
Michael Bramwell
Philip Mark Brazier
Dr and Mrs Bremner
G.C. Brickley
Eunice and Harry Brierley
Arthur Brookes
Margaret Brooks
Sue Brooks
Alex Brougham
Dr A.G. Brown
Mrs Brenda Brown
Karen and Ken Brown
P.R. and K.M. Brown
Dr Richard Brown and Family
Tom Brown
Valerie Brown
Mary and David Buchan
De heer J.G. Buitendijk
Mr I.P. Bulkley and Mrs Ann Bulkley
Tricia W. Burke
Mary E. Burkett OBE
David Burnett
Andrew J. Burns
The Rev'd David Burton Evans
David and Pauline Butler
Miss Beryl Cail
Miss Margaret Calow
Sonia Cameron-Jacks
Anna Campbell
Margaret Campbell
Miriam Campbell (née Arnold)
David and Diane Carr
Beverley and Joyce Carss
Dr D.J. Carter
Dr Joan Carter
Archdeacon and Mrs J.W. Carter
Patricia Carter-LeCompte
Sylvia Cathcart and Mary Elizabeth
Cathcart (née Moore)
Cathedrals and Church Buildings
Howard Cattermole
Dr W.B. Chamberlain
Gerald Champion
Barbara, Lady Chapman
Christopher Chapman
David J. Chapman
Sir David and Lady Chapman
Katherine Chapman
Peter and Joan Chapman
Rachel Chapman
Vicky Chapman
Rev'd M. Paul Chappell
Liz Charles
John and Margaret Charters
Robert Walmsley Chilton
Sarah Irene Chisem
Elizabeth J. Clapham
Allison Clark

Christopher M.G. Clark
Gordon Clark
Enid J. Clarke
Dr K. Clarke
Mary Morson Clarke
James F.E.J. Clegett
Rev'd David K. Clegg
Keith and Jen Close
Dick and Una Coates
Mr and Mrs E.W. Coates
Mrs J. Cohen
Rev'd Charles V. Cole
Mr J.A. Cole
Thomas E. Coles
Congregation of St. Peter's, Wolviston
Grace Connacher
Patrick Conway
Muriel Cook
Michael J. Cooke
Professor Helen Cooper
Joyce Cooper
Mrs Fleur E. Coppock
Dr and Mrs W.D. Corner
Dr and Mrs J.E. Cotes
Martin Cowen
Mr and Mrs R. Cowley
Mary Cowling
Paul R. Coxon
In memory of Rose Marie Crask
Benjamin Creutzfeldt
Adam John Crosby
Doreen and Mark Culling
Neil and Sue Cumming
Kevin T. Cummings
Ishbel M. Curr
Anthony Michael Cutbush
Jim Dale
Gail M. Dalley
Valerie Dalton
Mr and Mrs K. Dart
Gwenda Laidler Davies
Michael Davies
Mr and Mrs V.E. Davies
The Reverend Andrew Davis
Mr D.J. and E. Davis
John H. Davis
Maureen and Ray Davison
Molly and Fred Davison
Joanna and Peter Dawson
Maureen Dawson
P. de N. Lucas
J. Claire Dean
Philip Dear
M.H. and E.M. Defty
Olwyn Defty
Arthur Dews
Alex and Barbara Dickinson
R.M. Dipple
Alan and Anne Dixon
Alexander Scott Dixon
Kenneth Dixon
Frank and Hilary Donovan
Andy Doyle
Father Henry L. Doyle

Dr and Mrs Simon Draper
Anne and Dave Drinkwater
Mrs J. Linda Drury
Pauline Duffell
The Dumas Family
Kathleen J. Dumigan
Robert R. Dumigan
Denise Dunlop
Dick Dunmore
John Dunn
Judith Dunthorne
Benjamin Eadon
Pat Eames
Evelyn and Rose Ebsworth
Miss Ann Edgar
D.J. and J.M. Edward
Clive Donald Edwards
Geoffrey and Maureen Eggett
Mr Arthur Gould Elliott
Mrs Charlotte Maria Elliott (née
Johnston)
John S. Elliott
Amelia Grace Ellis
Peter Elsdon
Mr E. and Mrs J. Emms
Anne B. English
Peter and Pamela Errington
Dr Ruth Etchells
Richard Evans
Pat and Tony Everett
Neville and Anita Fairclough
Arthur and Lorna Falconer
Mr Michael Farrant
Miss Ann Farrow
Jill Farrow
Maureen Ferguson
Richard and Clare Firth
Mr and Mrs J.R. Flynn
Georgina Forbes
Margaret Forey
Mr and Mrs M. Forrester
Julia and Ian Forsyth
Jean and Geoff Foster
Julian P. Fowell
Rev'd Canon Dr James and Mrs Patricia
Francis
John Frearson
M.E. Frisby
Timothy Michael Frost
Joan and David Fuller
Susi Fuller
Mr M.J. and Mrs E.J. Furness
Col S.J. Furness
Anne Catherine Fylkesnes
Lynda Garcia
Jennifer Geard
The Rev'd Dr Anthony and Mrs Anne
Gelston
Dr Michael Gent
Patricia A. Gentry
Marjorie A. Gibbon
Frank and Jean Gibbs
J.E.P. Gilbert
John and Irene Gilbert

Kiki Ramos Gindler
Judy Goin
David A. Goodchild
Antony Norman Goodfellow
Canon Peter and Mrs Goodrich
Keith Gordon
Ian Gorrell
Mr H.H. Gossman
Derek Gowling
Alison Gowman
Kathleen A.H. Graff
Alice H. Graham
Mr J.M. Graham
Joan and Chris Graham
M.B. Graham
Ros and Ian Graham
A.G. Grant
A.S. Grant
Dr J.L. Grassi
Mr and Mrs Adam Scott Gray
Colin Gray
Dr M.E.S. Gray
Guy and Sarah Greenhous
Pearl Grieves
Elizabeth Griffin
Professor R.F. Griffin
Lilian Groves
Michael Groves
Yvonne and Ian Gustard
Keith Gymer
The Rt Rev'd Lord Habgood
G.H. Hails
Peter and Margaret Halling
Mr and Mrs K. Hamilton
Dr and Mrs T.R. Hamilton
Jean Hamilton-Proud
Mr A.S. and Mrs E. Hampton
Thomas Hancock
Miss M. Hanks
Professor Donald Hardie
Mrs Gillian Hardie
Master Sam Hardy
Aidan R.J. Hargitt
Nancy Marguerite Harper (née Moor)
Jean Harris
Ben Harrison
Elizabeth Harrison
Frank Harrison CEng (MIMM and M)
Rev'd Dr Helen-Ann and Mr Myles Hartley
Councillor Mary Hawgood and Dr John Hawgood
Elizabeth Hawkins
R. Hay
K.L. Hayton
Mr Brian Hedley
Robert L. Henderson
Rev'd Dr Marion Lars Hendrickson
Dr and Mrs Anthony Henfrey
Miss F. Hepburn
Christine W. Heron
Cnty Cllr Michael Heseltine
G.W. Heslop
Rev'd D. Hewitson

Mr Matthew Hewitt
Stuart and Marion Heywood
Colin J. Higgins
Rosemary Hind
Miss I. Hindmarsh
Canon and Mrs D.G.F. Hinge
Kathleen Hirst
M.U. Hirst
Jenny Hobbs
Canon Derek and Mrs Greta Hodgson
Ian Bramley and Dr Andrea Hodgson
John and Jane Hodgson
Stephen and Kelly Hodgson
Sara Hogden-Harris
D.J. Holme
Mr and Mrs E.N. Holmes
Ken and Judy Home
Richard H. Hopps
Leonard and Olga Horner
John Paul and Elizabeth Hoskins
Hazel Howard
Sarah Howard
The Rev'd William and Mrs Margaret Howard
Pam and Tony Howarth
Christine Howson
Mary Louise Hudson
Andrew and Ellen Hudspith
Mrs M.E. Hughes
Steve Hughes
Dawn Hull
Keith Humphreys
The Revd E.G. and Mrs K. Hunt
Malcom Hunt
Mr and Mrs Bill Hurworth
Michael and Sally Ingram
Dr Kathleen Irvine MBE
Rev'd H.W. Jackson
John G. Jackson
James and Doris Jackson
Richard Jackson
Mr and Mrs R. Jackson
Elizabeth Anne James
Helen James
Pauline and Dominic James
Miss Elspeth Jamieson
Alan and Mary Jarvis
Mrs Heather Jarvis
John and Margaret Jefferson
Margaret Jefferson
Paul and Margaret Jefferson
Mr D. Jepson
Miss A. Rosemary Johnson
Malcolm E. Johnson
Margot Johnson
Norman A. Johnson
Caroline Johnston
Margaret Johnston
Mrs Anna M. Jones
Jane Jones
Teressa C. Kavanagh
Allan H.H. Kaye
R.W. Kealey
Charles H. Keeling (Layclerk 1925–54)

Gordon Keers
Miss Jane Kellett
Audrey Kelly
Ann M. Kelly
Brian Kennett
M.P. Kent
Joan M. Kenworthy
Graham and Jill Kidman
N. and L. Kilner
Dr and Mrs J.I. King
Dr and Mrs J. Gordon Kingsley
Dermot and Christine Kirkwood
Patricia Kirkwood
Margaret Kirtley
Mr and Mrs Kirton-Darling
Brenda Kloed
L.A. Lacey
Mrs Nira Laing
Patricia Large
Mr and Mrs J. LaRue
Mary K. Fitzpatrick Lascelles
Cecil Laverick
Norma Laverick
Dr Uwe and Frau M. Lawrenz
Fenwick and Joan Lawson
Major Chris Lawton MBE
M.J. Le Fleming
Mr and Mrs David Leach and Family
Mr and Mrs Raymond Leach
Alan and Ruth Lee
Dr Donald Leinster-Mackay and Dr Maree Leinster-Mackay
Hilda F. Leith
Christopher Lendrum
Elizabeth and Mark Levy
Dr Ann M. Lewis
John and Margaret Lightley
Bill and Muriel Local
Michael Lodico
Colin Looker
Eleanor Lovegrove
Judge Richard Lowden
Mr and Mrs J.C. Lowe
Peter E. Lowis
J.R. Lucas
Mrs Barbara A.M. Luck
Elisabeth Luedemann-Ravit
Isabell and Robert Lunan
Dr J.F. Lund
Ron and Jennie Lund
Mrs Macartney
Brigadier R.B. MacGregor-Oakford CBE MC
Andrew Manson
Ian and Alicia Manson
Paul Manson
Tom Manson
The Venerable and Mrs G.J.C. Marchant
Mr E.G. Markee
Jenny Marriott
Mrs G.M. Marsden
Dr Geoffrey Marsh MBE
Gordon and Penny Martin

The Reverend John Masding, MA LLM
Mr and Mrs E.W. Mather
Margaret and Stuart Matthews
Jacqueline and Raymond May
Russell McAndrew
Mr and Mrs M. McConnell
John A.C. McGowan
Michael and Christine McMinn
Nigel and Elaine McMinn
Brian, Barbara, Naomi and Eleanor Meardon
R.F.A.S. Mellanby
Laura Wilson Messinger
Jean E. Middlemass
John A.D. Middleton
Rev'd D. Milburn
Gordon E. Miller
Ian T. Miller
Norman Miller
Maggie Mills
Mrs Lucy Mines
Andrew Mitchell
John and Jo Mitchell
Walter and Jennifer Moberly
Elizabeth Moffat
Robert Moor
Miss Olive Morgan
Gordon Morris
John and Stella Morris
Sandra Morris
Marian Morrison
Coral J.F. and Thomas J. Mosbo
George Souter Mullen
Stephen and Diane Murphy
Peter Murray
Trevor Musgrove
Dr Umesh Nanda
Ann E. Naylor
The Rev'd John W. Naylor
Mr R. Naylor
William Newby
Kenneth E. Nicholas
Edward and Anne Nicholl
Jim and Norma Nicholson
Sir Paul and Lady Nicholson
Charlton Noble
Roger Norris
John D. Norton
Rev'd Donald and Charlotte Nowers
Dorothy Jean Oliver MBE
Lady Openshaw DBE
Anne W. Orde
Lorna Osbon
Mrs Joan Oughton
Paul Overton
Alan Oyston
The Rev'd Canon K.V. Pagan
Donna M. Paige
Barnabus Palmer
Rev'd Margaret Parker
Janice L. Parkin
Stephen Parkin
J. Parkinson
Emma Charlotte Pascall

The Rev'd E.B. Pateman
Margaret and Chistopher Pattinson
Major Lisle Pattison
Andrew G. Patton
The Rev'd and Mrs M.T. Peach
Brian Charles Pearson
Donald Pelmear
Mr P. and Mrs P.E. Penfold
Mrs P.M.E. Penrose
Michael and Margaret Perry
John and Barbara Petrie
Mr Rodney Petty
Katarzyna Pindak
M.E. Pinkney
Rev'd Cannon L.A. Piper MBE
(deceased)
Mrs Mildred M. Piper
Julian and Amanda Platt
Heather Pollard
John and Celia Pottinger
Alexandros Poutachidis
Mark F. Pownall
Colin Neill Prentice
Michael Prestwich
Suzanne Louise Price and Barry Price
David Priestley
Dr Avril Lumley Prior
The Rt Rev'd John and Mrs W.
Pritchard
Charles W. and Mavis G. Pullan
Susan M.C. Pykett
Miss A. Radford
Frank Ralfe
David W. Ramsay
Gail and Paul Ramsey
Sir Vivian and Lady Ramsey
Tony Raymond
Donald Eastwood Read
Glynda Steele Readman
Ronald Reay and Audrey Reay
Hannah K. Redhead
John W. Redhead
George and Joyce Reed
Mrs Eleanor Reeve
Margaret A. Reeves
Thomas and Carol Rennie
Joe Parker Rhineheart
Professor P.J. Rhodes
Alan Ribchester
Alexander Richardson
William Richardson
Tony and Kay Richmond
Viscount Ridley
Pauline Rimer
S.C. Rioch
John Rippon
R.N. Rippon JP
Patricia Robbins
Gordon and Patricia A. Roberts
Richard A. Roberts Esq.
John P. Robertson
Anne and Bill Robinson
Evelyn Robinson and Keith Robinson
Brenda Robson

Joan Robson
Mrs Margaret Robson
Rita Robson
Susan Robson
Dorothy Rodgers
James E.J. Rodgers
The Rev'd Peter and Mrs Elizabeth
Rowe
Miss J.R. Rowell
Rhoda Rowland
Ruth A. Jones and Ian W. Rowley
Miss Margaret L. Rushford
Pam and Tony Russell
Moira Rutherford
The Very Reverend Michael Sadgrove,
Dean Of Durham
G. and E. Saint
Dr Thomas M.C. Saint
Dick Sale
Marjorie Sale
Robert Sale
D.C. Salisbury
Mrs Ælfwynn Sampson, BA Dunelm
Richard Christopher Samuel CMG CVO
Diana and Phil Sanderson
Aidan and Eileen Saunders
J. Robin Schofield
John and Edy Schofield
Mark J. Schofield
Angel Scott
Professor D.F.S. Scott
J. Scott
Lois and Keith Scott
Mr and Mrs Michael Scott
Lawrence A. Seman Esq.
Lorna Seymour
Mr and Mrs T. Seymour
M.F. and B.M. Sharratt
Sue Shaw
Jean Laidler Shepherd
Ian Sheppard
N. and H.D.F. Sherlock
Dr and Mrs A.M. Simper
Alan Simpson
Norma Simpson
Rev'd T. Eric and Mrs E. Simpson
Mrs M.A. Slack
In memory of Mr G.C.F. Sladden
David Slater
Eileen M. Slater
Alan Slomson
Caroline and Jason Smith
Mrs Dora E. Smith
R.O. and M. Smith
Joyce and Ron Smithson
David and Alison Snow
Dr James Snowdon Barnett
Dr and Mrs M. Souter
Alan and Margaret Spain
Dorothy W. Spaulding
L. Spencer
Dr Leonard James Srnka
Malcolm Stabler
T.J. and G. Stace

Miss M. Staddon
G.D. Stainsby
Margaret Stamp
Sheila Stanley
Dr M.M.N. Stansfield
Alan J. Stark
Mr R.W. and Mrs F.R. Stenlake
Anne Stevenson Lucas
Ian and Pamela Stewart
Patricia W. Stewart
Bill and Dot Stockdale
Tom and Eunice Stokoe
Mrs Constance Summers
Christine Sutcliffe
Frank and Mary Swales
Ken and Jean Swales
Marion Simpson Swann
Judith Sweetman
R.D. and M. Swinburne
David and Maud Symons
Christopher Taberham
Alan Taylor
Miss Carolyn Taylor
Christina Ord Taylor
John, Heather and Phillip Taylor
The Very Reverend Robert V. Taylor
Andrew and Johanna Teasdale
J. and J. Thackray
Professor and Mrs J.D. Thomas
Robert and Emily Thomas
Anne Thompson
Alison Thompson
Reginald and Gillian Thompson
Don Thomson
Jason Alexander Thomson
Gary Wayne Alfred Thorne
Dr J.S. Thorp and Mrs M.J. Thorp
Mr R. and Mrs M. Tindle
Elizabeth O. Tinker
Minas Tirith
Alison A.J. Todd
Joy Todd
Lady Tomlinson
Denis Trigg
C.E. Tristram
Douglas Turkington
Anthony and Daphne Turner
Arthur Mills Turner
L. Turner and M.J. Turner
Ushaw College, Durham
Eric Vallis
Hon. H.F.C. Vane
Catherine B. Veitch
J.C.H. Veldhuizen
Mrs Margot Waddle
Mr and Mrs B. Wake
Mrs Gillian Walker
Mrs Margaret Walker
Margaret Walker
Charles Pemberton Wallace
Mary and Ronnie Walters
Gordon Walton
John Walton
Margaret Walton

Frank Ward
Malcolm L. Wass
Mr and Mrs A. Watson
Derek Watson
J.M. Watson
Professor J.R. Watson
Richard and Teresa Watson
Dr Trudy A. Watt
Michael and Beryl Watts
David and Rosemary Way
Rennie Weatherhead
Miss Hazel Weatherill
Mrs Sandy Weaver
Mr Eric Webber
Reverend Toby Webber
Don and Dottie Weightman
Joan Weightman
Caroline Weir
John Welch
Barry Welsh
Kitty Werner
Anthony West
Mary Weston
Mr and Mrs M.P. Weston
David and Hildred Whale
J. and J.A. Whale
Frederick A. Wharton
John and Gisela Wheeler
Amber Whitby
Mrs Jean T. White
Canon M.H. Whitehead
Martyn and Melanie Whitehead
Anna L. Whitehouse
Shirley Whiteley
Dorothy Whiting
Jean Wiblin
T.J.N. Wickens
Mr and Mrs Stefan Wilczek
Norman Wilkinson, Sr
Dr Paul J. Wilkinson
John Aled Williams
Nora Williams
Mr and Mrs Magnus Willis
Dr Gillian Willmore
Dorothy Wilson
Mr and Mrs K.H. Wilson
Mr P.L. and Mrs Eva Wilson
C. and R. Wiltsher
Jack and Carol Winskill
John Wolfe
Peter John Woodhill
John Woodhurst
Audrey Woodward
W. Barry Woodward
Michael Bede Woolstenholmes
Ella W. Wright
The Misses S.A. and E. Wright
The Most Reverend Tom Wright, Bishop
of Durham
E. Harold and Joan Wykes
Margaret Wylam
Y. Yiannakou
M.M. Young
Dr J.C. Yule

INDEX

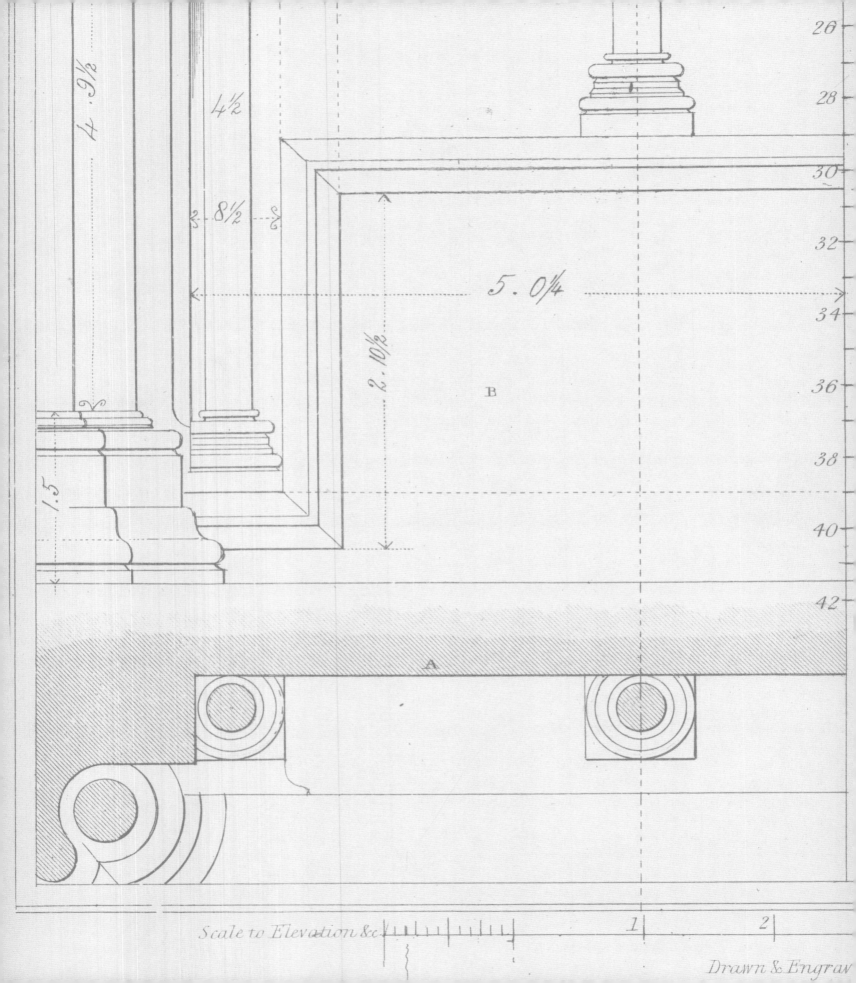

26

28

30

32

34

36

38

40

42

4 . 9½

4½

8½

5. 0¼

2. 10½

1.5

B

A

Drawn & Engrav